Can you smell Gas ?

Memories of a Town Gas Works

By

Paul Staniforth and
Claude Staniforth

Published by Paul Staniforth

Jacket Illustrations

Front Cover - Mr Therm; Treasures in Coal (illustrating the many useful by-products of the gas manufacturing process). Image courtesy of Transco National Gas Archive.

Back Cover - Manchester Guardian Gas Industry Supplement 1923. Image courtesy of Transco National Gas Archive.

Abbreviations and contemporary units of measures are:-

s = shillings 1/20 of a £, d = pre decimal pence[12d=s], I lb= I pound weight = 0.454kg, cwt means hundredweight 20 cwt = I ton, I cwt=112 lb=50.8kg, I qtr=28lb, I1"=eleven inches, I"=2.54cm, BTh U=British Thermal Unit, I therm=500 BThU (Ely). I therm = 200 cu ft. I cubic foot of gas was 0.005 therms at the Ely Works. kJ/l= kilo joules per litre

Can you smell Gas ?

Memories of a Town Gas Works

First published in the United Kingdom 2006

Copyright © Paul Staniforth

This book may not be reproduced in whole or in part,
without written permission of the author

Published by Paul Staniforth Bramerton Norfolk UK

ISBN 0-9554230-0-7   Soft back edition
978-0-9554230-0-0   Soft back edition

Printed by Info Print, Peterborough, UK

Autobiography– History, Business and Industry
London–England-History 1800-1950
Gas Lighting -England- London –History-19th Centaury
Great Britain-History-Victoria-1837-1901
London-England- Social Conditions

Further copies of this book may be purchased in Ely from Burrows Bookshop, your local bookshop
or by post direct from Paul Staniforth at: -

www.towngas.co.uk
&
By phone on 01508 538195

Every effort has been made to acknowledge copyright holders of material contained within this
publication. Apologies are proffered to anyone who has accidentally been omitted or who could
not be traced.

What the Book Reviewers say !

Maurice Martin, Curator of the John Duran, National Gas Museum Trust writes

Paul Staniforth's recollections in 'Can you small gas?' provides us with a real 'blast from the past'.

In his well researched book the author makes us marvel at how great an impact the gas industry had, not only on an individual and as a family, but also on the local community and the nation in general. 'Can you Smell Gas?' wonderfully illustrates the great debt society owes to the gas industry and provides us with an excellent historical record. Paul paints a most interesting picture of the development of the industry, linking it with social history. Unlike some historical accounts, he doesn't overburden us with precise dates. Instead he shows us the various stages of the industry's growth compared against national and world events.

An intriguing and intimate reflection on the gas industry, the people involved, social conditions at the time, and society in general, this book is much more than a report on the gas industry. It is a reflection on people's lives. Paul Staniforth uses characters from both within and outside of his beloved Ely gas works as a vehicle to give us an insight into the industry and social conditions.

This is no ordinary, straight forward written list of facts. Instead the author adopts an interesting and unique technique to present us with a very human story. His approach is to inform us of the magnificence of the gas industry, set against social conditions of the time, personal events and the impact these had on the emotional relationship he had with one man, his father. He lays these along side memories, writings and stories of several of his fathers fellow workers and associates.

In 'Can you Smell Gas?' Paul Staniforth has succeeded in producing a fascinating, accurate, in depth, yet warm and affectionate account of the gas industry.

Mike Petty, former senior librarian responsible for the Cambridge Local history collection and now President of the Cambridge Local History Society writes.

Nobody has previously researched the history of the Ely Gas Company until now when Paul Staniforth rectified matters with his magnificent study.

It is the story of the individuals who invested their money and expertise to bring gas to Ely. It details the production methods, appliances and the challenges of Nationalisation that were common to other gas works many of which still have a history yet to be told.

However it is not just the story of gas, for it embraces the river trade that brought coal along the fenland waterways, it tells of the impact of the first and second world wars and of the period of poverty in between.

But most of all it is the story of local people with reminiscences of the stokers, pipe fitters and gas users supplementing the personal recollections of the manager of the Company, Claude Staniforth and his son. Paul has supplemented them through detailed research into both the Company's archives, newspapers and photographs from the family attic.

This is a major contribution to the history of Cambridgeshire and a model for others to attempt to emulate. I am delighted to recommend it.

The City of Ely Gas Company
'embossing seal'

Memories of the Ely Gas & Electricity Company
1835-1959

(signature)	Own Ambrose.	Chairman of Directors
(signature)	Alderman Horace Martin.	Director
(signature)	Lt Col G L Archer.	Director
(signature)	Claude Staniforth.	Manager, Engineer and Secretary
(signature)	Charles Secker.	Distribution Superintendent
(signature)	Eric Ardron.	Works Superintendent

Signatures of Directors and senior staff at time of Nationalisation

To Celebrate the 50ᵗʰ Anniversary of closure of the works

Contents

The Story of :

From Boultons Market Place Ely

Ely from the air. estimated date 1923.

The gas works is in the lower left hand corner of the photograph. Three gas holders, and the office block are clearly visible as is the river frontage and the Cutter Inn in the bottom right hand corner where coal was originally off loaded from barges. The Woodall-Duckham vertical retort has not yet been built. A sharp eye may notice a purifier box just in front of a gas holder & a small square chimney to the left of the tall chimney which was the outlet to the steam raising plant.

13

Dedicated to my late father Claude Bertram Staniforth

by the little boy who longed to be loved.

Acknowledgement

I am greatly indebted to my wife Esmé for her patience and love in allowing me to absent myself, retreat to my library and for many hours engross myself for three years in compiling this book. It took three years to complete. I became totally enthralled by a journey of discovery, and in so doing my heart was for the moment totally lost to her. What a tremendous sacrifice she made for me for which I express my thanks. Like all good wives she came to my rescue many times when the going got tough as well as taking on responsibility for much of the photography and arranging the many visits we made to complete the research necessary. The dog meanwhile found life immensely boring curled up on her bean bag next to me while I rattled away on the computer and would so much have preferred to have renewed her acquaintance with the local smells of our riverside walks.

The late Andrew Armour, former city librarian of Cambridge City Library, and a longstanding friend was very supportive. The book as presented would not have been possible without recourse to research material from Cambridgeshire County Council Archives, Lincolnshire County Archives, Cambridge Local History Collection, The National Gas Archives in Warrington, The Ely Local History Society, Polly Hodgson (Ely Museum Curator), The Fakenham Town Gas Works Museum and The National Gas Museum. I would particularly like to thank Pam Blakeman, Sid Merry, Ann Powell, Robert Powell, Virginia Watkinson, Christopher Attersley, Audrey Longdon, G Leicester, Doris Buckingham, Lorna and Mike Delanoy, Beryl Lee, Mike Petty, and their respective families, all connected with or living in Ely for their support and contributions. Additionally many other people to numerous to name who have given of their time, advice and memories. Lastly, to Ken Golisti a retired British Gas Engineer in Beverley for his research into the Malam family and to John Horne a former British Gas Engineer in Southampton for his very detailed researches into the early history of the company a selection of works plans and aerial photograph. He also undertook the major task of proof reading Chapters 14 to 23 to ensure technical accuracy and he gave much advice which contributed greatly to the book. I am enormously indebted to him as he is one of a diminishing band of engineers who actually recall coal gas manufacture. Without the help of Richard Forster in Buckingham this publication would not have materialised for he gave invaluable advice on the computer technology which enabled me to deliver to the Printers a 'print ready' copy which relieved the costs of engaging a Publisher. Thanks also to Maurice Martin curator of the National Gas Museum Leicester who gave so much encouragement and to Dr Mike Bridges curator of Fakenham Gas Museum. Thanks, finally, to Maureen Harrison for proof reading the entire text.

Preface

In the 1970's I pleaded with my father to record for posterity his memories of his life as manager of the Ely Gas and Electric Company. Mindful of Dad's advancing age and with nothing written and no signs of my wish being fulfilled, I continued my pleas. My concern became ever more desperate after he experienced his first very serious heart attack, but to no avail. It was only after his second heart attack in the 1980's that he himself realised he was leaving the task perilously late and so whilst still in his hospital bed in the Old Addenbrooks, he started to write furiously, much to the curiosity of the nursing staff. Once out of hospital and many months later, his strength returned and he was able to devote time and research to complete his work. The papers were typed, bound and given to me in 1983, marked "Dedicated to my son Paul with much affection".

Mindful that I must be one of the youngest people in the country who has memories of a gasworks and how it functioned, all be it through the eyes and ears of a small child. It has always been my wish to record for prosperity, my recollections.

With much of the material for a book either in my head or penned by my father together with many documents, papers and photographs which I discovered in the roof of his house, then I had most of the material with which to make a meaningful contribution to the social history of Ely. I hope these writings will become a useful source of research material for those interested in the evolution of the Coal Gas manufacture in a typical small English Town in the late nineteenth and early twentieth centaury.

Compiling this account of Ely Gas works has been both practically and emotionally very challenging. The practical problems arose around the difficulty of combining the personal memories of Claude Staniforth the manager, my childhood memories, the archival history of the works together with the simpler technical aspects of coal distillation, all demanding very different styles of writing. None the less I have endeavoured to write in a way understandable to the lay person, retaining my personal experiences wherever I can as distinct from an authoritative but impersonal history.

The first half of the book is an auto-biography written by my fathers proceeded by some childhood recollections of my own. The second half comprises the researched history of the company drawn from directors board room minute books, documents found in our family home and the whole illustrated with photos mostly in my possession but supplemented by old photos kindly given to me and illustrations from the National Gas Archive. Within this I have incorporated the memoirs of Mr Attlesey, one of my fathers under-stoker stoker who before he died also penned the experiences of his life in the works yard.

I hope readers will find my Dad's personal memories fascinating, my own a good read and the history of the works a useful piece of local and social history. The latter chapters should provide for the interests of a small minority of technical experts fascinated by the days of Britain's heavy industry and in particular of town gas manufacture.

The emotionally difficult side to the task centres round the relationship I had with my father. On the one hand I am immensely proud of his achievements as a member of the British Institute of Managers, a chartered gas engineer and businessman. However, I confess to having received very little love and affection from him and actually being positively frightened in his presence. Indeed, he devoted so much of his time to running the gas works and at weekends, preparing sermons of the "Hell Fire and Brimstone" variety, for the local Primitive Methodist circuit, that he became my estranged father, something I have deeply regretted. My Dad later on in his life was also deeply saddened by the lack of a meaningful relationship with his son, so much so that my mother used to tell me, that he would weep frequently about me, when touched by past memories and regrets. Indeed he fasted one day a week for 7 years in the hope that the hurts of the past would be healed. His prayers were answered.

This book serves to illustrate that I had and still have a very deep yearning for my Dad even though he gave so little time to me.

Paul Staniforth   28 August 2006.

Introduction

The Ely gas works was built at a time when gas works were being constructed throughout the country. It was a small manufacturing plant when compared with its neighbour in Cambridge, ten times its size and a mere speck when compared with the large Gas Works to be found in London. The technical principles for making town gas from coal are the same and so an account of the design, running and modification of the Ely Gas Works serves to show, in layman's terms, how such a piece of heavy machinery functioned together with the immensely hard physical work involved, the scant regard for safety of employees as compared with standards we know today and finally the international, national and local politics of the time and how these impinged on the success of the business.

By 1933 the Company was in chronic financial difficulties but 16 years later witnessed meteoric growth and financial prosperity. Shareholders owning Ordinary Shares worth a mere £40 with an annual dividend of 0%, found them on Nationalisation in 1949 to be worth £102 10s 0d, yielding 10% dividend as compared with a Post Office Savings account of those days offering little more than 2½ %. This book records how it was done.

The history of the plant is taken from the Company Minutes commencing 1885, the latter part of which was written by my father when he joined the staff in 1933 at age 26. These papers together with a library of gas engineering books, gas journal directories, copies of letters he sent and photographs, have enabled this history to be compiled. No claims can be made as to the perfect accuracy of the text but I have made every effort to keep to the facts. I am sure that inaccuracies as well as omissions will be found within its pages and it is hoped that these can be sympathetically passed on enabling me to make revisions in the event of a second print run. The reading of hand written company minutes has posed occasional difficulties particularly in the correct spelling of names.

My personal memories of my father's works are confined to the period 1949-1955 when I was aged five to eleven. I doubt whether I would have been allowed anywhere near such dangerous machinery before the age of 5. By age 8, I was parcelled off to boarding school in Cambridge and saw little of the works after that date. In 1957 my father's job moved to the Cambridge Gas Works and my visits to the Ely plant came to an end. It was decommissioned some time after 20th January 1959 when a new gas main from Cambridge the manufacturing base was commissioned, (via Fordham, Soham, Ely) extending to Littleport. The Ely works were demolished in, I believe 1960. This accounts for why my memories are not as detailed as I would have wished, but still not bad for a 5-11 year old.

My fathers memoirs were written long after he had retired from the Eastern Gas Board, Cambridge Division, when he was 76 years of age. Fortunately, his memory was still very sound.

The Works as seen from Station Road in 1950
And the re-developed site in 2004

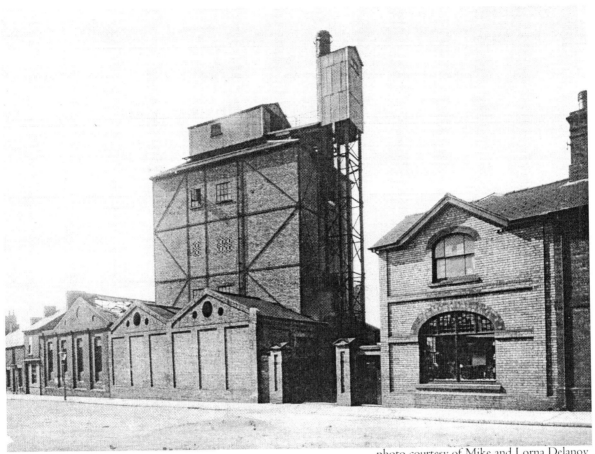

photo courtesy of Mike and Lorna Delanoy

The Vertical Retort (built in 1928) dominates the building complex. To the right hand side is the lattice steelwork of the steam driven lift behind which a gas holder can, with difficulty, just be seen. The lift was later 'boxed in' and electrified. On the street frontage a gas lamp stands in front of a single gabled roof which was the old retort house which contained the early horizontal retorts. In the foreground with the two gabled roof is the old coal store. The main gate is clearly visible with a small personnel door to the right. Visitors wishing to pay their gas bills or buy a new gas mantle or a pram load of coke would enter through this door. The showroom window with its arched top displayed the latest gas appliances. The Black Swan Public House was immediately to the right of the showroom.

Chapter I
Father's early career; pre Ely Gas works

From all accounts my father was a bright pupil at Yarmouth Grammar School. His primary education started at Doncaster where as I recall his telling me, he was taught to write on a slate. His family then moved to Hull and later Gt. Yarmouth where Dad's secondary education was gained entirely at Yarmouth Grammar School and the Yarmouth Technical School. Whilst there he gained the nickname 'lightning' for his quickness of thought and he won many prizes for his academic achievement and gained three Foundation Scholarships and exemption in Matriculation. Lack of finances precluded his considering a university place and instead he became an arti-cled clerk for 5 years at the nearby Gorleston Gas works under the guidance of the works manger Ken-neth Keeble. A copy of the 'Articles of Indenture' prepared by a solicitor, appear in the Appendix. Keen to continue his studies and en-couraged by my grandfather, John Staniforth, a teacher, he commenced a postal tuition course in Chartered Gas Engineering with the Gas Col-lege Halifax which on passing en-abled him to add Gas Eng. after his name. He then became a technical sales room assistant for three years. Armed with the necessary qualifications and experience of gas works management he applied for the post of Engineer, Manager and Secretary to the Ely Gas and Electricity Company. He was appointed in 1933, aged 26, the youngest gas manager in the Eastern Counties.

On arrival in Ely father sought lodgings at No 20 Prickwillow Road and in the ensuing years bought on mortgage No 36 Cambridge Road but I am unclear whether he actually lived there himself. He couldn't cook! The property was requisitioned by the Board of Health in 1940, leaving him with one other acquisition, a large garden along Lynn Road full of apple trees where he told me he used to sit. It was sold after he married in 1943.

During the ensuing years my Father became a Member of the British Institute of Management (BIM), Member of the Institute of Gas Engineers 1936, Member of the Institute of Fuel 1946, Associate Member of the Sales Managers Association, and a Member of the Institute of Public Lighting 1935 and a member of the London and Southern Juniors. He remained at Ely for 24 years until 1957 at which point he left to become the Commercial Manager to British Gas, Cambridge. Division based in Sydney Street, Cambridge.

Above

Claude Staniforth as portrayed in the Gas Engineer shortly after qualifying about 1933.

Below

The works from the air about 1923 published by Boulton of Market Place Ely

Chapter 2
The Ely Gas Plant

The Ely Company was, in the nineteen fifties a private concern directed by three prominent characters in the City, Lt. Col. Goodwin L. Archer a solicitor, Mr Owen Ambrose and Mr Horace J. Martin both farmers. Col Archer was a part time chairman of the Ely Urban District Council, a coroner and solicitor and had a great interest in cars. He was practically inclined and would my father told me, walk round the works. Mr Ambrose was a farmer from Stuntney who still used horses rather than tractors. He was said by my parents to be very astute with broad shoulders and twinkling blue eyes. Mr Martin too was a councillor on the Ely Rural District Council and farmed at Littleport. I was told he was a director of several companies. All were very reserved in their manner and my father addressed them with great caution and was I believe quite frightened of them, certainly early on in his career although not latterly.

The gasworks which I recall well, was located at the bottom of Back Hill near the intersection of Broad Street and Back Hill on the south side of Station Road about ½ mile from the Cathedral. It was situated barely ¼ mile from river and the railway station, both of which were the off loading points for all the coal used in the gas manufacturing process. Although called the Gas and Electricity Company, no electricity was ever generated. The name was adopted in the vain hope that electricity might one day be made for the city, but it never happened and indeed no machinery ever existed for this purpose.

The gas making plant was a prominent building complex when viewed in the 1950's from the road or indeed passing trains. It comprised a tall retort house containing four vertical retorts, later enlarged to six, (the previous plant had three larger ones) topped by a chimney, two gas holders, an office building complex, together with a range of machinery and equipment most of which stood out in the open, much of it in two large walled yards. The buildings abutted the public footpath alongside Station Road and were hidden from the public gaze by a tall brick wall. Within the wall were two dark green gates, usually closed. The first, a pair of double gates allowed entry of lorries carrying coal and coke and the second, a personnel door, enabled staff to enter and equally importantly the general public who visited to pay their gas bills, there being no other office in town for the purpose until some time later.

Once through the personnel door, the public could see a towering brick faced retort house to their left the height of say four houses with adjacent lift and chimney, an office complex to the right, ahead, a yard piled high with coal and beneath their feet the second largest cast iron weighbridge in Ely, the largest one being at the beet factory. The works was always a dirty place with coal dust everywhere and the pervasive smell of gas and by-products of its manufacture tainted the air. One got used to it and for me it was, well almost normal. Walking further up the yard, past the offices one could see the fitters' workshop to the right, the coke riddling plant to the left, the exhauster house also to the left and above it the wash facilities for the stokers. There were two large fuel piles in the yard, the first to the left was of coal to be used for gas making and the second to the right of coke, the by-product of gas making. This was used to fire the retort and the surplus sold to the public as a solid fuel to heat homes. Also tucked away within the building complex was a CWG plant which utilised oil to produce Carburetted Water Gas which was mixed with the coal gas.

The office block extended from the pavement frontage to the north three quarters of the way down the first yard. The building abutting the road was a showroom window in which new gas appliances were displayed. Advertising material, scant though it was, nearly always depicted the figure of Mr Therm with his flaming red coloured head and cheery smile. Next to this was a stairwell and adjacent to this the clerks' office where all bills were paid. Moving on, one came to Mr Charles Secker's office, then the laboratory and finally Mr Eric Ardron's office. Adjoining was the station governor room where the gas pressure on the 'District' was controlled. Beyond that was the fitters' workshop with a range of benches with vices, pipe threading and bending tools.

Above the offices was the Board Room a corner of which my father used as his office. His papers were stored all over the office in cupboards and filing cabinets. He was particularly fond of the boardroom table as he was with the six smoker bow chairs which surrounded it. It was on this table that he would play table tennis with me as a young boy, after office hours, of course ! I knew precisely which cupboard had the net and bats hidden away and, of course, the ping-pong ball. All the office building block was toasty and warm in cold weather as it was centrally heated from waste heat from the gas retort 25 yards away. In fact Dad's office was better heated than our home or most people's homes in those days. In less happy times I recall as an older school boy having to sit at this same table doing my Latin homework with my father breathing down my neck. I couldn't do Cesar's 'Gallic Wars' and Dad just terrified me.

The site of the gas works was unusual in that Little Back Lane ran right through the middle in an east west direction. The lane was very narrow, barely wide enough for a vehicle to travel down and was used primarily as a public path. This was later to be named Gas Lane. For safety reasons tall brick walls confined pedestrians to the footpath allowing no view of the premises.

The two sides of the works were connected by two solid personnel doors facing one another in the footpath walls. As we walked to the second site there was a clinker footpath running due south. To the left were the gas holders and immediately to the right were the purifier boxes made, I believe, of cast iron. They were set between two railway lines along which ran a travelling overhead gantry with block and tackle. This was used to lift off the heavy tops of the purifier boxes, one at a time, so the old iron oxide could be dug out and replaced with new material. The ground round the purifiers was covered with a deep brown red material, - the spent oxide. The purifiers my Dad used to tell me were used to remove the worst of the smell of the gas where layers of very damp iron oxide absorbed much of the sulphur, which otherwise became hydrogen sulphide, a toxic gas. From here gas went to the holders for storage ready for use.

A typical small Carburetted Water Gas (CWG) plant similar to the one in Ely. An enriched gas was made from 'cracked' light petroleum oil and blended with the coal gas. The Ely plant looked very similar and was built about 1953. It had a capacity of 300,000 cubic feet of gas per day as compared with the vertical retorts with a capacity of 405,000 cu. ft/day

The two gas holders to the left, the south east that is, were of differing designs. The one immediately to the left was of the open lattice type, which was built first and the second of the enclosed sheet steel type. Both rose and fell depending on how much gas was in store at the time. The lattice framed holder looked the more attractive but I was never taken to that one. The more modern holder called a spirally guided type was built under my father's direction to meet the ever increasing demand for gas. I recall the day when he took me on top. Firstly, we had to climb the vertical narrow rung steel ladder up the side, no safety rails if I fell off! Then once at the top we walked out onto the steel dome which contained the gas. It felt quite solid but with a hollow ring rather like the noise of hitting a large empty steel tank. A good view was to be had from this elevated position, not least, of the bathing beauties lying in their swimsuits around the perimeter of the nearby outdoor swimming pool. Not a bad memory for a boy of 7!

The works as seen from the direction of the old swimming pool looking North West. The last gas holder to be built a spirally guided one is in the foreground (50,000 cu ft). Ferro Construction built the concrete base tank and Firth Blakeley the holder. To its right the earlier vertically guided gas holder (114,000 cu ft). Behind that is the vertical retort house surmounted by the small structure at the top of the retorts where the coal was tipped. Just to its left the chimney to the producer gas furnace and hiding behind that the lift shaft. The white walled building in the foreground was not I believe part of the works. The holders have just been painted.

Starr and Rignall Ely

Plan layout of the north yard in 1949

1	Old Coal Store	20	Works Foreman's House	39	Condenser Air Cooled
2	Continuous Vertical Retort	21	Overhead tar storage tank	40	Scrubber
3	Carburetted Water Gas Plant	22	No 1 Gas Holder	41	Scrubber
4	Boiler House + chimney	23	No 2 Gas Holder	42	Cockley Washer
5	Meter House later shower room	24	Purifiers	43	New Coal Shed Potters Lane
6	Exhauster House mess room	25	Catch Box	44	Valve Pit for Station Governor
7	Coal Floor over Underground Tar tank	26	New Purifiers	45	Valve Pit for Holder Inlet
8	Coke Screening plant	27	New Purifiers	46	Underground Liquor Store
9	Coke floor over underground Water Tank	28	Underground Liquor Store	47	Platform around purifiers
10	Shower Room (later a show-room) + Store over	29	Old Coal Shed Potters Lane	48	Pipe Storage Floor
11	Enquiry Lobby	30	Compressor House	49	Valve Pit outlet from holders
12	Office, Board Room over	31	Store	50	Underground Waste Water filter
13	Office, Board Room over	32	Tar and Liquor Store	
14	Meter Store	33	Oxide Floor	51	Lift
15	Calorimeter Room	34	Garage	52	New Purifiers
16	Governor Room	35	Weighbridge	53	Electro detarrer
17	Gas fitters workshop	36	Store Shed	54	New Scrubbers
18	Maintenance fitters workshop	37	Transformer for Detarrer	55	Air Raid Shelter
19	Booster House	38	W-WD Detarrer	56	The 'Garden"

Plan layout of the works following Nationalisation 1949

With details of High Pressure integration main from Cambridge and supply provisions for Littleport detail of which was probably added in 1958/9- See Governor House at bottom of plan.

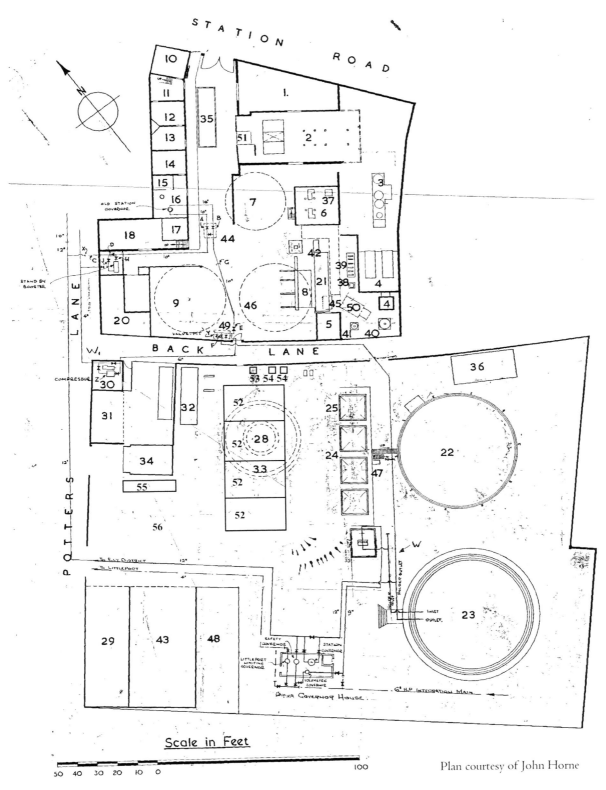

Scale in Feet

Plan courtesy of John Horne

Around the sides of the holder were water troughs which provided the gas seal and yet enabled the several sections of the holder to rise out of the ground unimpeded. It was rare to see a holder totally empty and I believe the City daily gas usage was enough to fill ½ or maybe ¾ of one holder. I know Dad always tried to fill both holders full just before Christmas day to ensure that there was sufficient gas to cook so many Christmas dinners. Most gas usage was for cooking rather than lighting. In addition, the stokers would not have to work flat out shovelling coal to keep up with the high gas demand. This enabled only one stoker to be on duty at any one time during Christmas day, instead of two.

Within the second yard were the scrubbers, purifiers and de-tarring plant. Gas from the retort was drawn by the exhauster pump and directed through the scrubber. Here water sprays, which I recall I could see through tiny portholes in the side of the steel case, were used to wash out some of the impurities and the water slowly became blacker and blacker turning into what was called 'gas liquor' an evil smelling concoction, which was disposed of into ponds and holes in the ground of any willing farmer prepared to take the stuff. Dad did try an experiment of using the material as a weak fertiliser and some volunteer farmer(s) were found to try out the material. I do not recall the outcome but know liquor is high in nitrates and may be a good many other things beside.

Before being distributed, gas was routed through the station governor which was situated within the office complex. Not a very sensible idea when one thinks about it. Within this small room was an inverted cast iron bell shaped dome which floated on a layer of water all contained within a larger cast iron vessel with a water seal much like a gas holder. This apparatus could be used to reduce in graduations the pressure of the gas from the holders as it was released onto the district. It was a silent piece of equipment and there was nothing exciting about it, but to say it was the seat of a fire which could so easily have destroyed the entire works.

Also on the south side of the site was the air raid shelter, a steel tube laid horizontally, with doors at one end and bench seats running along both inner sides for staff to sit on and 'sit out' a feared air raid. The structure was camouflaged to some extent by being covered in soil which had an established grass sward on top. Next to it was what I called father's garden, a bit of surplus land which Dad had landscaped and seeded to grass. Between jobs the stokers would keep the grass cut with a push mower and it looked every bit as good as a well managed domestic garden. To one side of this was a large wooden shed/garage but I am uncertain as to what use was made of it, coal or vehicle storage perhaps.

Main yard looking from the works entrance in Station Road towards Gas Lane. To the right is the office block with the Company Board Room on the first floor. In the middle distance are two walls running parallel to Gas Lane dividing the works into two sites. Only the forward wall is visible. The small door in the walls enabled staff to move from one yard to another. Just over the top of the wall in the centre of the picture is the flat top of the electro deterrer and to its left the scrubbers. In the middle ground is an elevator used for stacking coke and to its left a pile of coal waiting to be shovelled into the mobile bogey truck used & taken in the lift to be tipped into the retorts. One can just see the white wall of the exhauster house to the left of the coal heap above which had the stokers wash rooms. The purifier beds are behind the elevator and the wall and are not visible. The last of the gas holders to be built is just visible hidden in part by the steel framework to the lift shaft. The door to the left is the one through which members of the public went through to pay their gas bills. The 30 ton capacity 30ft by 8ft weighbridge is in the foreground.

Drawn Paul Staniforth August 2006

Chapter 3

How the plant operated

The day to day running of the gas works was entrusted to a team of stokers who maintained a 24 hour watch of the plant. Their job was probably the dirtiest of all tasks performed by staff and physically demanding too. During the day two stokers would be on duty but in the afternoon and at night one man kept a silent vigil. Their task was to shovel coal from the yard floor into a battery propelled rubber-tyred truck which had a capacity of about ¾ ton. This pedestrian controlled vehicle was steered into the ground level of the retort house towards the lift, the type with open trellis steel cage doors which I recall I could see through as the lift ascended. I remember the occasions when I was treated to a ride to the top. Father would pull the heavy steel gates open to let us walk in. They had to be opened one at a time and the lift safety system prevented it working if the gates weren't properly closed. There was no electric light inside and shafts of daylight would flicker in as we ascended. There were four floors including the ground and top floor. As soon as Dad opened the cage doors at the top we were often greeted by a sudden blast of fresh, sometimes very cold air. The warmth of the retort house was sufficient to heat many homes and the contrast on feeling fresh often breezy air 60 feet up was sudden and my instinctive reaction was always to hold on tight lest I get blown off.

Taken from the top of the Vertical retorts looking south east with it is believed the railway rolling stock buildings in the distance, beyond which is the river Ouse.
The tall circular chimney was not Ely Gas Co property and may have been part of the Water Board sewage treatment plant. The rectangular chimney In front of the gas holder may have been part of the works. Gas Lane is just visible in the foreground

1937

The stoker task would be to 'run out' the truck on a gantry at the top of the retorts. There were four of them in my memory and usually only three would be in use at any one time. The three were sufficient to supply the needs of the town leaving the fourth available for maintenance which was undertaken at about two to three yearly intervals and comprised re lining or repairing the firebricks within the retort. A stoker would propel the truck over the top of a selected retort, open a steel door to the retort and coal would then be discharged through the bottom of the truck. With the retort top closed the stoker would return to the yard via the lift to repeat the operation.

It was also the stoker's responsibility to empty the retorts of spent coal, now coke from the bottom. A second smaller hand propelled truck was used to receive the coke. This held rather less than the coal bogey, say 1/3 ton and was pushed into position beneath one of the three operational retorts. Then, by turning a steel wheel about the size of a car steering wheel at the bottom of the retort a mass of hot coke would fall into the truck. The stoker had to be quick not to overfill the truck! This now hot load had then to be pushed a distance of 20 yards and tipped into the feed hopper which was below ground level, of the coke grader .

28

Between jobs the stoker would operate this machine. It comprised a petrol engine and bucket elevator which made a great amount of noise and would pick up the coke from the hopper and transfer it across a series of elevated wire screens of gradually diminishing sizes. The coke was shaken mechanically along its path and would be separated and fall into one of several walled sections dependent on the sizes of the pieces, much as we would screen and separate gravel today. The really fine material known as breeze had no commercial value and every effort was made to mix some of the breeze with coke to use for steam raising. Ely was one of the few works in the country to use a breeze burning furnace in part because they were difficult to control, but it saved energy and added to the efficiency of the works.

Most of the surplus coke was sold to coke and coal retailers for later sale to the public and their coke was unsorted and stacked in a huge heap by means of a very tall petrol driven elevator in what was Benton's Yard. Meanwhile the graded material, a little of which was used either to fire the retorts, was put into sacks, weighed and sold direct to the public. Just after the Second World War when fuel allowances were limited, citizens eked out their fuel supplies by coming to the works on a Saturday morning with prams, pushchairs and home made carts to buy loose coke which was scooped up with a large tined fork and weighed out with a set of portable tipping scales.

Sometimes my father would walk up or down the retort house rather than use the lift. This I found immensely frightening but exciting at the same time. The steel stairs were made of open mesh tread between which, as a small boy, I could easily have slipped. Any way, I didn't, but I kept pretty close to Dad for I couldn't miss out on the excitement. Everything was covered in a black grime, much like a coal mine. Certain parts of the plant were very noisy particularly at ground level which I was told was the Producer Gas plant. Lastly, I must not omit mention of the heat in the building. It was always very warm in winter and roasting hot in summer. Heat emitted from the sides of the retort shafts, which inside were operating at 1,300 °C, made the first and second floors very hot places to be in.

Gas from the retort was sucked via what was called the 'ascension pipe' by one of two steam driven pumps located in a dedicated building near the coke grader called the Exhauster House. I so loved going in this building. It was always warm and I recall the timber floor. The engines were made of cast iron and massive by modern standards. Each had a flywheel of about 4 feet diameter connected to a piston driven by steam. Unlike a steam railway engine the exhauster pumps were very quiet but they did make a lovely rhythmic throb as the flywheel spun round controlled by a lifting ball centrifugal governor mounted on the top. In later years I have often wished I had taken measures to buy one of the engines when the works was dismantled, but what would I have done with it and how could I have ever made it work again?

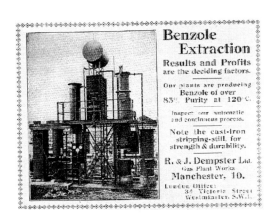

Schematic diagram to illustrate the
varying plant and processes used in gas manufacture

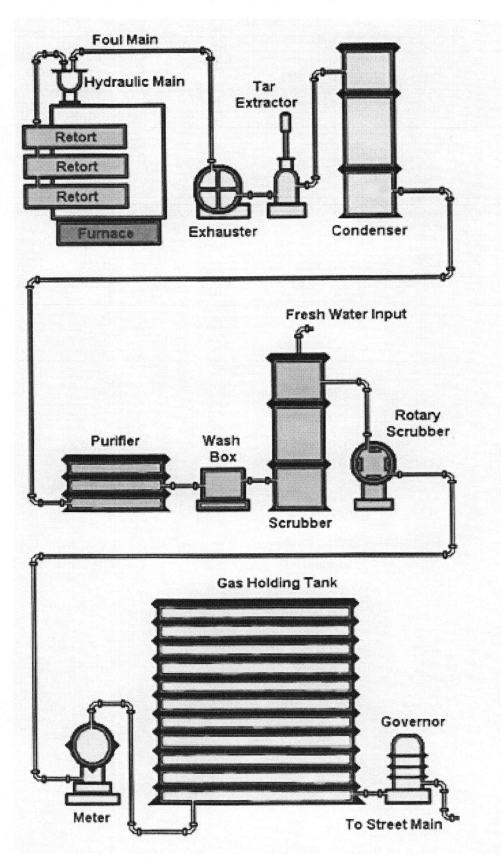

1. Board Room and Managers Office

2. Store over Showroom below

3. Access for visitors to General Office to pay gas bills, buy coke or gas mantles

4. Meter store later offices

5. Access to Calorimeter Room and Foreman/ Assistant Engineer's office

6. Station Governor located in here when the works nearly caught fire.

7. Fitters workshop built here in 1908

8. Valve pit to Station Governor

9. Gasholder. The third to be built- A very early design

Photograph courtesy of Mike and Lorna Delanoy and probably taken by Star and Rignol

The main office block constructed in 1903 at a cost of £500. Station Road is to the right and a building on the north side of that road is just visible. Potters Lane runs behind and parallel to the office block. Bensons Yard is immediately to the left occupied in part by the gas holder which was demolished in 1937. The weighbridge has not yet been installed. The retort house is to the right of the camera man. A small stack of coal is visible in the foreground and coke to the right. The works clock hangs in the window. Date of photo 1903-1908, probably 1903/4.

Flow diagram to illustrate: -

The route of coal and coke to and from the works gas production,

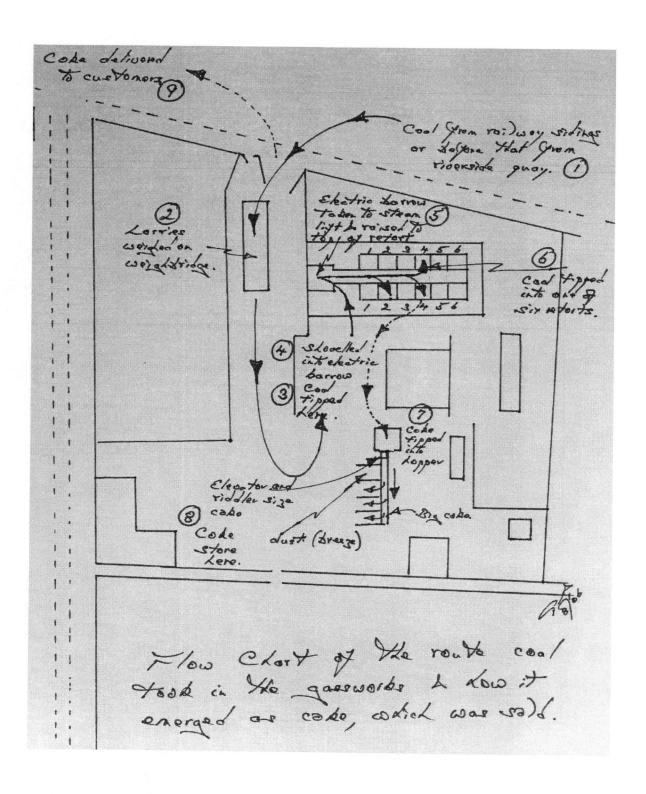

Paul Litton-North ELY GASWORKS YARD – about 1950

My memories of the main yard looking north to the main entrance with the houses of Clayhythe and Gas Green in the distance. To the left, was the office block with the iron weighbridge just in front. A large pile of coke stands on the left. To the right is the towering vertical retort house next to which is the open lattice framework of the lift shaft. The vertical retorts are just visible through the entrance to the building. The coal for the retort in the centre of the picture was tipped by lorry as close as possible to the entrance to the retort. To the right, is the coke breaker and screening machine which riddled the coke into separate bunkers according to size. The battery driven pedestrian steered coal truck is in the foreground.

33

The Exhauster House
Starr and Rignall Ely

1. Overhead steam pipes

2. Cast Iron Flywheels

3. Gas discharge from pump to scrubber, purifiers meter and holders

4. Steam engines each with a single large piston operating the exhausters pumps

5. Rising ball governor

6. Exhauster pumps Waller/Dempster

7. Pressure regulator for gauging vacuum on ascension pipes from the retort like a mini gas holder.

8. Just visible through the window, the south end of the office block. and the outside stairway/ hand rail up to the wash room above the exhauster house.

34

Chapter 4
Characters I remember

There was an enormous amount of checking and documentation of the operation of the plant undertaken in part by the stokers but I suspect mostly by the company engineer a Mr Eric Ardron. I didn't see very much of him but I was always fascinated by his hobby of making model planes which he flew by radio control. Quite a sophisticated interest in the 1950's. Anyway it was his task to ensure gas production proceeded smoothly and the plant operated at maximum efficiency. Indeed, it is partly due to him that the Ely Works was rated year on year as the most efficient of the small works in the Eastern Counties. My father received the praise but his right hand man deserves some credit as well.

My father used to explain to me that it was essential the retorts were maintained at their most efficient operating temperature for the extraction of as much gas from the coal as possible. It was Mr Ardron the assistant engineer who had the technique off to a tee. Much to Dad's jovial annoyance because Ardron wouldn't tell him how he did it. Basically, as I remember, the temperature of the red hot retorts had to be measured regularly with an instrument known as a hot wire pyrometer. It was used as follows: Each retort had a small say 2" diameter sighting hole in the side. One of these would be opened, and the instrument placed next to the orifice in in such a position that the user could look through a small optical viewfinder and simultaneously see the glow of the retort behind. Inside the optical part of the instrument was a thin wire which using battery power could be made to glow. By adjusting a rheostat on the pyrometer the electrical current could be varied so the wire glow with equal intensity to that of the retort. From the dials a temperature of the retort could be measured. This was the easy bit which my father like Ardron could accomplish. Adjusting the temperature was another matter and more akin to 'black magic' than refined technology. Nearby was a firebrick in the wall of the retort which was movable using a long iron rod. My father would either push or pull the brick an inch or so. How it worked I have no idea but I guess it may have controlled the air flow to the flames of the producer gas furnace and operated rather like a the air inlet on an enclosed solid fuel stove. He never did master the trick but tried very hard to emulate Mr Ardron who was fittingly so master of the gas plant for which he was responsible.

A presentation by Mr Hunter-Rioch (my fathers boss) to Mr William Taylor to mark 28 years service and retirement. He was congratulated on his recent marriage. He had just moved to 26 Station Road.

To the left the manager Mr Staniforth and to the right a very young Mr Ardron, Engineering Assistant.

Ely Standard 24 July 1953

The retorts were heated to their very high temperature by burning producer gas which was made in a separate piece of plant called a Producer located near the foot of the lift shaft. It made a great deal of noise. Its fuel was coke and the resultant inflammable gases produced were piped to burners alongside but integral with the retorts where they burnt at a much higher temperature than the earlier coke hearths could achieve.

Another of Mr Ardron's tasks was to check the calorific value of the gas at regular frequencies. The calorific value is the scientific term for the heating capacity or richness of the fuel. The task of the works manager was to produce gas which just and only just complied with statutory legislation which specified the minimum standards which must be maintained. An inspector from the Board of Trade, would call regularly and check the laboratory tests and reported findings which Mr Ardron maintained. The Inspector's visits were always greatly feared as the works could be fined very heavily for infringement. To my knowledge, they were only once found wanting in the gas quality, but the visits of the inspectors kept everyone on their toes.

Ely Standard Friday 10th 1953

To do this work, Mr Ardron had, in addition to his office, a small laboratory with a range of copper calorimeters, Bunsen burners, glass tubes, bottles and thermometers. He also undertook regular checks on the amount of sulphur in the gas. In addition to recording gas quality, a huge register was kept and updated several times a day with such information as, temperature of retorts, gas produced, gas pressure on the inlet main, pressure on the district main supplying the public, height of both gas holders signifying gas in storage, 'make' of gas in the proceeding period taken from the station meter and so on. This my Dad checked on most occasions when he took me with him to the plant to ensure everything was running correctly.

The company secretary was a man called Mr Secker, a quiet, gentle and, I believe, extremely reliable member of staff. He laboured away writing lots of letters, I don't know what about and Dad frequently mentioned him over meal times when I was little.

Most of the revenue for the works came from the sale of coke and gas. Most people had a prepaid gas meter and these would have been emptied by a visiting Collector at regular intervals. For those with non pre-pay meters the same inspector would take a reading from which Miss Redman would raise an invoice. Miss Redman was a clerk who was responsible for collating all the payments and sending out bills. She was on duty whenever the works was open. A customer entering the works to pay a bill would knock on her small office window, there upon, she would slide back the window and speak to the caller, take money, answer queries and even sell you a gas mantle. These came in varying sizes the Bijou and Number 2 being the most frequently requested sizes. Miss Redman doted on my father, almost worshipped him, but sadly she contracted cancer and died. She liked me very much and would always talk to me through her funny sliding window.

Whilst my parents were at work, (my mother taught history at Ely Grammar School opposite St Mary's church), I was cared for by Ken and Grace Thorne. I addressed Grace as Nanny and spent my days with her at New Barns Avenue where she lived at No22. Their Council home was lit by gas and I recall of an evening Ken returning from the sugar beet factory and lighting the light. A chain to one side of the pendant glass bowl was pulled, so turning on the gas and a lighted spill offered up to the gas mantles which would go 'plop' as the gas lit and after a few seconds later the gas mantle emitted a warm glow. They were both quite frightened of gas but Grace did cook her Welsh Girdle Cakes on one of two separate gas rings [see insert] but oven cooking was done with a paraffin heated oven.

A gas ring of a type used by my nanny together with an all rubber flexible connection pipe with push fit

Of all the gas fitters working for dad, the one I knew best and who was a clear favourite was Mr Partridge. He was a jovial, well built gentleman who was always clad in a pair of dungarees. He, like all the fitters would go from job to job around Ely fitting new gas appliances. Transport for fitters was by bicycle and each carried on his handlebars a big canvas bag some 28" long full of tools, copper or brass pipe solder, a methylated blowlamp and pliers and assorted spanners. My memories are of Mr Partridge steadily pedalling along balancing his load and always with a cherry smile for me and a courteous hello for my Mum. He came to our house many times to install appliances.

Most mischievous of all was probably Mr Harry Martin, a fitter who also came to our house at 23, Orchard Estate near the RAF Hospital. He did his tasks well but nearly always had a cheeky crack to make with all who he met.

160 FAMOUS COUNTY RECIPES

Chapter 5
Our home and its gas appliances

The principal perks of my father's job, and there were many, were his entitlement to as many gas appliances at no cost as he could cram in his house and free gas to power them together with coke for Christmas. As a result we had everything from gas lights (as aback up system should the electricity fail) to a gas iron, pokers to clothes drying cabinets for nappies. Geysers for hot bath water and an Ascot for sink water, a fridge, radiant gas fires in four rooms, a Live Water Washing Machine and, of course, a gas cooker. We had everything that was going 12 appliances as I recall including a Halcyon warm air heater a modern innovative heater in it's time. Dad did tell me he had seen a gas fired radio but he did stop short of acquiring one!

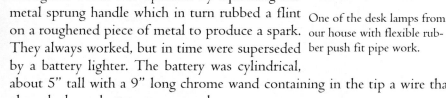

One of the desk lamps from our house with flexible rubber push fit pipe work.

Ignition of our gas appliances was nearly always done with 12" long white wax tapers which were lit from the pilot light of the Ascot. In the bedrooms we used a flint lighter which was operated by squeezing the metal sprung handle which in turn rubbed a flint on a roughened piece of metal to produce a spark. They always worked, but in time were superseded by a battery lighter. The battery was cylindrical, about 5" tall with a 9" long chrome wand containing in the tip a wire that glowed when a button was pressed.

A Gas Radio in the John DoranLeicester Gas Museum. The 'gas' parts in the foreground with the loudspeaker behind.

Not all these appliances were very effective and by current day standards of health and safety positively dangerous. The gas iron whilst a great improvement on the earlier cast flat irons, which were left on the top of the stove or later gas cooker to heat up, it had one major drawback. Carbon soot particles which developed round the gas jets always fell off onto the very washing one had just cleaned. The gas poker used in our solid fuel stove worked well at igniting the coke, but it was continually burning away at the tip and having to be replaced. Both these appliances relied on a flexible initially rubber tube from the gas tap to the appliance, but a later version did have a spirally wound metal sheath around the rubber. Woe betide anyone using such an appliance should the rubber hose become detached from the tap by an inadvertent tug. The whole house could go up in flames!

The washing machine made of a non corroding copper encased in sheet steel was also fired by gas which heated the water tub. Agitation of the soap suds was achieved with a lever which projected out of the top of the appliance, hard work, the modern equivalent of the 'wooden dolly stick' with which Nanny used to clean

Ken's overalls. A tap at the bottom enabled the dirty water to be drained into a bucket to be tipped into the sink. A cast iron framed mangle used for squeezing the water out of the clothes was mounted on the side of the tub and very cleverly it folded up when not in use and disappeared in the washtub. It had a long crank handle for turning the wooden rollers which did what a spin drier does today but nothing like as well. My mother didn't like the washing machine and who can blame her and preferred to send our clothes to the Ely and District Laundry barely ¼ mile up the road. The drawback to the washing machine was that all the flue gasses entered the kitchen which today we would call carbon monoxide poisoning. Indeed, few gas appliances in those days had a flues excepting fixed fires and most, but not all, water heaters, so we breathed much of the products of combustion discharged into the house.

The Electrolux gas fridge which used very little gas was extremely reliable but it did need to be defrosted at regular intervals. Hot water for the sink came from an Ascot water heater, wall mounted just above the sink. Bathwater came from the C28 Circulator, the forerunner of central heating which was flued and effective but ignition was always a problem. We lit it with a 12" long wax taper. If the bi-metallic strip controlling the pilot light malfunctioned, which it did daily, turning on the full flow of the gas before lighting the by-pass, then ignition was accompanied by a loud explosion audible throughout the house. I recall sticking a small 2"*2" advertisement from Prudential Insurers which I found in a stamp book over the ignition hole where my father would find it when he did his next a light up. He was not amused!

The gas lights were in the lounge. Three of them, one a standard light and two table top lights were all enveloped in fabric light shades like an electric light today. They were only rarely lit usually on the nostalgic whim of my father. They gave a quaint wispy light, more orange than the electric lights but most noticeable we could hear the gas whistling through the air jets on the way to the gas mantles. mother hated the gas lights as the flue products which came into the room blackened the ceilings. Indeed the heat from the lights not only smelt, but was sufficient to heat the room.

We all loved the Rainhill gas cooker. It was white and blue enamelled. Again my father somehow managed to get at no cost, a brand new cooker for his wife shortly after they got married during the Second World War. He certainly knew how to pull strings. What we particularly liked about the cooker was the taps situated under the hob. They were of a lever design but most significantly as they were turned from full on - to off, the array of gas jets would reduce to only four which then slowly diminished in size. The taps enabled very accurate control of the flame size and the simmering of pots was extremely easy. The small oven had a door hinged to the left with a big knob and a mechanism which latched the door shut, rather like a gate. The oven was maintained at a constant temperature with a device called a 'regulo' which was positioned outside the oven on the right hand side. Come to think of it the oven tap was next to the regulo, not as one would find it today next to the hob taps. Cookery guides

"NEWHOME" COOKER WITH EXTRA WIDE OVEN, IN GREY MOTTLED ENAMEL. ALSO "WATER" GREEN AND "NANKING" BLUE SELF-COLOURS

In 1938 the manager instigated a special promotion of GLC enamelled cookers later to be named the ELY No 1 at a rental of 1d per day.

always gave an oven temperature on a scale of 'regulo setting 1-9. Eventually the cooker was superseded by a cream coloured New World cooker, much larger than its predecessor also built of cast iron, unlike pressed steel cookers made today.

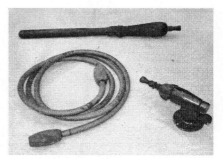

The five gas fires were all very different. The most used was the living room fire in the back room which was called a 'Radiant'. It was a dull gold in colour and made of cast iron. Unusually its ceramic elements were horizontal bars about 10" long there probably being about 9 in number. Periodically these would fracture because of incessant heating up and cooling, and had to be replaced. The front room contained an open coke grate on which we had an open 'coke' fire at

One of our surviving Gas pokers with flexible spirally wound steel pipe with push on rubber connectors and next to it a quick release fitting for detaching it from the permanent house pipe work.

Christmas. A built in ignition system, much like a built in poker, enabled very quick lighting of a coke or for that matter a coal fire. For most of the year a gas fire stood in front of it. The flue had been extended from the fire so products of combustion did go up the chimney. The 8 or so ceramic radiant were vertical, about 10" high and 1" across. They were like hollow tubes, the front

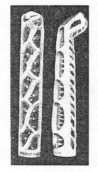

bit of which was like an open lattice so the radiant heat 'shone' into the room. The illustration shows a vertical radiant made of fireclay which was fragile and easily broken.

My parent's bedroom had an identical fire whilst the back bedroom had a small 'built in' fire. Occasionally, we would also use a portable 'bowl' gas fire. The bowl of the gas radiant reflector was a half sphere, about 10" diameter with a shiny chrome inner reflective surface. In the middle was a carrot shaped ceramic heating element within which the gas flame would play. They were not very powerful and more significantly had no flue! They like the iron had a rubber pipe from the gas tap to the appliance.

Photographs of Walter Partridge at his retirement E.G. News 1987

This proliferation of appliances was, I imagined, seen as extreme affluence by our neighbours and necessitated regular visits by fitters to install them. As a small boy I had a natural bent for mechanical things and would sit with the fitters as they plied their trade. Walter or Mr Partridge, as my mother called him, always fascinated me with his blowlamp which was fuelled by mentholated spirits. Attached to the small burning wick was a steel pipe of 1/8 inch diameter to which was attached a rubber tube which he placed in his mouth. By blowing down the tube he could direct the flame onto the lead joint he was preparing. To my intrigue, he could blow constantly down the tube and like a trombonist take breaths at the same time so maintaining a constant blue flame on the solder joint to be wiped. Only forty years later did I read that Mr Par-

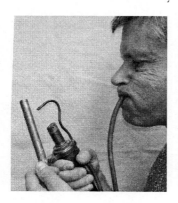

The Author with a similar meths blow-lamp to that used by Walter Partridge. The fore runner of the modern butane gas blowlamp.

tridge did play the euphonium! Mr Partridge and Harry Martin did nearly all our domestic work which even extended to erecting a clothes line comprising two gas pipes held vertically at each side of the garden each with pulleys mounted at the top to enable the line full of clothes to be hoisted like a ships bunting.

As if our house hadn't got enough gas associations, I should not omit the garden. My father loved gardening or to be more precise, looking at flower gardens, for he was no good at actually growing things. To satisfy his interests he employed Townsend of Fordham to dig up the entire garden, front and back and landscape it and finally plant it up with shrubs, herbaceous plants and bulbs, a very expensive luxury in those days. The front garden at No 23 Orchard Estate, Ely, had a natural depression about 18" deep in the middle for most of its length and he capitalised on this by having a sunken garden constructed with retaining walls about 2' tall built in sweeping curves. The grass was in the sunken bit and the flowers round the perimeter. The walls, believe it or not, were made from disused silica bricks from the retort house of the gas works. They were hard and excellent at frost resistance.

Ely Standard 13th May 1949

Like most managers my father was entitled, I discovered to yet more perks, the most financially advantageous of which was, free rental and rates on the property the family occupied. Additionally, we had provided not one, but two telephones, the second being in the bedroom, justified no doubt on the grounds that father could be contacted in an emergency, which did actually happen. My mother took a very passive role in affairs concerning the gas works and confined herself to stipulating we had an ivory white phone in the bedroom, very unusual instead of the standard black phones, none of which had buttons or even dials which we know today. Calls were very expensive and a 'trunk' call, meaning a long distance call to grandparents in Yarmouth or Portsmouth cost two shillings and six pence for three minutes at which moment the three 'pips' would sound to tell callers their time was up and any excess time would incur an additional charge.

41

Chapter 6
Childhood memories of my Father

My father was the only person on the works staff who had a car. The Gas Company owned 66% of its value and my father the remaining 34%. He would, from time to time, drive around the small City of Ely to see how work was progressing with the many projects he initiated. In the evening he used to make a point of checking that all the gas lights were working and during the day he would drive round checking on the progress of repairs to gas leaks, occasionally taking me with him. When leaks were being repaired the smell of the escaping gas was very pronounced. I must have taken a shine to watching men digging holes in the road as I recall how they used to do it.

Lamb Corner as we called it was the most frequent place for main fractures. There was so much heavy traffic turning at the traffic lights next to the Lamb Hotel on its way down the A10, that the cast iron pipes beneath the tarmac were for ever cracking. Repair was made worse by the proximity of the excavations to the traffic lights at what must have been the busiest spot in the town.

25 YEARS IN THE GAS INDUSTRY

Father receives his 'gong' for 25 years service to the Industry- a Certificate.

Ely Guardian 2 April 1954

The task of locating a leak was not very refined. Firstly, every effort was made to narrow down the search area by human smell. Having confined the search zone to say 10 yards of piping, holes were driven through the tarmac pavement or road with a long handled hammer and a steel spiked chisel of about 2' length. An instrument was then set atop of each hole in turn about the size of a Faraday Gas lantern and with this the strongest gas concentration could be determined. Main layers would then proceed to dig up the road with pick axes and shovels to expose the main, hopefully, in the right place, to find the fracture.

Once found, a by-pass pipe would be temporarily installed to enable the repair work to proceed without disrupting the supply and cutting off consumers. To do this, holes would be drilled in the cast pipe a yard or so above and below the crack. The holes were then threaded to take the temporary pipe which bridged the fault. Once complete, a further two holes would be drilled one below and a second above the bridging. Into each of these would be stuffed a pigs bladder, sown up, of course. Once in, these were inflated with air, like a balloon, to seal off the gas supply and enable the damaged section of pipe to be removed and replaced whilst the temporary by-pass ensured continuity of supply.

The rear yard formerly an orchard looking east from the corner of Gas Lane hidden by the wall to the left and Potters Lane. The structure in the foreground is the bed of Purifiers running alongside which was an overhead gantry and pulley block system for lifting the heavy steel tops off to replenish the iron oxide.

Just beyond the door in the wall, which lead to the main yard, is the electro de-tarer housed in a brick building, which my father refers to as being potentially lethal if mishandled. Beyond that were two scrubbers for washing the gas with water producing the infamous Gas Liquor.

To the right is the last holder to be erected. As it sank into the ground it gradually rotated in a spiral fashion. The other gas holder rose and fell guided by the four lattice steel framed towers.

The retort house is clearly visible towering above the wall to the left.

One of the principal users of gas in the town was the Ely City Council who contracted the Gas Company to light the City's streets at night. It was therefore necessary to regularly check the functioning of each light. By the time I was born all the lights had been switched over to clockwork driven mechanical lighting systems so the days of the gas lamp lighter had long since gone. So valued was this contract that the glass sides of the gas lights were regularly cleaned and at the same time the clocks would be wound at, I believe fortnightly intervals. The gas lighters engaged for this purpose would cycle around town with their short wooden ladders balanced on their shoulder, steadied by one hand, whilst they used their other hand to steer and balance their bicycle. On the handlebars they balanced their bucket of water and glass cleaning cloths. They seemed as I remem-

43

ber to pedal round effortlessly in fact they seemed to have a grace in how they 'set off' from a standing start and pedalled down the road.

The gas lights down Lynn Road were spaced out at greater intervals between lights than in the centre of town and along Orchard Estate there was either just one or certainly no more than two lamp standards. I remember how the lights used to slowly flicker maybe about ten times a minute. My father told me this was because of trapped water which had settled inside the gas pipe, condensed from the gas itself, and which would move within the pipe rather like the tides in the oceans so causing the flickering. I think they sucked it out from time to time, possibly where it settled at purpose made road siphons.

When the gas lamps were eventually dismantled, to be replaced by electric lighting, I asked my Dad if for nostalgic reasons, he would keep a gas standard, the post that is, together with its gas light. He agreed and told me he had put two aside. A fortnight later, I was told that the scrap metal merchant had called at the works to collect all the redundant street lights and seeing two lamp posts set to one side, picked them up and added them to the scrap he was taking away. I was so sorry that I never did get my lovely copper lamp on what today would be a very short lamp post with its two projecting arms near the top for the lamp lighter to lean his ladder on.

The largest gas consumer by far was the Royal Air Force Hospital situated on Lynn Road. Its usage was so high for those days that a separate high pressure pipe was laid to serve the hospital needs. A separate meter house was built for the purpose and periodically my Dad would, as it was close to our house in Orchard Estate, go across before mid-day lunch to read the meters. I used to accompany him on these brief forays.

It is worth recording that as I became proficient at pedalling my trike, my parents entrusted me to cycle on my own, aged about 8 from Orchard Estate to Cross's Shop, what we would call a 'Convenience store' today, located on Lynn Road opposite the alleyway to New Barnes, in order to buy provisions my mother had run out of. By age ten, I had a Humber bicycle and was allowed to cycle on my own all round the town. Probably my most responsible errand then was to 'pay in' my mother's school teachers pay cheque to Lloyds bank, a task I did many times feeling enormously important.

1953 saw the Coronation of the young Queen Elizabeth II and the country rejoiced in celebration with street parties the length and breadth of the land. Ely was not alone and I recall my father acquiring from somewhere a large supply of flags and bunting with which to decorate either the gas showroom in High Street or the works frontage. We had so many flags that the surplus came home and were artistically draped over the porch to our front door. I got to keep a large white ensign, fitting, I thought, as my mother's father had fought at the battle of Jutland.

For reasons that I cannot remember the works lift had a major service, indeed, it may have been rebuilt or enlarged taking several weeks. Mindful that its daily operation was essential to enable recharge of the retorts, then alternative measures were planned by my father. To do this a scaffold was erected on the south side of the retort house right up to the top. It was of sufficient size to support a small petrol driven lift, compromising an open platform with no sides, large enough to hold just one wheelbarrow. With the main lift out of commission this makeshift arrangement was used to convey wheelbarrow loads of coal to the retorts. With one stoker at the bottom replenishing empty barrows, and a second at the top wheeling the barrows off , tipping them into the hoppers and back to the lift, two men were able to fuel the retorts as fast as Ely citizens burnt the gas produced, so maintaining continuity of gas supply to the City for a month or so.

This was not the only improvement project that I recall in my infancy. One day my father announced that on Saturday morning a mobile crane was coming to the works to lift two tanks into place and I was to come with him to watch operations. This was an unusual treat and we duly drove to the works, parked up and walked through to the second site beyond Gas Lane. Here a large, very large in those days, mobile crane had been positioned near the purifiers. In the intervening weeks, I had seen on several occasions several brick piers being built with a concave top cradle into which the tanks were to be lifted. When all was ready the crane started to lift the tanks, delivered on an equally large low-loader, on to the cradles. It seemed that a lot of gas staff although not on duty, turned up to watch what was an unusual event. I believe there were even some members of the public from Potters Lane who crept in the works yard to watch the excitement. The tanks were to be used for the storage of gas liquor.

My father enjoyed many perks to his job. The most public of which must have been his car. Whilst gas lighters were peddling cycles around town and fitters pushing a truck laden with gas cookers up Back Hill, the manger was enjoying the luxury of a Standard 14 which he drove to work each day and parked in the road outside the show room window. The car, black, they were all black in those days, did not have a heater, a luxury only afforded to the few limousines, non of which existed in Ely in those days. Not to be beaten Dad did have an electric heater especially made which worked off a second battery stored in the floor well behind the driver. Its size necessitated lowering the floor well which made the car prone to grounding and hitting bumps in the road. I can recall many times calling out to my father as we drove over rough ground, "Mind the battery box".

Use of a Company car (KVX 852) gave Dad an automatic entitlement to Petrol Rations during World War II and the Suez Crisis. These he used very frugally but somehow he managed to drive to work each day. When rationing was lifted he drove home for lunch too. To the left is a sheaf of ration books which he chose not to redeem to support the country through the acute fuel crisis.

In time my father decided to replace his Standard 14, the one with a crank handle if the battery failed, with a shining brand new Vauxhall Wyvern (CJE 865), which had no crank handle. He bought it from Henleys Garage London for £800, 66% of the cost being funded by the gas undertaking. It sported a bench seat at the front and steering column gear change. This enabled room to be made for me to sit on the front seat on top of a hassock, between my parents, so I could see out of the window which I loved. No seat belts in those days! As I grew older (8-9) this unashamed luxury became an embarrassment as my parents would occasionally, when it was raining, take me to school in the car, driving past some of my playmates who lived further down the road who had no alternative but to walk the mile to school.

A further memory I recall was the periodic trips we would have on a Saturday afternoon to go and see the gas liquor pond into which my father had gained permission to tip the gas liquor. This arose when the fields were wet at a time when it became extremely difficult to dispose of this obnoxious product and one of the Directors had agreed to accept the material on his farm. Father claimed business usage for visiting the site to check that rain had not overtopped the pond and Mum and I went along for the ride. It was only when we used the car for family occasions dad had to reimburse the company for private mileage.

Not content with one car, my Father started up a taxi service in Ely. He employed two people as drivers and confined his commitment to financing the purchase of two cars rather than day to day running of the business. He told me the venture was not a success and sold the cars neither of which I can actually remember.

One story I recall my father recounting concerned the Works 'clock-in clock' which was attached to the wall near the fitter's workshop. When coming on duty at the beginning of their shift stokers, fitters and manual staff had to insert their time card in a slot in the clock where it was automatically franked with the time and date. This procedure was repeated when staff finished their shift or overtime. The time cards measuring about 3" by 2" were stored next to the clock. The cards of all the staff were collected weekly so the wages clerk could calculate the wages due to each individual for the time they had worked.

Realising the old clock had seen better days my father bought a new clock. The old clock was put out for scrap but one of the stokers asked if he could have it, to which Dad agreed. All went without hiccup until one day my father noticed that one stoker who should have been on duty was not about the yard but more worryingly Dad found his docket had been stamped to say he was present. Father was not slow to realise that the person to whom he had given the old works clock was franking his dockets at home. Amused by the workman's guile, Father summoned him and extracted a full confession whereupon my father demanded the return of the old time piece to prevent further temptation.

Catching his staff out when committing misdemeanours was not unknown. I recall the conversation over evening dinner one day when my father full of laughter recounted how he had 'caught out' one of his fitters. In the proceeding weeks he had had installed an intercom system throughout parts of the works, enabling him to talk to staff from his office, be they in the rest room, workshop, and other quieter parts of the works. Well, one day he had said something to one of the fitters which didn't go down very well. The conversation terminated and Dad returned to his office and the fitter to his colleagues in the workshop. Unbeknown to the fitter his colleagues had accidentally nudged the switch of the workshop intercom to 'on'. As a result the dialogue between the fitters having a gripe about my Dad was fully audible to my father in his office. He listened in for 30 seconds or so and then spoke over the intercom to the fitter with whom he had just had words suggesting he switch their intercom 'off'. There was stunned silence at the other end. They had been well and truly rumbled.

Before nationalisation gas was 'charged for' on a cubic foot basis but that later changed to a charge per therms used. In both cases all gas consumer consumption was measured volumetrically with a meter. This would have been either a 'slot' or pre-pay meter, as we would call it today or a standard meter. My 'nanny' living in New Barnes Avenue had a slot meter and I remember how it would clonk quietly as the mechanism inside slowly rotated as gas was consumed registering usage on a series of about 4 small external dials 1 inch in diameter. The meter would only accept one-shilling pieces and just before the money ran out the gas flame on a light would start to flicker and a cry

46

would go up "Quick! Have you got a shilling for the meter". If one was quick, a shilling inserted and a dial rotated the gas would continue uninterrupted. If one were slow, the supply would be cut off, and very often we had to go round to a neighbour to borrow a shilling and then needed a candle or accumulator to see to put the shilling in. Thereupon the gas light had to be re-lit.

Finally I feel it is worth recounting a story that happened in Cambridge long after my father had left Ely. One winter evening when I was seventeen, I came home from school clutching a pair of Start Rite shoes which my mother had just paid to have re-soled. Like any schoolboy of that age I was very absent minded and I put them down on the most convenient flat surface and went out. A little while later my mother, called out "What is that terrible smell? Paul go quickly and find out" To my horror and great shame I discovered I had put my lovely shoes on the top of the now very hot coke burning stove and the house was filled with the stench of burnt leather. The shoes had round holes in the new leather soles. I was extremely ashamed of myself. My mother was petrified my father would arrive home to discover my accident and that he would as usual go ballistic. In order to avert detection she instructed me to open every single window in the house. Not content with this she then proceeded to turn on several gas taps in the house. Within minutes the house reeked of gas whilst the coke stove was burning fiercely in the breakfast room. Minutes later a passing pedestrian knocked at the front door to advise us that we had left all the windows open on what was a cold night. Mother mumbled something and then proceeded to close the windows. Just as she had finished, my father arrived from his Gas Board office, smelt the gas and demanded to know what was going on. We had by then turned off the taps but my father, rightly so, - went ballistic after all. "What are you trying to do?" he balled, "Blow us up!" He never did discover the truth, we were too frightened to tell him. Although I felt extremely contrite at my actions, I never was rebuked by my mother. A minor accident which could so easily have turned into a tragedy with headline news in the local and probably the national press!

Which reminds me of another happening concerning my father. Well, one day we all sat down to mid-day lunch prepared by my mother. When setting the table she had added a bottle of vinegar as a dressing to the salad. My father sat down full of enthusiasm to tuck into his lunch. He rather overdid meals. As he reached out for the vinegar bottle which he was about to sprinkle on his salad, my mother suddenly realised she had hidden her secret supply of whisky in the vinegar bottle. "Oh Claude dear", she said, "don't use that, I forgot I have some much nicer white vinegar you should use"! Grabbing the bottle from his hand she fled into the kitchen to substitute the bottle contents for real vinegar. I should explain my father in his youth signed t'he pledge' meaning he was a teetotaller. My father never did know what happened. Again we were too scared to tell him.

Chapter 7
A brief history of the gas and Electricity Co
By Claude Staniforth

The discovery by Murdoch that an inflammable gas could be obtained by subjecting coal to intense heat in the absence of air gave the world a new and wonderful fuel and more flexible source of power which today has resulted in pipelines across the whole civilised west conveying gas, not only from coal, but from oil and reserves in the frozen north and the torrid wastes and now even from the ocean floor.

But first the implication of the discovery struck London and gas making was set up there to light the streets of the capital. The London and Westminster Gas Company (later to be called the Gas Light and Coke Company) was established in 1813 and one can reliably assume that Westminster Bridge was bright with gas light when the nation celebrated Wellington's victory at Waterloo. Soon the new vogue was sweeping the country as far as the remote fens of Ely, where a gas works was set up in 1835 by George Malam of Spalding.

The early days of the Ely Gas Company were far from calm. Five years later it was put up for sale, its income then being a mere £250 a year in rent. Apparently it was bought by a 'London Gas Company' and it settled down to a period of silent service.

But not for long. In 1868 a public notice announced a sale by auction under a 'distress' of all stocks of coal, coke, and tar. A rumour flew round the City (of London) that "gas was seized by fits" meaning a Sheriff's officer named Fitzjohn. However, the sale notice was withdrawn presumably because the 'distress' of the London gents had been relieved in some other way.

By now the local gentry were aroused to attempt to take over the gas concern and turn out the London 'foreigners'. Within two months a committee of local notables appointed Mr Muriel to confer with the London Gas Company, as an engineer, with a view to purchase.

The 'new' gas company decided to offer the old company £6,000 for the works and the whole outfit of mains etc. When this offer was rejected the new company threatened to build a rival works for an estimated £7,500. The London Company demanded £9,000 but reached no agreement.

Somewhere along the line the name was changed from plain 'Ely Gas Company' to 'The City of Ely Gas Company' for we learn in the local newspaper of 1880 that the City Of Ely Gas Company gave notice that they would apply to the Board of Trade for a provisional Order to supply Gas in Ely and enlarge and alter the works in Station Road. Nothing more is recorded in the local press of this aspiration. From now onwards until Nationalisation in 1949 the fate of the gas undertaking remained in the hands of the local shareholders and its history is an account of the varying fortunes usually associated with public utilities of the period.

Initially the purpose was to supply an illuminant for the streets and homes of the city. A 'batswing' or flat flame burner giving forth a yellow light was the characteristic form of illumination but when combustion technology advanced considerably Dr Bunsen found an intensely hot blue flame could be achieved by introducing some air required for combustion, prior to the burner nozzle and Von Welsbach used this discovery to invented the gas mantle which was dipped in a solution of thorium oxide. An incandescent light of considerable power was produced and gas became even more popular.

Yet not a minute too soon for electricity had been discovered, its method of continuous manufacture and distribution mastered and the electric light bulb invented. Then began the intense struggle between gas and electricity for the public's custom. Although the demise of gas was confidently predicted, still even today it is neck and a neck race in the realm of heating.

Wishing to profit from both sources of power the City of Ely Gas Company in1913 gave notice to the Ely Urban District Council of its intentions to apply to the Board of Trade for powers to generate electricity and distribute it within a radius of ½ mile of the "centre of the west gate of the cathedral". Two conditions were laid down before the approval of the Council could be given. The price per unit had to be reasonable and the whole work completed in five years. But on a vote the resolution was defeated.

The gas company besought the Board of Trade to dispense with the permission from the Local Council, which stung the same council into protestations that only the centre of Ely would be catered for, that no price per unit had been granted and that in any case efficient competition between the two services of power would be impossible if both were supplied by the same undertaker.

In response the Gas Company quoted a figure of 8d per unit and said that it was prepared to extend the cables to supply the whole of Ely, Stuntney and Chettisham all in vain. The council withheld consent and the Board of Trade refused to proceed with a provisional Order. Not many years after that, a public electricity supply was brought to Ely from the power station near Bedford. Meanwhile, the gas company had to rest content with the name only - The City of Ely Gas and Electric Company to which it had altered in anticipation of success.

Although real competition began between the two services of energy supply, the output of gas did not fall materially as a result, for in place of lighting roads, gas became more popular for heating, cooking, water heating, space heating and the odd gas engines (for a few years). Street lighting remained the public realm of combat. In 1934 when the Urban District Council were prepared to grant a 5 year contract instead of the annual one, the gas company relighted the centre of Ely with high powered lights and in the rest of the city, lamps were fitted with clocks, battery ignition and reflectors. The role of the lamp lighter on foot carrying his lighting pole had come to an end.

The siteing of a gas works is of great importance. Not only should it be at the lowest point of the area to be supplied but also easily accessible for receipt of coal and disposal of by-products. Hence the position of the Ely Gas works at the foot of Back Hill which enabled the gas pressure to seemingly rise 10% as it progressed uphill (due to the fall in atmospheric pressure). Also it was conveniently near the river from whence came coal in barges loaded at the Kings Lynn from coasters loaded at Goole in the Humber. When some years later the railway arrived at Ely and coal came by rail wagon, the works was near enough to the rail head to cut transport to a minimum.

Reliability of coal supplies, their quality and price were of fundamental importance. The miners strike of 1921 compelled the importation of Belgium Coal both inferior and dearer than Yorkshire

The Works Staff in about 1945

A The works staff photographed in front of the exhauster house above which was the mens' wash rooms. From left to right. Middle row Walter Partridge, unknown, Charles Secker, Claude Staniforth, either Jack Hacon or Mr Gould, Sid Merry. Front row all apprentices. Back row fifth from left Harry Martin, seventh from left Mr Binge. Flat capped staff are believed to be all stokers or under-stokers. For staff to be dressed in suits rather than work wear indicates this was a n unusual event to occur.

coal. The rail strike of 1924 failed to lower gas pressure thanks to the huge stocks of coal that had been laid down in anticipation. During the First World War, prices were controlled in 1915 by an Act of Parliament but in general the rate slowly increased from 13/6^d per tonne delivered to Ely station in 1886 to 35/1^d in 1923 although they drifted down to 26/6^d in the depression of the 30's. In part this was due to the company buying its own rail wagons so saving the rental on rail company's wagons.

The Coal Strike of 1926, (together with the General Strike), necessitated the importation of Silesian coal costing about twice as much as English fuels and then stocks fell from 9 weeks to 3 weeks usage. Coke stocks of 300 tons were abruptly cleared out after 8 weeks and it needed Government restrictions on gas usage to save the day, throughout the country. In general it was easy to sell unbroken coke until the erection of coke ovens in the Midlands which flooded all south east England with well graded coke at reasonable prices. This compelled the Ely works to install cutting and grading plant as well as one of the largest platform weigh bridges in the area.

Tar once assured of a ready market for road gritting came up against keen competition from imported asphalt and a dehydration plant had to be erected in Gas Lane. Even that was not enough and Prince Regent Tar Distillers at Peterborough took the surplus by rail tank, a 2" pipe being laid from the gas works to the rail head.

But the most intransigent problem was the disposal of gas liquor- or ammoniacal liquor to give it its correct chemical name. For many years it was piped to the riverside for loading onto special barges which took it to West Norfolk Farmers Manure and Chemical Company at Kings Lynn. Here the product was refined to produce ammonia sulphate a widely used fertiliser. was extracted and treated with sulphuric acid to form the popular farm fertiliser Ammonium Sulphate. In those days the gas liquor was not an inconsiderable source of income but when the Mond process became more widespread whereby ammonia could be derived from atmospheric nitrogen, the sale of liquor slumped. The Kings Lynn factory refused to take anymore. Neither was it possible to jettison it into the river for fear of killing off the valuable fish which were suffocated due to the deoxygenation of the water. Efforts were made to spray it onto agricultural land, untreated, to act as a cheap fertiliser. Every effort was made to reduce the quantity manufactured and at one time it was conveyed and pumped into a very large pit in the Fens out of harms way and with the consent of the farmer. But the problem was never satisfactorily solved until gas making ceased at the Ely works when they were supplied with gas from Cambridge.

Gas outputs slowly but steadily advanced until it became necessary to build a unit of vertical retorts (continuous) in 1927 and to shut down the horizontal retorts which had been shovel fired. The new plant was completely rebuilt and doubled in size a few years later. Gas making in 1900 was nearly 20 million cubic feet and on Nationalisation just over 100 million per annum.

Plans were in hand to double it's size yet again, when the State took over the ownership and a gas main laid from Cambridge gas works to meet the demand. By about 1960 the Ely works had ceased entirely to produce gas and nearly all of it was demolished.

Chapter 8
The Ely Gas works in action

The manufacture of town gas, until recent years, was based on the principle of subjecting coal to a temperature of 1000° C and above, in vessels sealed off from the air. Under such heat the coal substance broke down, about a third passing away in gaseous form and the rest remaining as coke, some of which is employed afterwards to heat the coal in the furnace sited under the closed vessels.

A bench of five retorts at Fakenham Gas Works, which would have been similar to those found at Ely.

These originally were horizontal fire brick retorts about 8' long, D shaped (the D lying on its back, the flat side) and supported along their length by vertical walls spaced about 2' apart to allow heat from the furnace beneath to rise and circulate around the body of each retort. The back end of each retort was sealed whilst the front end was fitted with an iron mouthpiece complete with openable door and off-take pipe.

In the first place such retorts were hand charged, the stoker shovelling coal from a barrow and throwing it into the blazing hot retort, a feat that required strength and skill as well as an endurance against the heat. When the lower half of the retort was filled, the door was closed and issuing gas was passed away by a vertical ascension pipe to a horizontal tank on top of the bench, through which flowed a stream of weak ammoniacal liquor. Some ammonia from the gas was dissolved and the heaviest tar was also deposited.

From here via the 'foul' main the gas proceeded to the condensers, usually air cooled to lower the temperature and brought down, meaning condensed, some more tar. From there the partially cleaned gas was drawn to the exhausters, steam driven pumps which proceeded to push the gas through the rest of the plant. First, there were the scrubbers which removed most of the remaining ammonia impurity as well as the tar that was left, then came the purifiers, boxes about 6' deep with 10' or more square sides.

Usually there were two layers of iron oxide here, supported on wooden grids. The oxide absorbed the hydrogen sulphide remaining in the gas, turning from black to brown in the process.

The now purified gas passed through the station meter which indicated its volume and so on to the gas holders which stored it. From there it passed out onto the district through a station governor which maintained an even pressure on the whole town system of mains, provided that they were of adequate size to cope with the maximum demands.

Such in brief, is the process but it is subject to many controls and adjustments to ensure, not only that there is no hold-up anywhere along the line to remove all impurities but also to guarantee the resulting product is of a certain heat calorific value to ensure steady burning in all the many types of gas appliance to be met with on the district. But for that, a rich gas would soot up cooking utensils, fires and water heaters and poor gas would 'light back' at the burners so giving out very little heat at all. Recordings were taken every hour and often between times when alterations in the controls have to be made.

A gas examiner called three times a quarter in a small works. He called without warning to test the heat value of the gas then flowing onto the district, its purity and pressure. Heavy penalties are laid on gas undertakings for the slightest deviation from the norm.

Over the century and a half of the British Gas Industry's life many changes were made. In the retort house of the largest works, retorts were doubled in length and fitted with a mouthpiece

Sketches of retort house workers 1880 courtesy of the late David Loverseed

and off-take pipes at each end. This permitted the use of a charging machine which pushed out the red hot coke at one end while admitting coal to replace it at the other. The extruded coke was guided to a water filled trough for quenching and conveyance. The furnace was redesigned so as to divide the combustion process into two stages. By restricting the initial air intake, producer gas was formed and led to flues to points adjacent to the retorts where the remaining air was admitted and the intense flame generated. Silicon bricks were introduced to permit high temperatures which enabled a greater yield per ton to be achieved.

But the greatest advances occurred when retorts were 'up-ended' so to speak. By erecting vertical retorts, coal could be fed in at the top continuously, no gas escaping or heat being lost. The charge would steadily slide down 20 odd feet of retort increasing in temperature for half of the length and then steadily and continuously discharge into cast iron coke boxes at the bottom the heat having been extracted by steam and finally water spray. Heat losses were halved at a blow and efficiencies raised from 50%-60% to 75%-80%.

At Ely, continuous retorts were installed in 1927 but as this was one of the very first small gas works to adopt this ultra modern plant, a serious mistake was made. There were only three large retorts built which allowed insufficient flexibility. Later these were pulled out and four smaller vertical retorts installed in the same retort house. With increasing popularity of gas two further vertical retorts were added.

Coke, the main by-product of the whole process was initially drawn red hot from the horizontal retort by the use of long rakes operated by sweating stokers. It had to be quenched there and then before it could be moved and this was done by buckets of water flung onto the blazing heaps - sending up clouds of steam. This quenched, but still very warm coke, was moved into the coke yard and sold to merchants and private users in its irregular lumps and sizes - from large pieces probably 6"-8" cube to ¾" cube or less.

When coke ovens in the Midlands started to sell well-graded coke, the Ely undertaking installed a coke grading machine itself consisting of a bucket elevator, crushing machine with spiked rollers and a reciprocating shaker supported on division walls so that the fuel could be separated into 'nuts'(¾"-1"¼"), broken (1¼"-2") and large (over 2"). Then what was left was sub-divided by an under-slung screen into (dust) 0"- ⅜, and large breeze (⅜"- ¾"). To make maximum saving the dust section was burned with unscreened coke in the producers and the large breeze on the Cornish Boilers. Should breeze appear in the nuts or broken the whole bunker was emptied and passed again through the screens. Such was the strict control exercised over the principal by-product. One merchant said it was the cleanest and most closely graded coke from any works in the country.

In the matter of purification, to completely eliminate tar vapour which used to get through the washing plant and even the oxide purifiers onto the district (to be picked up by the siphon emptier, who cleaned siphons in the street mains of condensate), an electric de-tarer was installed which worked at a very high voltage- several thousand volts - and had to be treated with great respect because of its lethal powers.

As gas outputs increased due firstly to the London evacuees who arrived in Ely during the Second World War and also the gas tariffs near the end of the war, it became necessary to increase the storage capacity. Another gas holder of the spiral type was built alongside the column guided holder. It was half as big again. The spiral guided holder was the only piece of works machinery left in operation when the works was pulled down in about 1960.

To improve pressure on the district a medium pressure gas main was laid from the works to the RAF Hospital, feeding back into the low pressure main at that end. Also Broad Street main was relayed. Many other streets saw the relaying of mains.

Provision of power was most important. The two original Cornish Boilers were supplemented by a waste heat boiler which extracted heat from the spent furnace products after heating the retorts and en route to the main stack. Eventually, electric power was also introduced.

Finally the efficiency of the Ely Gas Works was amongst the highest in the 'Nationalised' Eastern Gas Board and sometimes the very highest - topping 84%.

Coal gas was eventually replaced by natural gas- or North Sea Gas as it was called- but it is by no means certain that coal will not again be employed when natural gas is exhausted but the process will be very different. (With global warming I have my doubts Dad!)

Reverting to the performance of the Ely Works itself, one might well ask - in view of the description of the gas making plant revealing it was very similar in broad outline to other gas works using continuous retorts - How were the surprisingly high efficiencies achieved, which escaped the efforts of most of the other works?

The answer, I think, is that the very latest control equipment was installed which many other works (even the large ones) did not trouble to learn about or install, plus meticulous care over the use of these units. This must largely be credited to Mr Eric Ardron, Assistant Works Engineer.

Primarily profits are made in the retort house, i.e. the carbonising process, and to its perfection Mr Ardron and I bent our efforts. It is difficult to describe to the uninitiated general reader without going into technical details and using technical drawings. So I must generalise.

Firstly it is vital to have the right carbonising system. There have been stop ended retorts, 'through' retorts, horizontal retorts, inclined retorts, static retorts, vertical retorts and continuous vertical retorts. In my opinion the last named is easily the most manageable and efficient. These within limits can be speeded up and slowed down, to make varying volumes of gas per day.

The right size and number of retorts is also vital allowing 15%-25% of the plant capacity can be kept under heat as a standby

Clearly the quality of the coal is another vital factor. The Silkstone seam in South Yorkshire yields excellent gas making coal which not only has a high volatile content when carbonised but leaves a coke which is burnable and lively in domestic grates. Also the sizing of the coal is important. I found 2" doubles ideal. If smaller, the charge tends to 'hang up' in the retort; if larger is slides through too swiftly and comes out only partially carbonised.

The Ely retort plant was of an ideal size to suit the demands of the City for gas and experience had shown that coal from the Briley pit with a small addition of Maltby Main suited the plant.

But this was only the start. You can have a powerful and well-designed racing car, but unless it has very exact controls and is well driven, it will not be a winner. Temperature is all important in carbonisation. To get best results the flues on the outside of the silica retorts need to be about 1,400°C. To be on the safe side the makers specify 1,350°C – 1,380°C, for silica starts to soften at about 1,430°C and once this happens the retort inside surface forms very slight bulges which cause the descending coal charge to stick, causing the temperature to rise even higher and then one is in real trouble for the width of the retort is only ten inches

We ran the retorts at 1,400°C and the flue temperatures of each retort were read every morning, first thing and the results reported to me. To get these four temperatures (for each retort) to correspond within 10 degree Centigrade was an art which Mr Ardron had mastered and very few engineers ever do. If the temperature fell below 1,390°C I knew fuel efficiency was suffering. If they rose above 1,410°C I was alarmed lest irreparable damage was about to occur. We ran the works on our nerves.

One vital piece of equipment was installed on the entrance to the chimney stack, which is not often found on such retort systems. This was an outsize chimney damper which was so extremely sensitive that it would slightly open and close with as little variation in chimney pull (at the top of the stack) as 1/100th (one hundredth) of an inch water gauge, as much as a gentle breath. Thus, if a storm blew up in the night and there was a large increase in chimney pull, then the damper moved slightly towards the closed position - and all was safe - otherwise the heightened flue pull could burn out the retort plant in the night.

While extracting the most gas per ton from the coal, we also had to reduce to the minimum the coke used on the furnaces or producers as they were called. This was done by fitting doors in front of the step grates forcing air in by the steam jets. The pressure on these jets determined the quantity of producer gas made and so of coke used. The steam pressure had to be controlled by an exact steam regulator.

Further controls were achieved by dampers between the producers and retort flues, the whole being a precise balancing act.

To still further save coke consumption, fine coke dust from the coke screening plant was admitted to the producers but excess of this quickly dampened the fire and increased clinker formation. Coke breeze used to be sold at a low price for breeze block manufacture and to greenhouse owners was now consumed on the works saving valuable coke which would have otherwise been used to heat the producer.

Another unusual practice adopted at Ely was a modification to the Retorts. These furnaces are made of hundreds of silica bricks cemented together. During use and the inevitable heating and cooling of the structure, small cracks occur in the retort walls and between the firebricks and coal gas leaked through the fissures into the atmosphere instead of being contained and directed to the gas holders.

To overcome this, I discovered that a rival firm of retort makers - Glover West - had devised a small pump which would blow into the retort a fine silica powder, when the retort was standing (idle). The powder in trying to escape through the cracks in the walls, fused and blocked up the cracks. Although my Woodall Duckham retorts were in competition with Glover West retorts, the makers of the latter very nobly allowed me to use their system. This made a noticeable contribution to the carbonising efficiency of the Ely plant, nor did I ever learn that any other works (not using a Glover West plant) on the Eastern Region adopted the system - at any rate as early as Ely did. It also made the retorts last so much longer that, when it came to shutting down for the normal re-building; the retort setter said that it was a shame that retorts in such good condition should have to be pulled down. However, I had to obey the rules of the Gas Board.

Another innovation at Ely in the retort house, was the introduction into the un-purified coal gas stream (at about 520 BThU's heat value per cubic foot), Producer Gas in small quantities at about 130 BThU's per cu ft. I could have diluted with 'Blue Water Gas' by forcing more steam into the base of each retort, but this has various disadvantages. The Producer Gas has first to be washed from its contained coke dust before insertion into the coal gas stream. I only knew of one other gas works which adopted this method of dilution - many years after it was started at Ely. In my pursuit of efficiency, I paid attention to the consumption of coke, not only in the producers, which heated the retorts, but on the boilers which provided steam to run the various engines.

With so much heat going to waste up the stack, I had a multi- tubular waste heat boiler fitted to the retort house to intercept this heat, but it was not quite powerful enough to run the works without some aid from the Cornish boilers which had served many years, nor would it have been wise to rely entirely on just one boiler. So a Cornish Boiler was kept under slow fire using coke breeze burned in a special grate so designed that air could be blown through channels in the bars to aid combustion.

All exposed steam pipes were lagged even in the retort house, to save heat losses. That still left some exhaust steam blowing to waste. Some of this was turned into boxes at the foot of the retorts

Letter headings of some Gas Companies around 1930-45
(with whom the manager corresponded)

THE TAMWORTH GASLIGHT & COKE COMPANY

L. B. RUSTONBHAM
ENGINEER & GENERAL MANAGER

TELEPHONE
No. 44

GAS WORKS
TAMWORTH

YOUR REF

DATE 4. 7. 44.

Cambridge University and Town Gas Light Company.

TEL. 3389.

A. E. KING.
SOLICITOR & SECRETARY.

8, Market Hill.
Cambridge.

ALL COMMUNICATIONS TO BE ADDRESSED TO THE GENERAL MANAGER AND SECRETARY
AT THE HEAD OFFICE.

Cambridge University & Town Gas Light Company.

CHIEF SHOWROOMS 52, SIDNEY STREET TEL. 54005 (3 LINES)
BRANCH SHOWROOMS { COTTENHAM. TEL. 9.
{ WILLINGHAM. TEL. 10.
SIDINGS: R. & S. R. & H. & S. &c.

HEAD OFFICE. TEL. 5/006 (3 LINES)

52, Sidney Street.
Cambridge.

OUR REF. YOUR REF.

J. HUNTER RIOCH, M INST GAS E.
CHARTERED GAS/GAS ENGR
ENGINEER, GENERAL MANAGER
AND SECRETARY

TELEPHONE: GORLESTON 81.

GORLESTON & SOUTHTOWN GAS COMPANY,

E. F. KEABLE,
M. INST. GAS E.,
ENGINEER AND MANAGER.

*Gas Works,
Southtown,
Great Yarmouth.*
E.W.B./D.R.

6th
November,
1931

GORLESTON & SOUTHTOWN
GAS COMPANY

E. F. KEABLE, M. INST. GAS E.,
ENGINEER & MANAGER

TELEPHONE: GORLESTON, EIGHT ONE

*Gas Works
Southtown
Great Yarmouth*

TELEPHONE 3451
R. BRIDGE M. INST. GAS. E.
GENERAL MANAGER & SECRETARY

SHOWROOMS WESTGATE

PETERBOROUGH GAS COMPANY

ALL COMMUNICATIONS TO BE ADDRESSED TO THE GENERAL MANAGER & SECRETARY

NEW ROAD
PETERBOROUGH

OUR REF YOUR REF DATE

379

THE LAMBOURN GAS, COAL & COKE CO.

NEWBURY STREET, LAMBOURN
Telephone
LAMBOURN 44

GAS WORKS
LAMBOURN
BERKS.

F. C. WAGG
Engineer and Manager
STEVENS

to assist in the quenching of the hot coke and make blue water gas Some was employed in providing hot water for the stokers shower baths and some for heating the offices via radiators. Practically all the exhauster steam was consumed.

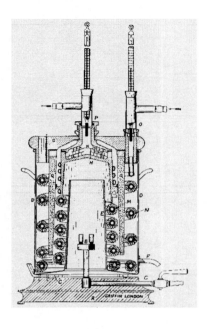

A Boys calorimeter for measuring the quality of the gas. Photographs both from the Fakenham Gas Museum

The calorific value of the gas as it left the works was tested daily with a Boys calorimeter, a very accurate measuring instrument, but to obtain the maximum yield of gas, it was necessary to check the gas as made as it entered the gas holder. For this purpose, a Sigma recording calorimeter was used, the aim being to achieve an almost perfect straight line between 495 and the 505 (BThU's per cu ft) line. To rely on the chart being read every hour was not good enough. Accordingly, I had a device fastened to the Exhauster house wall, which I could see through my office window. When the value fell below 495 C, a red light came on, and when above 505 C, a green light. Either light showed adjustments needed to be made at once to bring the value midway between those two points. I left the stokers to make the necessary adjustments, but if either light remained on for too long, I went out to enquire the reason.

Lastly, mention should be made of the workshop of which I was proud. It contained a lathe, a metal saw and pipe cutting and threading machine, all electrically driven as well as the usual bench range of tools. Many larger works were not so well equipped.

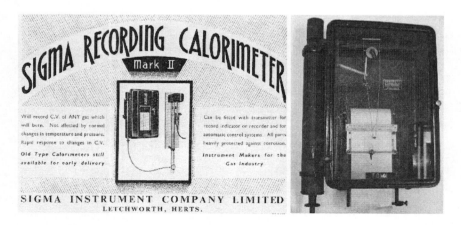

1. Electric Motor to ley shaft and flat belt drive to lathe

2. Bench with fire-bricks on top for welding

3. Stove for heating workshop

4. Pipe support

5. Reciprocating pipe cutter

6. Belt Driven lathe

7. Work bench

8. Electric Pillar Drill

9. Gas light

10. Grinder

11. Vices

Starr and Rignoll Ely

The fitters workshop

59

Chapter 9
Recollections and reflections of an Ely Manager

My twenty four years as Engineer and Secretary of the Ely gas and Electricity Company were easily the most varied, adventurous and interesting of my life, upon which I look back with pleasure. It was a priceless experience.

I little realised when in 1933 at twenty six years of age (and, so I was told, the youngest gas manager in the Eastern Counties) as I first entered the gates of the gas works in Station Road, that it would take nearly twenty years to turn a very sick undertaking into a highly prosperous one. There were nine months of unpaid bills awaiting me, a dividend of only 2% being paid out of losses and disastrous technical results from the works.

The value of the Original Capital Stock in 1933 was £40 per £100 nominal. On Nationalisation it was worth £202.10s.0^d reflecting the improved results and prospects.

But what could have been better for an ambitious young man to show results? I had three wonderful directors (Mr Owen S Ambrose, Mr Horace J Martin and Col. Goodwyn L Archer) who backed me to the hilt. Also I had a very wise accountant, Mr Bunney of Messrs Wood Drew of London, an excellent Chief Clerk in Mr Secker and by and large a good labour force, on works and district. What more could I ask? We all pulled together and heaven provided the blessing. But which events in those years are likely to be of sufficient interest to the general reader? The following is a selection.

By Act of Parliament every gas undertaking had to maintain a minimum general pressure in the gas mains, of 2 inches water gauge. One day I ordered the new foreman to clean out the station governor that maintained an even pressure on the district for which purpose it was situated on the outlet of the gas holder. It was fitted with an inlet and outlet 10 inch valve plus a by-pass valve. Of course the by-pass should have first been opened before the others were closed and I left him to take the obvious precautions. About half an hour later came a telephone call from a lady in St Marys Street to say that she could not get her cooker burners to light. The by-pass had not been opened and for a few minutes gas was cut off from the whole of Ely!

The supply was quickly restored, but all that day I was under strain least there should be an explosion or gassing somewhere on 'the District', due to the extinguishing of all by-passes. Not until nightfall did I realise that the mishap had passed without incident.

Equipment was very primitive in the 1930's. New cookers for fixing, plus tools had to be pushed up Back Hill in a barrow by the gas fitters - a strenuous effort. All road breaking apparatus was similarly transported by the service laying gang. As for personal transport, the men had to use bicycles. Not until much later was a motor van purchased.

Repairing leaking service pipes necessitated opening up the roads with a pick and shovel — hard work indeed. Later a mechanical drill was obtained but this caused heavy vibration to the operator's arms.

On the works itself coal from the vertical retort plant had to be taken up 60ft to the top of the hopper in steel bogeys which were shovel-filled each night, each with 14 cwt. The stokers had to push these heavy containers from the yard into the lift cage, then at the top from the cage to the hoppers in all weathers -an arduous task.

About once a month one of the four purifiers which removed sulphur from the crude gas, had to be emptied of the fouled-up iron oxide and refilled with revived oxide. This was a particularly odious task and no special clothing was then provided.

Eight members of the Ely Gas Works staff receive awards for 25 years service from the Eastern Gas Board together with a £5 in cash. Presentations were made by Mr J Hunter Rioch Divisional General Manager assisted by E. H. Winch [Group Engineer] and Mr C. H. Stanley [Divisional Secretary] Mr C. B. Staniforth [Works Manager] gave a personal appreciation to those receiving awards.

Mr Rioch in making the presentations commented that Ely staff had the second highest percentage of certificates, one in four of the staff. [There must have been 32 staff at this time] of which 25 appear in this photograph.

Recipients were C.M.Secker 35 years [Ely Gas Co Secretary], W.J. Taylor, C.J. Lee, R.W. Liles and G.F. Oakey [all stokers]; W. Cross [32 years cleaner and lamplighter]; W.E. Partridge [fitter]; and J.H. Barton [works cleaner and former lamplighter].

Also to receive Certificates were Mr J. Beardshall, a CD General Instructors Certificate; Mr M. Thorpe a Safe Driving Badge, Mr Skeels [a mains and service layer] who following an injury retired, a clock from colleagues and Mr A. Wilden [coke yard worker] who last year fell ill and retired, a fire screen from colleagues.

Ely Standard June 27th 1952.

Top photograph
1st from left front - Mr Staniforth	18th from left front — Mr Secker
8th from left front -Eric Ardron ?	17th from left - Mr Chris. Lee
9th from left back -Harry Martin	25th from left front — Mr W. Partridge
15th from left front — Mr Hunter Rioch	26th from left front - Mr Winch

A similar ceremony held the same day at Littleport for employees in of the works.

Dealing with the tar and gas liquor was an equally filthy job and could give rise to skin cancer of the hands: not until the early 1940's were shower baths installed. I pay full tribute to the endurance and faithfulness of all those men, who received little more than a farm labourer's pay to keep the homes of Ely warmed and lighted and meals cooked and all without strikes, insubordination or refusal to help in times of emergencies- the unsung heroes.

Mr Charles Secker my chief clerk merits a special mention. He was utterly honest, a good time keeper and an excellent executive and typist. He kept the ledgers so accurate and tidy, that the Gas Board auditors said they were the best of any small works around Cambridge.

I was fortunate to enjoy the services of two first rate engineers who also acted as foreman. They were Mr A. K. Gould and Mr Eric Ardron. The latter eventually left to be a Gas Examiner in New Zealand and later an independent manufacturer of gas making plant, using oil as fuel stock. In the interregnum the works were served by Jack Hacon a very loyal and conscientious foreman who left me to become manager of a works at Maningtree in Essex.

Gassing was always a danger and several times I had to go into the trench in the roadway when the service layer or mate was very groggy due to escaping gas. I was able with the aid of a small cylinder of compressed oxygen squirted into their mouths to stimulate breathing and so ensure recovery.

The vertical retort house could be a dangerous place too and on one occasion young Peter Crawford was so badly gassed that I feared he would not survive. But the RAF hospital pulled him round. Sadly it was not for long as he joined the RAF and was shot down during manoeuvres - a real loss to us, as he was skilful, ingenious and very good-natured.

One prayer of mine was certainly answered. I never lost a man by death or serious injury whilst in my service. One injured man recovered but left of his own volition.

But we had some narrow escapes on 'the district'. On one occasion in the depth of winter, two or three very young children came to the office to say that they could smell gas in their house and that their parents were ill. I hurried down to their house in Broad Street and found the parents unconscious in bed, which was stained with vomit. The gas had entered the cellar by way of a drain pipe. Both people were saved, but it was a close call.

Gas is not the only hazard on a chemical works. Coal, coke and tar are also inflammable and electricity has to be treated with care. The tar dehydration plant started spluttering badly one day and fearful of an explosion everyone kept well away until the fire in the furnace had burned itself out and all was safe. Several times the purifiers overheated and had to be 'smothered' by steam injection.

One winter's night the duty stoker telephoned me to say that crude gas was issuing from the coal in the large top hopper. Apparently, heat from an empty retort, which was being 'scurfed' from retort carbon, had so heated the bottom of the hopper only 8 feet above it that the coal therein had started to smoulder. These fumes of choking tarry gas rose through the superimposed 40 tons above and filled the coal house above. Men commenced to dig out the coal, but had they continued would have been choked to death before reaching the fire. To have called the Fire Brigade would have been to invite a torrent of water which whilst quenching the fire would have ruined the silica brickwork of the white hot retorts. The foreman suggested using a fine spray of water, which would evaporate before reaching the retort. Though it was a very slow process it worked. Otherwise the gas supply from the plant could have been interrupted for days and possibly a beacon of

1. Retort House

2. Chimney to steam producing Cornish Boilers

3. Top of condensers on the north side of Gas Lane

4. Wall backing on to Gas Lane

5. Clapham pumpless ammonia washers

6. Tar tank

7. Building housing Whessoe electric detarrer

8. Power line post and electric control box on wall

The Wessoe Electro de-tarrer and gas scrubbers

The back of the works looking north east. The electro detarrer is contained in the brick building and the two scrubbers to the right. The water jets washing the gas were visible through the six port holes. The underground tar tank is in the foreground. The little personnel door in the works wall was just to the left of the brick building

Starr and Rignoll Ely

63

blazing coal to be seen, atop the plant, for miles around. The incident illustrates the care and attention to detail that has to be given to every part of the gas making process.

Another piece of plant that had to be treated with extreme care was the electro-detarer, designed to remove every globule of tar mist from the 'foul' gas. This worked at very high voltage - I think from memory 20,000 volts. When it had to be shut off or opened up, the greatest care had to be taken when putting it back on stream that no air whatsoever was inside. Occasionally, electro-detarers had blown up at other works, with devastating results

A really devastating fire occurred in the main office block on the Sunday morning before Christmas day, one year. [23rd December]. Due to my forgetfulness to instruct the stoker, he started the compressor an hour too soon in the morning. The gas travelled through the high pressure main to the RAF Hospital and then started to return via the low pressure main towards the works. Normally it would be used up before arriving at the works, but it was so early in the morning that the citizens of Ely were not awake and so the gas arrived back at the works, blew the seal on the station governor and caught fire. Most of the wood of the office was of pitch pine and had the fire taken hold the building would have been gutted with all the records therein.

The stoker telephoned me. I leapt out of bed and clad only in pyjamas, a jacket, top coat and shoes, tore down to the works in my car. Through the half light and mist I could see before me the ghostly figure of the fire engine - which had also been called out, descending Back Hill. The next few minutes saw intense activity as the fire was doused and the building saved.

Chris Lee the stoker had stood within feet of the flames to phone me and the Fire Brigade and only in the nick of time. A few minutes later the telephone was incinerated. For this devotion to duty, he was duly recognised - as he deserves to be, but I used to laugh afterwards to think that the man who (inadvertently) caused the fire, received an award for helping to extinguish it.

This was not the only fire on the works for there was a much smaller fire in November 1947 at a time when the vertical retorts were being modified from four in number to six. A workman from Woodhall Duckham, the contractors, managed to cause a fire with his oxy-acetylene welding gear. Fortunately little damage was done but the local Brigade arrived on the scene to quell the flames. The waste heat boiler was slightly damaged but it was an incident a manager could do without.

CITY NEARLY HAD GAS EXPLOSION

Danger Averted By Prompt Action

A WORKMAN'S DISREGARD FOR DANGER, and the fire service's prompt action, averted the possibility of a serious explosion at Ely gas works while townsfolk were still in their beds on Sunday morning.

Just before 7 a.m. a stoker discovered that the station governor, a delicate piece of equipment controlling the supply of gas from the holders to the mains, had caught fire — pressure having blown out the water seal inside the governor.

The stoker—Mr. Chris Lee—at the risk of injury used a telephone in the room housing the governor to inform the fire service and the local manager, Mr. C. B. Staniforth.

The call was answered by a water tender and pump escape unit. Before their arrival, workmen made unsuccessful attempts to put out the flames with a foam extinguisher.

CONTROL IN 20 MINUTES

Directing water from the tender and a hydrant through a window, the fire-fighters were able to gain control within 20 minutes, though they had to remain on the scene until 11-20 a.m. The room in which the governor is housed was severely damaged, and the ceiling was burnt.

But for the speedy action a serious explosion might have resulted. Immediately above is a store-room containing wash-boilers and cookers; had the flames obtained a stronger hold the ceiling might have given way and caused the appliances to fall through. They would have smashed the governor and allowed a large amount of gas to escape.

Mains pressure in the City was not affected by the incident.

When the fire was discovered the Police were mobilised, to prepare for the possibility of evacuation of the area.

Ely Standard 28th December 1951

GASWORKS STOKER HONOURED

Chris Lee Stoker second left receiving a presentation of a Rolls Razor from Mr J Hunter-Rioch General Manager Cambridge Division of the Eastern Gas Board in recognition for his devotion to duty. Mr Attlesey the under-stoker gave assistance using fire extinguishers.

Ely Standard Jan 18th 1952

65

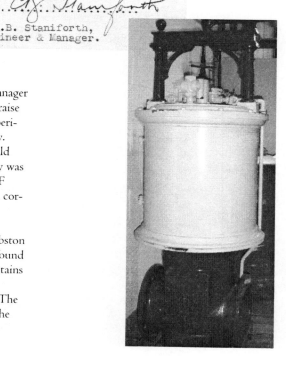

Following the potentially catastrophic fire at the works the manager
issued more precise instructions for the stokers as to when to raise
or lower the gas pressure on the District dependent on the experience of varying demand by consumers at differing times of day.
This practice ensured there would be no repetition which would
give rise to blowing the seals on the station governor. The City was
served exclusively by the low pressure system where as the RAF
hospital had its own high pressure gas main. The hand written cor-
rections were made after the fire.

The insert photograph taken at the National Coal Board's Snibston
Colliery Museum is of a Gas Works governor similar to that found
at Ely which was at the seat of the fire. The white cylinder contains
within it an inverted bell. Attached to the bell top are variable
weights which press the bell down to increase the flow of gas. The
red pipe work beneath was the outlet pipe from the works to the
district.

Mentioning this large office building reminds me that the first floor housed a most impressive Board Room, one of the best in the Gas Undertakings in the Eastern Division. And in the Board Room was a very extensive Board Table. In 1940 when the air raid alerts were sounded, I slept on the table with the telephone at my side, and a wire overhead reaching out through the wall to a steam whistle on the roof of the coal store roof. When the red alert was rung through on the phone, I reached up to the wire from my horizontal position on an air cushion and sounded the siren note to warn citizens living in the lower parts of Ely of a possible air raid. I shared this duty with the foreman for several weeks alternating with him.

About 1938 I bought a very large 6ft diameter cylinder of ½" steel plate. When war preparations were generally underway, this cylinder, lying horizontally behind the Potters Lane wall with a heavy steel circular door at either end, was turned into a comfortable air raid shelter with seats along each side and a gas heater beneath. The whole was covered with grass turfs and it was intended for the protection of any gas employees on the works at the time of a raid. One night when I was on fire guard duty, I thought to look into the shelter, not having been in since it was redesigned. To my astonishment I found it full of householders from Potter Lane quite unconnected with the gas undertaking. My permission had certainly not been sought, but I had no heart to turn them out.

An auspicious occasion. A visit to the Ely Works by Sir John Stephenson, Chairman of The Gas Board. Left to right Mr Hunter-Rioch Cambridge, Claude Staniforth Manager Ely, Sir John Stephenson , Mr Kincaid representing Eastern Gas workers representative and to far right Mr E H Winch (Cambridge).

The photograph is taken in the old orchard yard looking north west towards Potters Lane. In the foreground can be seen the recently created garden and behind it the air raid shelter covered by a bank of soil and landscaped. The entrance to the shelter is on the left.

Starr and Rignall Ely

The winter of 1947 is unforgettable for weather. It was called Shinwell's winter because 'Manny' was Minister of Fuel at the time, in the first Socialist Government since the war. Coal output from the mines in 1946 was too low to meet an average winter's needs. The London Power Stations and Gas works in November were warning that their coal stocks were vanishing, but Shinwell did nothing effective. He should have rushed in supplies from overseas.

Having no faith in socialist politicians I took warning from the chiefs of the London large coal users. How could I keep Ely supplied if my coal ran low? For years I had kept some of my old horizontal retorts undemolished and quite unheated, of course, as a standby. Here

The southern yard during what must have been a formal occasion. The manager stands second from left with the general store in the background just to the right of the 'garden' shown below.

was the emergency. I had one bed of eight retorts heated up (a process taking several weeks). Then I fitted up an old tank with a pipe leading down to the retorts. The tank was filled with paraffin (or light oil) and more kept in reserve. By January, I was all ready to make a rich gas by running oil into the horizontal retorts, and mixing this gas with the main stream.

No one who lived through 1947 will forget how severe the weather was. Coal was very scarce. The government demanded all gas works to reduce pressure to conserve fuel supplies. But in Ely oil gas supplemented and mixed with coal as - in the right proportions - kept up the pressure in the mains so that no one had to go short.

The garden at the back of the works. Looking south. Potters Lane is to the right of the photographer.

Spare section of mains pipes are neatly stacked in the distance.

The dark building in the background was a general store and garage. To its left is the new meter house an inside picture of which appears in this book.

Starr and Rignall Ely

Many Gas works ran right out of coke. At Ely we opened the gates each Saturday morning for retail sales limited to 28 lbs each. Queues formed on the path of Station Road with prams, cars, barrows, bicycles and boxes on wheels to take the precious commodity. The coke was graded, screened and de-breezed. Handouts of ¼ cwt lots were served each Saturday morning and on the heaviest day 990 odd lots were sold. There was no time to weigh each item. The coke men just used their large forks - and so many forkfuls for 28lbs - and I doubt if any one was under supplied. What with the gas and coke we felt we had saved Ely from the wretched winter.

I was even a hoarder and could not bear to sell off odd pieces of sheet or bar steel from demolition tasks or surplus to construction jobs. Being mostly second-hand it was not taken into stock but was a hidden asset. During the first or second year of Nationalisation, the new Eastern Gas Board chairman desired to look over the ninety odd works appropriated under the 1948 Gas Act.

Knowing my works would not show up well against works of better appearance but poorer efficiency, a month before a routine inspection I spent lavishly in labour, polishing machinery and painting iron and woodwork and general tidying up. But quite an area of the second half of the works was rough ground and I knew that my officers over me at Cambridge would not dream of sanctioning expenditure on landscaping. Now at last I could fall back on my stock of old scrap. This was promptly sold and the money used to pay Townsend's of Fordham to landscape our rough land and insert instant plants. So the place was embellished without direct expense to the Board and our honour saved.

I made great efforts to increase sales of gas, firstly by sales of our appliances. The first exhibition took place in the spring of 1934 in the Women's Institute in conjunction with a cookery demonstration. A full range of appliances were on view and much curiosity shown in a wireless set where the electric current was derived not from the mains, or battery or accumulator but from a set of thermocouples energised by a gas flames.

Learning that the gas company started in 1835 I suggested to the directors a Centenary Exhibition, which was held in 1936. The chairperson was Lady Rothschild and the opener, Cannon C Raven. Cookery lectures were again the main attraction

Ely Standard Friday 1st April 1955

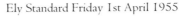

THE
EASTERN GAS BOARD
Is pleased to announce that the
New Gas Service Centre
at
7a, HIGH STREET
ELY
Is now open
Hours of Business:
WEEK-DAYS (excepting Tuesdays)
9 a.m. to 1 p.m. — 2 p.m. to 5 p.m.
TUESDAYS: 9 a.m. to 1 p.m.

WASHING MACHINE
DEMONSTRATIONS
WEEK COMMENCING 4th APRIL
★
EASTERN GAS BOARD
Telephone ELY 2100

Photograph
supplied by
John Horne

69

A Cookery Demonstration. The speaker is believed to be Canon Raven and the lady to the left seated probably Lady Rothschild

Starr and Rignall Ely

The women's folk were invited to look at the home laundering appliances, all gas heated some with powered agitators, one in fact with no moving parts at all in the clothes drum, washing being accomplished by an electric pump. Special demonstrations had proved popular. The hot water section seen at the far right end of the photograph displayed the latest wall mounted water heaters. A range of all fuel economy grates was also on view, one in operation to encourage the use of smokeless coke. A gas fridge is visible on the right of the photograph.

The First Gas Showroom opened in Ely High Street on 15th April 1955. The shop was very narrow in relation to its depth. It displayed a wide range of cookers in gleaming white enamel and subtle cream effects which had largely superseded the black cookers common twenty years previously.

Photographs courtesy of John Horne

An official opening ceremony was undertaken to which many of the eastern gas managers attended.

EG News

About two years afterwards, learning that Messrs R and A Main were producing two specially low priced enamelled cookers for mass sales by the then Gas Light and Coke Company, and called GLC N°1 and N°2, I begged them to grant me the same privilege and name them the Ely 1 and Ely 2. This they did and they were sold in Ely for the ridiculously low price of 1 shilling per week on hire purchase. They proved a great success.

In addition, I persuaded the local editor Mr W Green, of the Ely Standard to let me use two 8 inch column advertisement spaces each week in his paper. They were in prominent positions and I strove to change the wording every week to avoid boring repetition, but it was quite an effort to provide 100 different advertisements each year.

But the most effective measure in raising gas sales was the introduction of the new Two Part Tariffs. For years I had followed the arguments of those in the Gas Industry who favoured the Step Rate method of charging for gas to domestic consumers as against the supporters of the Two Part method of charging favoured by the Electricity Industry and I filed away many cuttings from the technical press on the subject.

Eventually I determined that the time had arrived when something spectacular could be done. The evacuees from London had raised gas sales in Ely by probably 30%. This extra revenue plus economies from higher efficiencies in manufacture provided that little extra margin of profit that could be introduced - for the flat rate of 17^d a therm was too high - but as well as giving a real shot in the arm to sales, it had also to avoid bankrupting us and of course the final plan would have to be 'sold' to my Board - and to the accountant and auditor who was a very cautious man.

For a complete month I concentrated on various schemes. I did nothing else each day, save opening the post, for I knew that I could either ruin the Company or give it perpetual prosperity. I read through stored cuttings and tried them out in theory using Ely Gas figures.

Then came an inspiration from an experiment tried out in another town in England. It was not quite suitable for Ely but could be adjusted. Where as other schemes would only benefit the really high user of gas, this would benefit 75% of consumers. The commodity price of gas could be halved (the balance being incorporated into a standing charge) but it involved the considerable labour of getting each consumer to sign up to an individual contract. The benefit to the consumer

71

was only available if more gas was consumed, but that benefit began with the very first additional therm.

It was a gamble, but a sure gamble and I received permission from 'The Board,' and approval from the auditor. When the public realised that the gas extra to that which they consumed in the standard year would be at half price, sales roared ahead. The Gas Board took over the scheme but when it came to standardising prices over the whole area, it was too revolutionary to adopt and a simpler two part tariff was instituted. Sales of gas at once declined.

Coal supplies to the top of the vertical retort house were taken up each night in bogeys by way of the one and only lift and emp-tied into the hopper from where is slowly slipped down through the white hot re-torts. The lift ropes were regularly examined and re-placed if they showed signs of wear. For years all went well. Sud-denly, one night a lift rope broke and the cage would not move, so threat-ening the manufacture of gas and the whole supply to Ely.

Tear off here and tuck in

Printed Paper Rate

Ely Gas & Electricity Co. Ltd.
Station Road
ELY
Cambs.

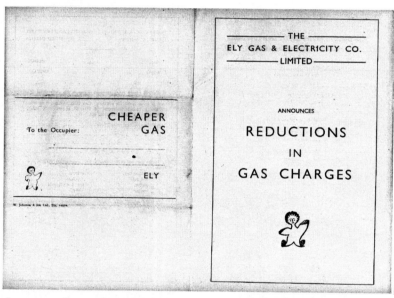

CHEAPER GAS

To the Occupier:

ELY

W. Johnson & Son Ltd., Ely, 44204

THE
ELY GAS & ELECTRICITY CO.
LIMITED

ANNOUNCES

REDUCTIONS
IN
GAS CHARGES

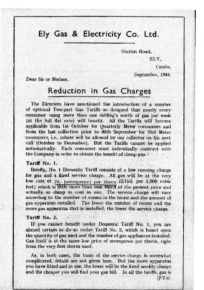

Ely Gas & Electricity Co. Ltd.

Station Road,
ELY,
Cambs.
September, 1944.

Dear Sir or Madam,

Reduction in Gas Charges

The Directors have sanctioned the introduction of a number of optional Two-part Gas Tariffs so designed that nearly every consumer using more than one shilling's worth of gas per week (at the full flat rate) will benefit. All the Tariffs will become applicable from 1st October for Quarterly Meter consumers and from the last collection prior to 30th September for Slot Meter consumers, i.e., rebate will be allowed by our collector on his next call (October to December). But the Tariffs cannot be applied automatically. Each consumer must individually contract with the Company in order to obtain the benefit of cheap gas.

Tariff No. 1.
Briefly, No. 1 Domestic Tariff consists of a low running charge for gas and a fixed service charge. All gas will be at the very low rate of 7d. (sevenpence) per therm (2/11d. per 1,000 cubic feet) which is little more than one third of the present price and actually as cheap as coal in use. The service charge will vary according to the number of rooms in the house and the amount of gas apparatus installed. The fewer the number of rooms and the more gas apparatus that is installed, the lower the service charge.

Tariff No. 2.
If you cannot benefit under Domestic Tariff No. 1, you are almost certain to do so under Tariff No. 2, which is based upon the quantity of gas used and the number of gas appliances installed. Gas itself is at the same low price of sevenpence per therm, right from the very first therm used.

As, in both cases, the basis of the service charge is somewhat complicated, details are not given here. But the more apparatus you have fitted and in use, the lower will be the fixed weekly charge and the cheaper you will find your gas bill. In all the tariffs, gas is
[P.T.O.

It was a time when steel was very scarce, all but rationed. Furthermore, time was a vital factor. Stocks in the top hopper would not last more than 36-48 hours. I was in despair and I knelt down to pray for help. Then I remembered that years earlier a Yorkshire manufacturing company had done extensive repairs to the cage. It was late at night and I knew it was impossible to phone the manager until his office opened next day and even then what immediate help could he offer?

I risked it and rang the telephone exchange of the northern town and explained the position. The telephone operator not only knew the firm but knew the manager's name too and rang his number. He came to the phone and explained that I was lucky to have caught him. I explained the dire situation of the Ely works and begged for a new steel rope knowing that delivery could be many days at best. He said he would do what he could. The next day by teatime the rope was delivered to my works and shortly after the fitters arrived to fit it. It took all night but by the dawn of the following day the lift was working and the Ely gas supply saved.

Meanwhile within an hour of the breakage I phoned the Divisional Office for help. Two days later they rang through to say that the earliest delivery period was two weeks. I told them not to worry, as a new rope had been fitted and the lift was working. Just another illustration that the big battalions are not always the most effective - but limitless is the power of prayer.

The public were well protected by legislation against inadequate service. Not only was there a minimum gas pressure but a minimum heat, or calorific value. This was tested each month and the average of three tests per quarter had to be 500 BThU's or above. No warning was given of the arrival of the Gas Examiner and as the quality could vary from hour to hour I was several times in great trepidation as to the result. Only once did the value fall below the 500 average mark for the quarter and that resulted in a penalty of £3.3^s 9^d calculated by the Gas Reference. As this was supposed to be returned to the consumer or deducted from shareholder's dividends then as it was too small to be divided, it appeared on the balance sheet for years, a visible blot on my escutcheon.

Sulphuretted hydrogen had also to be eliminated from the gas. This was thoroughly done through the oxide purifiers. A very puzzling incident occurred on one occasion. Tests showed the absence of sulphur on the outlet of the purifiers yet present on the outlet of the gas holders. Where had it come from and how could it be eliminated? Fortunately, I was able to call on a central laboratory in the Gas Industry and learned that some micro-organism in the water of the gas holder tank were breaking down the dissolved mercaptans in the water and releasing hydrogen sulphide. The remedy was to dissolve a chemical in the water (zinc oxide, I think), which cancelled out the efforts of the micro-organism and thus another threat to the purity of the gas supply was eliminated.

One of the problems that plagued me for years was the disposal of the ammoniacal or gas liquor resulting from the washing of ammonia from the crude gas, after the West Norfolk Farmers Chemical Manure Company stopped taking it away (by barge). Some of it just had to run into the sewers but the percentage was much too small to cause harm to the river fish. Co-incidentally it so happened that the Ely Sugar Beet Factory was being sued by a Mr Nichols for pollution of the Ouse so causing death of the fish - harmful to the sport of fishing. In defence, the factory pleaded the water was already polluted before they received it.

There was a High Court case, which I attended as an observer and when a chemist from the factory was called to the witness box, he held up, for all to see, a small flask containing a black fluid - tar which he claimed to have collected at some river outfall in Ely and which must have derived from the Gas Works. The Beet factory escaped incrimination but for quite a time I feared that a claim would be taken against the Gas Company. This did not ever occur, but in 1947 the Local Authority forbade me to let any effluent whatever to enter the sewers. For a whole month, I could not even let the boilers be 'blown down' which should be done daily. Had they 'packed up' gas supply to Ely would have come to an end. From my memory, it needed the intervention of a third party to lift the ban.

On the whole, I was fortunate in labour relations. When I arrived there were about thirty five employees of the Gas Company in total and I was surprised to find that at the age of twenty six I was practically the youngest. During my time the labour market fluctuated. One morning when I went down Downham Road to arrange for the extension of the gas main, I was shocked to find a row of unemployed men, standing by the side of the path in the hope of being given work as labourers. It brought home to me, as never before, the plight of the out-of-work people in the thirties. The word had got round of this minor project and here in their silent vigil was an eloquent testimony to the wretchedness of unemployment.

Not that men could not sometimes exact what they thought were their rights. In an attempt to reduce the cost of emptying the purifiers of the smelly fouled iron oxide and replacing fresh material, I was offered a lump sum for the job and took on two or three men on that basis. To my astonishment, they took half the time usually consumed and I realised how much extra effort could be put out when the incentive was good enough. Therefore when another purifier had to be so treated I tried to alter the terms by lowering the figure a little, which would still have been a bargain for the labourers. The men point blank refused to do the work at all, accusing me, by implication of foul play. I stood rebuked and have always felt since, that I had let them down.

During the war labour was very scarce indeed and I was lucky to obtain the services of two prisoners of war. One was a Northern Italian and the other a German. They were both good workers, cheerful and willing. Both were trustworthy and the Italian would go round Ely Streets quite unsupervised cleaning the gas street lamps when street lighting was restored.

Occasionally, so I was told, tramps entered the works by night and kipped down on top of the Cornish Boilers - unobserved- where it was comfortably warm without being dangerous. They were not welcome.

About the end of the war, there was money enough available to provide the stokers with a mess room and shower baths over the exhauster house where the steam from the engines provided hot washing water and hot radiators.

A few years later a pension scheme was introduced to include all manual and clerical staff. Specialists were called in to calculate, not only the weekly contribution from men and employer, but to decide the lump sum necessary to commence the scheme. Very few gas companies offered this benefit at the time and nearly all were larger and wealthier undertakings. Yet not all of our men welcomed the idea of contributing from their wages although the benefits offered were considerable. Eventually the nationalised Gas Board took over the scheme without loss of benefits. Credit was given for years of service before inauguration of the scheme and there are still ex-employees alive benefiting from this addition to their state pensions.

Looking back I can see that I ran the Ely undertaking on my nerves, but I felt that I really lived through all those years.

constant

hot water

at your sink

The 'Ascot' Gas Sink Water Heater gives you hot water at the sink whenever you want it — every time and all the time. In gleaming enamel, it fits over the sink, neat, smart and ready for instant use.
Simple to fix, cheap to run and *now — so easy to buy.*
See it at your gas showrooms.

The popular 'Ascot' Gas Sink Water Heater (Model 503/0) — supplied and fixed complete for

10'- down

1'9 a week

NO EXTRAS!

EASTERN GAS BOARD

Ely Standard 26th March, 2nd, 9th, 23rd, 30th April and 7th May 1954

Many efforts were made to reduce costs. At one time, I thought to lower the water charge by sinking a borehole within the works boundary, if sufficient supply was available at not too great a depth. Accordingly, I invited a water diviner to investigate and indeed he did discover two streams that ran under the works yard. Unfortunately the risks and costs did not seem to be worth the exploitation of this natural water supply.

But I shall never forget his visit because I was fascinated to see the small forked twig suddenly turn upwards when directly over a water supply, that I asked to be allowed to try with the same twig. Of course, nothing happened, but as soon as he laid his hands on top of mine, without touching the twig, it flew round and turned upward with so much force that I just could not turn it down again. Dousing is certainly a mysterious but real craft.

To lower the transport costs of coal from South Yorkshire pithead to Ely railhead I attempted to negotiate with the Railway Company. When that brought no results, I wondered whether I could return to the old style of waterborne coal by utilisation of river barges But an interview with an officer of the Great Ouse Catchment Board showed me that there were too many expensive obstacles in that direction.

One of the largest bills the Company had to pay was that of rates and it was due to the excessively high rateable value placed on the undertaking in the days when it was prosperous. This figure had been over £1,000 but after protest some years earlier was reduced to £850. In principal it should be related to the rental a willing tenant would pay to take over the undertaking and run it.

In 1933 the undertaking was making so little profit that it could not pay any dividend and would not do so for years. Now was the time to put a strong case to the rating authority of the Isle of Ely. Accordingly, the Directors commissioned Messrs Ryde Sons and Brown, rating specialists, to present the case. It was not easy going but the injustice of the £850 and earlier, still higher figures was clear for me to see. The Company had really been unfairly treated and justice was demanded. Finally, a figure of £150 was proposed as a rateable value and although we thought this too high, we were told that it would be kept down to this figure for some considerable time to come. Over the years that followed, this saved us many thousands of pounds.

When I arrived at Ely, I found the streets lighted but learned that the public lighting contract was decided annually and there was a perpetual threat that it might be lost to electricity at any time. To lose lighting would herald the loss of much domestic lighting and as Ely was largely lighted throughout by gas the loss of gas sales might be crippling.

A family-size oven

We've built the oven roomy enough to take a family-size meal, with a flat base for slow cooking, a drop door and Mainstat oven heat control. We've given the hotplate four fast boiling burners (which equally well simmer) and a large quick-heating grill—all designed to save time and gas. To simplify cleaning we've rounded all the corners and made all the hotplate parts to lift out. There's a removable double platerack, too. It's the world's cleverest, cleanest cooker—

THE MAIN No. 20
CENTURY
GAS COOKER

Yours for a few pence a day!
See it at your Gas Showrooms

Ely Standard October 2nd 1953

This public lighting had to be retained at all costs - but how? It was obvious that the centre of the city was quite adequately illuminated. The same small square lanterns being employed as in the side streets. I worked out and priced up a re-lighting scheme for High Street, Fore Hill, the Market Square, Market Street and part of Lynn Road, using lanterns with 6 light N°2 size mantles, in lieu of the 3 light bijou mantles and these to be set up on high lamp columns.

But before the company could offer this improvement there would have to be a five year contract instead of the precarious one year contract in order that some at least of the extra capital cost could be recovered. I knew that some of the Councillors were strongly in favour of electricity and would need a lot of persuading before they would commit the city for a full 5 years to the despised incandescent burner.

I took the matter up with prominent members of the Rate Payers Association and asked to put my case for gas before them, for amongst their numbers were some of the City Councillors. Eventually they agreed to a debate between a representative from the Gas Company and one from the Electricity suppliers. I carefully prepared my speech and on the appointed night in the spring of 1934 entered the Central Hall.

THE "WEST MINSTER."

Drawing courtesy of
The John Doran Gas
Museum Leicester

To my astonishment, nobody seemed to speak up for electricity and I had the floor to myself. All I now remember of it was the last sentence. Having described how the historic centre of London was gas lighted I said "If it is good enough for Westminster it is good enough for Ely". The Councillors took the hint. The Company received a five year contract. The centre was relighted and all the other square lanterns were fitted with reflectors, automatic ignition and with clock controllers. The latter were of the latest type fitted with dials which altered the time of ignition by the usual two minutes per night due to the varying times of sunset, so that the only manual attention they needed apart from cleaning the glasses was the winding of the clock fortnightly. This spelt the termination of the duties of the two lamp men who used to walk the streets twice each night, once to turn on and ignite the lamps with their poles and once to turn them off at eleven o'clock. Instead they cycled round to ignite any odd lamp that failed to come on.

The five year contract terminated in 1939. It was renewed for a further five years but a fortnight after the commencement of the second contract, the Second World War necessitated the lamps to be extinguished. On V J Day (Victory over Japan) the second contract was started up again and gas lighted the Ely streets until 1950 when electric lighting was installed throughout. That one lecture in 1934 had in effect delayed the take over by electricity of the public lighting system for sixteen years.

One severe handicap for appliance sales was the absence of a showroom in the High Street. In view of the competition it was too much to expect customers to walk right down to the gas works in Station Road to select a gas cooker, a fire or a water heater.

The company had no suitable shop or site available and I had to be content to run exhibitions in the Women's Institute every few years with cookery demonstrations to draw the ladies. Also a door to door salesman was signed on and especially low priced appliances were offered on seven year higher purchase terms.

Then one day (or night) there was a fire which gutted Russell Wight's Butchers Shop with a 41 feet frontage, thus this site became available in 1938. Mr R. N. Barwell purchased it for £800.

The arrival of war and lack of immediate capital made it impossible to build a really modern showroom. Further more I learned, rather belatedly, that my plan to turn the rear of the shop into a gas fitters workshop from which barrows with appliances would be wheeled along the Cathedral Walk would be prohibited by the Dean and Chapter.

In 1945 when plans were being tentatively sketched out for the future of parts of Ely, it became apparent that the area including the showroom site might be altogether cleared of buildings. This was the last straw and in the next year when capital was needed to extend the gas works itself, it was decided to sell the site. Mr Barwell received £1,000 for it.

Source unknown but almost certainly a 'Punch' cartoon making fun of the new street lights in the capital

As a sideline it might be worth recording that the metal detector now so successful in detecting ancient coins and artefacts in the ground, had mixed success for company use. For a time I tried to use one to discover in doubtful cases, precisely where the gas mains were under the street surfaces in order to save reinstatement costs when opening the ground merely to probe around. The trials were abortive. With two foot cover of road material the signals were too faint to be certain and even these sounds were 'fogged' by the sound given by countless other tiny metal pieces in the ground.

Perhaps my last word should be very personal. To serve such a fine public service as the Gas Industry has been a privilege which I have greatly valued and enjoyed. But to have served such a city as Ely, within the shadow, so to speak, of that beautiful and inspiring Cathedral, has satisfied my dearest wish. I felt 'called' into the Gas Industry. I felt 'directed' to Ely.

My record is not without blemish, alas, and I am conscious of some lamentable shortcomings, being something of a martinet in matters of discipline. I believed in my main decisions and those of my Directors, in relation to the fortunes of my staff and the gas consumers of Ely whom I served. Also I wish to acknowledge the trust bestowed on me by the shadowy figures the shareholders who waited for me to secure their just rewards having waited so long for a reasonable return on their investments.

I write in all humility - the benefice of a higher power which has seemed to watch over and guide me.

The last Directors' Board meeting held on 30th April 1949 after which the company was nationalised and taken under the control of the Eastern Gas Board. Left to right Alderman Horace. J. Martin (Director), Mr C. B. Staniforth (Engineer, Manager and Secretary), Mr Owen S. Ambrose (Chairman), Lt-Col. G. L. Archer (Director).

Ely Standard 6 April 1949 Starr and Rignall Ely

The last Directors Board meeting 22 April 1949 before the company was Nationalised to become British Gas– Eastern Region

The following is taken from the company minute book at the time.

At the close of the meeting Mr Staniforth the engineer manager and secretary voiced a few words. Of farewell to the Directors he considered that the interests of the shareholders had been well served and guarded. The latest methods had constantly been introduced and the Directors had furiously perused a progressive policy of installing additional plant as demand had warranted it and of maintaining other plant in good condition.

The Consumers interests was always to the fore and extensive main laying had been done and that it could now be claimed that gas pressure was nowhere unreasonably low. The fact was that in general Ely Gas consumers were well satisfied.

Employees had not been neglected. Not only was there provided a good mess room and washroom but the Directors had launched a most generous pension scheme for all grades. Employees generally were satisfied that they were being fairly treated.

Shareholders consumers and employees could vouch that the stewardship of the directors had been carried out with great dignity and wisdom and had been marked by progress and success.

Speaking for himself Mr Staniforth expressed his appreciation of all the kindness and consideration he had personally received from the directors and the perfect freedom he enjoyed to attend whatever meetings, visits or exhibitions etc. he had liked. Particularly was he grateful to the support he always received when urging introduction of new plant and new methods. He had been very happy serving an appreciative board.

In reply the Directors thanked the manager for his remarks and for his service. They wished their thanks to be conveyed to the staff and in particular referred to Mr Secker.

In this happy atmosphere ended the last meeting of the Directors of the Ely Gas and Electricity Company

Chapter 10
Nationalisation—1949

And so my fathers memories end and I take up the story once more.

The City of Ely Gas Company, which was founded in 1835, became in 1881 under the authority of the Ely Gas Order, a private company with a Board of Directors from the Ely area, financed by shareholders, who I presume were largely from the locality. All that came to an end almost seventy years later when on 30th April 1949, under the Government's Gas Act of 1948 the Industry was nationalised and the Ely works and staff taken under the umbrella of the Eastern Gas Board.

A press cutting from the Ely Standard dated 6th May 1949 records that ownership of the gas undertaking passed unceremoniously to the Eastern Gas Board on 30/4/49. At the final Director's meeting held in the Board Room in Station Road, the Ely Standard reported that the manager Claude B. Staniforth thanked the three Directors Mr Owen S. Ambrose (chairman), Alderman Horace Martin (Director) and Lt. Col. G.L. Archer (Director) for their ready advice and support and for their stewardship, marked with diligence and wisdom which saw so much progress and success. Their progressive policies had resulted in the dividends on shares rising from very low levels to the legal maximum and the condition of the plant was now 'very fair'. The press went on to say that the very pleasant atmosphere at that meeting epitomised what was best in British business life; "of good treatment and a fair balance between the competitive interest of the consumer, staff and shareholders".

John Bunney in retirement 1968

The Gas (Stockholders) Regulations of 1948 required a final auditing of accounts of the Gas undertaking. This was presented on 5th December 1950, by John Bunney, the company accountant, who had been so respected by my father for his wise council. Negotiations with the Minister of Fuel and Power had resulted in the following valuations.

Additionally a sum of £1,086 13s 4d. Gross; (£597.113s 4d net of tax) was paid by the Eastern Gas Board representing interest on these stocks and shares up to 30th April '49. This money would have been distributed to shareholders.

The 'take over' did not bode well for local works managers particularly Ely, my father now finding himself accountable to management teams in Cambridge, who knew nothing about the Ely works for which they were now responsible. The days of the directors with their local knowledge were greatly missed. In November 1949 my father in a confidential letter expressed his frustration and disillusionment with his new bosses.

He stated that whilst formerly he served three directors he was now accountable to no less that twenty officials at Divisional level, all of whom were less qualified than he and none of whom could have done his job; but who at the same time tended to look down on him and all the smaller works managers.

Dad discreetly berated the Divisional managers who since Vesting Day had demanded a bewildering amount of detailed desk work and he gave examples of how the changes had frustrated the fortunes of the Ely works. Firstly, he cited a new main laying scheme which necessitated about ten times the amount of planning as would have been necessary under his former Board of Directors. Secondly, he quoted an order placed by him in January 1949 for new gas making plant, only now to be told that the Cambridge Works was in greater need for the financial resources and gas making capacity. Why argued Father, had the Cambridge manager and Board of Directors not had the courage and foresight to expand their plant in the days of free enterprise, as the Ely Directors had done.

Original Capital Stock	per £100 Unit of Stock	£202	10s	0d
Additional Capital Shares	per £10 Share	£14	4s	0d
4% Redeemable Debentures	per £100 Unit	£100	0s	0d
5% Preference Shares	per £10 Share	£12	10s	0d

Claude Staniforth
The Manager

A reference written for Claude Staniforth by the Master of Christ's College Cambridge University.

THE LODGE,
CHRIST'S COLLEGE,
CAMBRIDGE.
TEL. 54153.

11 Sept.

Gentleman,

I have known Mr. C. B. Staniforth for some years, & when I lived in Ely saw a good deal of him & of his work. He is a man of the highest character, a sound administrator & organiser, happy in his relations with colleagues & subordinates, efficient & wholly reliable & with a touch of imagination & insight which lifts him out of the ordinary run of managers. It is hardly too much to say that he worked a revolution in the gas company in Ely. I should have no hesitation in commending him for a post of high importance. For in addition to his personal qualifications he has a thorough knowledge of his profession & wide intellectual interests.

Believe me to be, gentlemen,

Yours faithfully
C. J. Raven
Master of Christ's College
Cambridge
Some time Canon of Ely
Cathedral.

I should not omit mention of my father's nomination by the National Gas Council to attend the National Training Centre at Brooklyn College, Weybridge. This course for aspiring managers was a residential one of six weeks, a long time in those days. Dad was the oldest pupil on what was the

Retirement comes to most of us
.
Claude Staniforth departing for his last day of work for Eastern Gas Cambridge Division. He originally occupied an office in Sidney Street opposite the gas show room on the west side. Later he was to have an office on the works in Newmarket Road.

In the background is the second Humber Hawk saloon he owned with which he used to visit coke distributors and gas showrooms throughout the Division.

ninth course and much to his delight was elected top pupil. He was also thought by the staff to have been one of the top pupils on the entire course and particularly gifted in public speaking, possibly because of his weekly lay preaching. Before the close of the course fellow managers dressed in makeshift Arabian turbans celebrated my father's success one night by raiding his dormitory after dark and parading him on his bed around the college precincts calling " *Hail Ozymandias King of Kings".* The photograph of pyjama-clad managers bears witness to the night of celebration.

Right—Fifteen course members celebrating on the terraces of the House Of Commons before visiting Strangers Gallery to listen to a debate on the Homicide Bill 1ˢᵗ Feb 1957. Father second from right.

Right the same managers with father on the bed.

Below Brooklyn College

My father's staunch beliefs in pacifism and his endeavours to practice what he preached should not go un-recorded. Whilst in Ely he had the humbling experience of being physically assaulted (23/3/1944) in his offices by Mr A J B——— a member of the public living at 1a, Potters Lane adjacent to the works. My childhood memories of the incident are that Mr B——— came round to the works to complain about the dust emanating from the works and the distress and frustration this caused when they hung their washing out to dry. The ensuing discussion resulted in my father being assaulted. He was psychologically very shaken. As was usual for him he prayed quietly at home after the event and decided to ask the individual for an apology. None was forthcoming so he then went to his solicitor who advised that "as my father had sought mediation by way of an apology then he could no longer seek redress for assault". Whether in hindsight this was correct advice I have my doubts. The Company Directors were very anxious my father did not make an issue of the affair and the matter was dropped, but not before Directors agreed to heighten a wall and roof over the coal store to lessen the problem. A year later Mr B——— complained again of coal dust in his house and dairy, caused by

> Records of 1894 reveal that Mr A E Varell requested to be relieved of his tenancy of a company house and it was re let to a Mr B— In 1909Mr B——— of Potters Lane was in arrears of annual rent of £17 to the company and that having failed to pay arrears of £35 10s he was given 12 months to vacate the house and yard.

the crushing and stacking coal in front of the coal shed. Minutes record (August 1945) that the Directors decided very quickly 'to eliminate further trouble with B——' and pay Boulton and Paul, a large timber company from Norwich, now defunct, to erect a timber roof over the coal stacking area at a cost of £418. It seems Mr B—— had grounds to be angry but not to assault my father.

Only respect for the family prevent my naming the individual in full.

The war years were particularly testing for our family. My dad had for many years belonged to the Peace Pledge Union and as war approached his pacifist views became more confirmed. He preached weekly in the local Methodist Circuit.

His beliefs were put to the test when men were called up for active service. My father was told he was in a reserved occupation and his services were more important at home, running the gas works. Being a man of principal he decided to announce publicly his opposition to the taking of life and going to war. The result was he was called before Judge Lawson —Campbell in the High Court to declare his beliefs. Father never did have to carry arms and continued his gas works manager's duties but from then on the family were heavily despised in the City. My mother recounted many times how members of the public would not talk to her in the shops and there was a silent disdain for the family. On my mothers ninety third birthday 19 June 2006, she recalled walking into Leggs shoe shop to be greeted and then in a voice loud enough for everyone else in the shop to hear was introduced to an assistant with the words, "Oh this is Mrs Staniforth who's husband is the paci-fist". My mother was very upset by what was an intentional snub. Whilst dad seemed to weather the storm my mother certainly felt deeply hurt. After the war the public feeling towards us gradually mellowed.

Many years later in about 1950, I recall our house being burgled. An intruder entered via the french windows and left a trail of struck matches around the house. We lost both my father's still and cine camera, some postage stamps, a travelling alarm clock and our family sweet ration. Most telling the intruder left a white feather. Whilst I can sense both sides of the argument as to whether or not the Nation should go to war, or its civilians conscripted, the fact remains my father had the courage to state his beliefs which he didn't have to disclose. Some of the men who carried arms might not have had the courage to challenge authority and face the social stigma that society imposed. Their courage in fighting on the front line must also be respected and honoured too. Additionally dad gave nearly all his salary to charities for his entire life.

Of the many responsibilities that befell my father in Cambridge was the rather distasteful task of representing the Eastern Gas Board at Coroner's inquests when citizens were found gassed in their homes. In term time Cambridge was awash with students and sadly a few either by accident or intentionally were gassed to death. The pressure at end of term exams caused some students to put their heads in a gas oven, usually on a pillow, before turning on the gas. Others lost their life when flues to bath geezers became blocked and they died of carbon monoxide poisoning. I remember forty seven years ago, on one Christmas afternoon when the phone rang, the family were about to listen to the Queen's speech and then open Christmas presents. It was the police to report another suicide. Father left immediately to visit the scene. The student's family were not the only ones to have sad memories of that Christmas.

OZYMANDIAS

I met a traveller from a far off land

Who said; Two vast and trunkless legs of stone

Stand in the desert.... Near them, on the sand,

Half sunk, a shattered visage lies, whose frown,

And wrinkled lip, and sneer of cold command,

Tells that its sculptor well those passions read

Which yet survive, stamped on these lifeless things,

The hand that mocked them and the heart that fed;

And on the pedestal those words appear:

"My name is Ozymandias, king of kings;

Look on my works, ye Mighty, and despair!"

Nothing beside remains. Round the decay

Of that colossal wreck, boundless and bare,

The lone and level sands stretch far away.

P B Shelley

Dad loved poetry and would certainly have known of Shelly's writings. How fitting it was to be for him to have been hailed in a college prank as Ozymandias when he had made his life's work the rebuilding of the Ely Gasworks. Like the great king's empire nothing now remains of my fathers 'works'. The college escapade was like an omen of things to come.

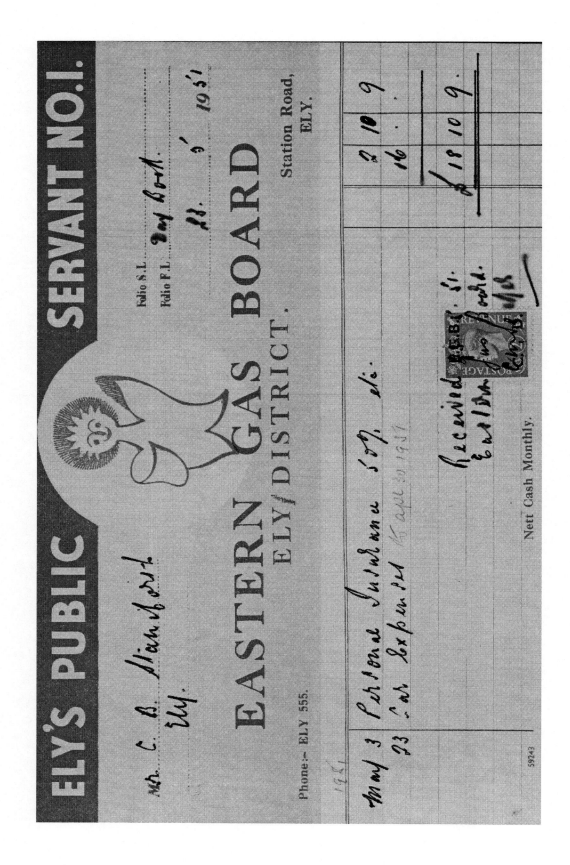

ELY'S PUBLIC SERVANT NO.I.

EASTERN GAS BOARD
ELY DISTRICT.

Phone:- ELY 555.

Station Road,
ELY.

Mr. C. B. Mandont
Ely.

Folio S.L. ....
Folio F.L. Day Book.

Ll. 3 1951

1951				
May 3	Personal Sundranc 5/9, etc.	2	10	9
23	Gas Expenses to April 30 1951		16	.
		£ 18	10	9

Received E.G.B. £1.
£ 18/10/9 with thanks
4/58

Nett Cash Monthly.

59243

Chapter 11
The Manager's Farewell
1st April 1957 The Cutter Inn

In 1957 my father was offered promotion to the post of Commercial Manager to the Cambridge Division based in Cambridge and it was with sadness that he relinquished his post in Ely to move with the times. To mark his departure he organised a farewell dinner at the Cutter Inn for thirty three staff, mostly people in post and a few who had recently retired. I along with my mother was invited and sat at the top table with my fathers work colleagues all around. I felt very bemused by the size of the gathering but do remember my father's long farewell speech. (He was known for his long sermons.) I also recall his thanking everyone there for their loyal service and his going round the room saying something personal to everyone who had worked for him. I would not say my father was liked by his employees but he was respected, was scrupulously honest and he tried very hard to be fair.

The Farewell Dinner at The Cutter Inn. I am the little boy at the top table.
Top table R to L- Mrs Secker, Mr Secker, the author aged 12, his mother, his father, Mrs Ardron, Mr Ardron and Miss Redman Mrs Searl?, Mr Searle? Left Table 3 down Mr Binge?, 5 down Harry Martin, 2 down Walter Partridge, 3 down, Mr Attersley. Right table 2 down Mrs Tibbs 4 down Sid Merry. Who else do you recognise ?

87

In Cambridge my father was responsible for the 'Sales' and 'Servicing' of all appliances (for which he had a team of fifty plus fitters), as well as 'Sales of Coke' throughout the Cambridge Region. In total he had ninety staff, a big jump from the thirty five at Ely. It was not the job he would have liked which was making gas for which he was eminently qualified. The work was immensely demanding and after about ten years in the job, it was split into three, each with its own manager. He

took charge of coke sales. Within twelve months his two colleagues managing the other departments had heart attacks, which they did survive but father looked back with relief that he had relinquished responsibility for two thirds of the workload but was immensely sorry for his two colleagues. Retirement came in January 1970 during which he pursued his love of gardening, reading poetry and travel. He died in April 1984 aged 76.

Attendees at the Farewell Dinner at the Cutter Inn 1957

Name	Job and any other information	Address	Left/Retired
Mr Claude Bertram Staniforth	Manager	23 Orchard Estate	
Mrs Beryl Olive Staniforth	Wife -History School mistress Girls Grammar School St Mary's Street	23 Orchard Estate	N/A
Master Paul Staniforth	Son	23 Orchard Estate	N/A
Mr C. Secker (Charles)	Chief Clerk	17, Prickwillow Road	3/1959
Mrs Secker (Nancy)	Wife	17, Prickwillow Road	N/A
Mr A Ardron (Eric)	Foreman and Assistant Engineer (10 years)	1, Potters Lane	6/1957
Mrs Ardron	Wife	1, Potters Lane	
Miss D Redman (Doris)	Secretary. Cheerful, loyal willing wonder	123, Lynn Road	Died 1958
Mr E Searle		15, Hill Row Haddenham	
Mrs Searle		15, Hill Row Haddenham	
Mrs B. Stearman	Typist	41, Back Hill	
Mr E. Binge	Salesman	50, West Fen Road	
Mr S. Merry (Sid)	21 years fisherman and drinker	31, Willow Walk	
Mr H. Newnham		58, St John's Road	
Mr B. Liles (Bob)	Stoker	70, Broad Street	11/1958
Mr C.J. Lee (Chris)	Stoker commended for his actions helping extinguishing the works fire joined 1921 (31years)	55, Waterside	11/1958
Mr E. Clarke		47, St Ovins Green	
Mr J. Day	Stoker	7, Newnham Street	

Mr G. Oakey (George)	Stoker v. conscientious	83, Newnham Street	11/1958
Mr R. Attlesey (Ronald)	Assistant Stoker helped at fire Chairman of Social group Retired 7/79 from Cambridge (after 27 years service)	120, St Johns Road moved to Cambridge Works	12/57
Mr J. Martin	charming Irish Ways	Lark Bank, Prickwillow	
Mr E. Martin	safe driving cert.	121, High Barnes	
Mr P. Hood		Prickwillow Road, Adelaide	
Mr A.C. Williams	loved emptying purifiers!	56, Walsingham Way	9/1957
Mr N. Osbourne	Hobby - cooking	Chettisham Hill, Ely	
Mr T. Youngs		165,New Barnes Av	
Mr W. Partridge (Walter)	Fitter and Trombonist	19, Hills Lane	1958+
Mr H. Martin (Harry)	Fitter and Salesman- good with people apt 8/35	52, Back Hill	1958+
Mr G. Sewell		15, High Barnes	
Mr P. Elsden		165, New Barnes Avenue	
Mr A. Collett (Archie)	Fitter then Service and Main layer from Newcastle joined 1947 ret 1964 17 years	63, Broad Street	1964
Mr E. George		Lower Road Stuntney	
Mr J. H. Barton (Jack)	Works cleaner former Lamplighter.	168, New Barnes Av	9/1958
Mr W. Starling		The Shade, Soham	
Mr T. Staines		29, Victoria Street	10/1956
Mr L. S. Cummins		70, St Johns Road	
Mr J. C. Skeels	Mains and Service layer. Retired but called on to find pipes in road	2, Newnham Street	
Mr W. Cross (Walter)	Retired cleaner/ Lamplighter of 32 years	3, Potters Lane	1952
Mr A Wilden	Coke Yard worker		
Mr M. Thorpe	Driver		
Mr B. Taylor (Old Bill)	Stoker working horizontal retorts joined 1925 28 year service age 65 at retirement		1/1953
Mrs Tebb	Typist 1951-1957		1957
Mr J. Beardshall	Certificate as Instructor		

Images from the National Gas Archive Warrington

Chapter 12

Record of my work as an under-stoker for the Ely Gas Co by Ronald Attlesey

Employed as under-stoker working on thirty two inch continuous vertical retorts, chief job of which was called 'rodding' to keep a regular flow of coal through the carbonising retorts. This had to be done every hour and every two hours the coke had to be emptied from the collecting chambers at the base of the retorts onto a handcart then taken out to the coke grader.

Coal from the retorts was loaded onto an electrical buggy and taken to the top of the retort house to the hopper via a lift. In the early days this was operated by steam governed by a rope. 'Push' the rope down to go 'Up' and visa versa. The buggy was loaded by hand via a shovel and the load was approximately fifteen hundredweight of coal. The coal had previously been delivered to the works by lorry to the coal yard adjoining the retort house. In the summer the under-stoker on the morning shift (6am-2.00pm), sometimes had to help with the loading and unloading of the coal.

Other jobs were to maintain the smooth running of the exhauster. This is more like a pump which draws the gas from the retorts and sends it through a series of appliances including the de-tarrer, washer, and oxide boxes, namely purifiers and then to the holders for distribution to customers. A record was maintained each hour of the amount of gas made (by meters), the temperature and the calorific value.

Steam was produced via a waste heat boiler besides the retorts. The source of heat to the retorts was what was known as a producer. At Ely it was called a step or ladder producer and burned coke in an enclosed furnace. This had to be de-clinkered once a shift and long steel rods of steel were used to break off the clinker working from the back of the grating.

Operating the coke grader was one of the jobs for the daytime under-stoker and some times on Saturdays had to serve coke to customers. Other times weighing coke for delivery and help to deliver to customers. At other spare times in the summer I've helped to lay mains, dig the trenches for them, also services to houses and to help fit cookers and fires in customer's houses. Also fit and 'burn off' the old type gas mantles for aged customers who could not do it for themselves. I have sold cookers and fires by direct contact with customers. This was before the reward for propositions materialised and sales came about.

One dirty job was emptying the oxide boxes usually pick and shovel work, and then having to put it through a breaker to aerate it ready for reuse. The smell of the oxide was "a job in itself" to get rid of. Whilst at Ely, I organised a social club, thanks to a hard working committee, and when we had to give up due to Cambridge taking over the supply of gas, we closed down by having a slap up dinner at the Lamb Hotel. I was Chairman whilst it lasted.

Chapter 13
Memories of Ely residents

Mr Jack Hagger aged 90 former Personnel Officer to the Gas Board (Eastern Region) recounted 11/Feb/2005:

I knew your father very well and remember you as a young boy. - You must not omit mention in your book Charles Secker you father's right hand man. He was a wonderful chap who took responsibility for all the bills that went out, all the coke sold and all the meters that were read. I recall one day arriving un-announced at the works and walked into the enquiry office to be greeted by Charles Secker. On seeing me he said" -'*One moment I'll call Mr Staniforth*' (on the intercom). Your father replied" -'*Oh send him up*'. "Ely" Jack told me "was the only works in the Eastern Region to have a two way intercom system on the works enabling staff to summon or consult with one another whilst at their work place". Jack told me, "Your father, used it primarily to talk to Charles Secker his chief clerk on the floor below. Whenever I visited Ely I was assured of your dad and Cyril Secker's welcome and co-operation.

Do you recall", he asked, "Doris Redman a woman of slight build with a pale complexion?" 'Yes' I replied to which Jack said "did you know she had pernicious anaemia and kept fainting? Your father usually had the job of bringing her round each time! " (*I sensed a slight chuckle as he recalled the memory*). I had to visit all fourteen of the works in the region on staff matters. I never knew what I would find, but remember visiting the Sandy works to discover Mr Stocker the Manager fishing in the river.

Mr Winch was an ubiquitous gentleman. He was chairman of the Cambridge Division of the Eastern Gas Board and was the proto-type higher manager. His knowledge and dedication was outstanding and he was largely responsible for the integration of the Divisions mains with the control centre in the Cambridge Works. (*After Nationalisation but before North Sea Gas.*) I recall he would call me into his office and I would find him sitting at his desk fumbling with his solid gold propelling pencil whilst a gold hunter dangled from his waistcoat. He was a kind and deeply religious man.

I am ninety now and with failing eyesight have just had to stop driving which I miss very much. I used to have a new car every year for thirty years. Harry Mortimer (manager from March) always drove a Bentley. Sometimes when I went to the March works I would find him under the bonnet. Mr Winch Chairman of the Cambridge Division had a Jaguar (FCE 611). What was your father's Car?" 'Well in Cambridge he drove a Humber Hawk', I replied. "Yes that was a splendid car too" he replied.

Mike Delanoy who used to live at No 9 then 5 then 3, Railway Terrace later renamed Castlehythe opposite the works wrote (Jan 2005)

I have three vivid memories of the gasworks which for my early years dominated the landscape and were very much part of my life.

The first which was a permanent feature was the noise, especially audible in the long night hours. The coal was taken up to the top of the building, it being a vertical retort, in an external steam driven lift which produced a 'chugging' sound. When this stopped there was a clatter of a sliding doors and a silent pause as the coal container was pushed a short distance before being tipped to feed the coal into the top of the retort. The falling of the coal made a considerable noise which would have woken anybody not used to it.

The second memory is of Saturday mornings- coke day! Coke could be purchased on a Saturday morning which helped considerably with the fuel ration. I constructed a small trolley/barrow from an old tea chest, a length of 3inch by 2 inch fixed to the bottom onto which was attached a pair of push chair wheels. From whence these were acquired, memory fails me! Two sturdy handles (not of matching timber), multi nailed to the tea chest, produced the required coke transporter which did marathon service for many years. We bought a ticket from the window

Not the Ely Works but the photograph illustrates a weekly scene which would have occurred every Saturday morning at Ely during the winter.

Photo courtesy of the National Gas Archive

of the general office, having queued for some considerable time, went down the yard to where stood a large pile of coke and a large set of scales. The coke was shovelled up into the scoop of the scales till they thumped down. The scoop was then tipped into your container and it was considered a major catastrophe if any odd pieces should miss your barrow and roll back into the base of the heap!

The third memory is one of the smell! The unique coal tar/gas oil smell which pervaded the air around the back of the gasworks, especially along the lane which runs from Potter's Lane to the Angel (Back Lane). It completely obliterated the chlorine smell from the nearby open air swimming pool!

Despite the noise, smell and the fact that we had recently been at war, they were Happy Days which were typified by the cheerful conversations whilst waiting in the coke queue on a Saturday morning."

(The Author thinks the sound of tipping of the coal into the top of the retort must have been so clearly audible and the sound carried, because the operation took place well above roof top level of nearby houses).

Coke scales Fakenham Gas works

92

Mrs Doris Buckingham of 32, Wisbech Road Littleport writes (Dec 2004)

My brother was a fitter who died 3 years ago. Dick Brunby worked in the yard. I went down there as a kid to buy a huge bag of coke for 6d.; Mother found the biggest chaff bag she could find; so I had some pram wheels; then I bought some for the neighbour; pulled that all up Back Hill from the back of the gas yard; which was a narrow lane to Chettisham. Saturday mornings. I'm 92 years old so I can remember". *(The distance from the Works to Chettisham must have been 2 miles!)*

Mrs Audrey Longdon formerly Reynolds phoned 11/Feb/2005 to say:

My father Earnest worked as a stoker on the works but only for a short while before he was killed in a motoring accident in about 1936/8 leaving our family of six children aged 2½ to 12½. We lived in New Barnes Avenue near the Cemetery and I recall my father using a wheelbarrow to collect coke but we young girls did not go with the men to fetch it.

G. S. and D. Spencer of Littleport wrote on 14 Feb 2005.

We lived on the corner of Broad Street and Castlehythe No1 right opposite the works from 1950 to 1962 and I remember the Gas Works well. We purchased our coke on a Saturday morning after obtaining a ticket from the office which we believe was 2/-, then going down the yard and exchanging it for the coke. We recall your father, Mr Secker, Mr H Partridge, Mr H Martin, Mr E Searle, Mr E George and Mr T Young. We remember one occasion when the works caught fire one Sunday afternoon when all this black smoke came out of the top of the plant and with the wind being in the south east, all that smoke, dust and grime came right down onto our house, the smell was awful. The problem went on for the entire day. We believe the coal was fetched from the goods yard at Ely Railway Station by the employees of the Gas Company but as time progressed the coal was brought in by Coote and Warren road contractors.

(The fire referred to must have been the fire in the vertical retort plant described by my father which was extinguished not by the fire brigade but by the works staff using light sprinklers. These avoided damaging the silica bricks within the retort the repair costs of which would have been extremely high).

Sid Merry junior, aged 74, of Waterside, better known as the Eel Man of Ely, said to me on 24 August 2006 -

My father, Sid Merry, used to work at the gas works. He was a mains layer and a relief pipe fitter. When the Broad Street main was being re-laid by an outside contracting firm, work stopped because they did not have a pipe tapper. Several people were on site and one said to Mr Staniforth "Well, the best pipe tapper you could have is standing right next to you". At this point Sid's eyes glazed over and tears trickle down his cheeks as he recollected with pride that this was his father.

After re-composing himself he said I recall Tom Youngs, a lamplighter who came from Littleport and Harry Martin also a lamplighter who additionally emptied the slot meters. As a boy I remember traipsing down to the gas works on a Saturday mornings with a barrow to collect the weeks supply of coke.

Mr Merry junior recalled that his father said "Mr Staniforth was known as a fair, honest and good employer so long as you did an honest day's work". Sid recalled Mr Staniforth taking his father Sid and himself in his car to a gas workers darts match. He was always smartly dressed.

Chapter 14
The National Evolution of the Gas Industry

There are many historical references to seepages of natural gas and its 'eternal' flames. In the 17th and 18th centuries a number of experimenters became aware of what happened when coal was distilled in an enclosed vessel, but they did not see its practical values. It took the inventive genius of William Murdoch (Murdock) who in 1792 lit his house in Redruth with manufactured gas. Samuel Clegg his pupil and another eminent pioneer in the early manufacture of gas, lit in 1805, one of the cotton mills in Halifax. By 1810 Parliament had given statutory authority for the formation of the 'New Patriotic Imperial and National Light and Heat Company' later to be known as the Chartered Gas Light and Coke Company which was approved in 1812. By 1819 there were 12 companies making gas for public lighting. These included Bath, Birmingham, Bristol, Cheltenham, Edinburgh, Exeter, Glasgow, Leeds, Liverpool, London, Preston and Manchester.

Running in conjunction with the many new gas companies was a host of new inventions essential to the industries meteoritic growth. Clegg invented the 'dry' gas meter in 1815 and the following year the wet meter. Reuben Phillips introduced in 1817 gas purification with slaked lime and by 1820 fireclay retorts were in use in Edinburgh. 1823 saw the invention of the first waterless gas holder and the following year the first gas cooker was made. Leeds claims title to having the first telescopic gas holder. In 1835 in the excitement of all these discoveries the Ely Gas works was founded. So fast was the clamour for new lighting that by 1875 there were 66 undertakings. By 1943 there were 1,079 gas undertakings despite many having been merged.

By 1849 iron oxide was in use for gas purification purposes and the first bath heated with gas jets is documented, the gas jets being underneath the bath. By 1851 one, Ebenezer Goddard demonstrated his East Anglian Gas Cooking Apparatus and the following year we know that gas cookers provided 1,000 gallons of soup per day to the newly opened City of London Soup Kitchens.

There then followed a swathe of Government legislation to regulate the expanding industry. The 1847 Gasworks Clauses Act assisted those applying to Parliament for the building of gasworks for the supplying of gas to towns and embodying powers to lay pipes, limitations on profits, annual accounts, recovery of damages and penalties. (This Act and its constraints on profits to shareholders became very pertinent to the Ely undertaking in its boom years in the 1940's-1950's). Four years later the Great Central Gas Consumers Act of 1851 included standards of lighting and testing. The Sale of Gas Act (1859) regulated the measures used in the sale of gas. The Metropolis Gas Act limited the amount of sulphur permissible in gas and by 1868 the City of London Gas Act regulated prices. In the year 1871 Parliament began to impose 'obligations to

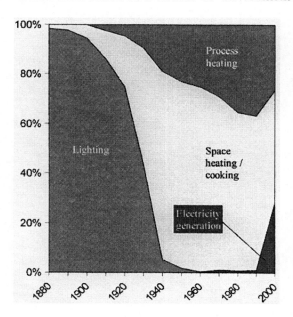

supply', on gas undertakings and a requirement that all undertakings publish formal accounts. The Ely works was the subject to its own bit of legislation, part 37 of the Act1871, which basically put the works on a legal footing.

The British Association of Gas Managers was founded in 1863 and the first examinations in gas manufacture were introduced by the Royal Society of Arts (1874) and later taken over by the City and Guilds Institute. The National Union of Gas Workers and General Labourers was founded in 1889 and after many years, they successfully negotiated an eight hour day.

The development of improved appliances resulted in increasing popularity and greater demand for gas. The original gas light was little more than a smoky flame from a small pinhole but a gas version of the Clegg's Argand burner was an improvement as were the Cockspur and Batswing burner which provided for a slot in place of a single small jet. The invention of the Bunsen burner followed and in 1884 or 1887 Carl Auer (later known as von Welsbach) introduced the incandescent mantle made of cotton soaked in thorium nitrate and cerium, transformed the industry and gave it a greatly extended life in its competition with the electricity generators.

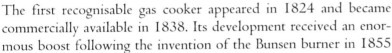

The first recognisable gas cooker appeared in 1824 and became commercially available in 1838. Its development received an enormous boost following the invention of the Bunsen burner in 1855 which brought great improvements in the design of the heating rings. A cooker grill was added in 1886, a regulo for controlling oven temperature in 1923 and the first completely enamelled cooker by the manufacturer, Main in 1927.

Gas fires and water heaters made a similar evolution. Fires in full Victorian decoration were on the market in 1853 but radiant fires did not appear until 1882. The earliest geyser for instantaneous water heating is recorded in 1868, the multipoint water heater in 1899 and the famous Ascot water heater in 1920. 'Mr Therm' the salesman's friend was first introduced to domestic appliance marketing in 1933 but was laid to rest on 13th July 1964. When shares in the new British Gas provocation were advertised on our television screens "Sid" encouraged the public to subscribe.

In conjunction with these developments I should not omit the introduction in 1887 of the slot meter for the prepayment of gas constructed to supply gas, in 'pennyworths' and the subsequent Metropolis Gas (Prepayment Meter) Act of 1900 which regulated gas charges for prepayment meters, at least in London.

As gas appliances developed so too did the plant used for manufacture. Early retorts settings contained varying numbers of horizontal retorts made initially of cast iron which varied in shape but which were usually of an inverted 'D' in cross section. These were filled or charged manually by stokers who

An exhibition of the work of Eric Fraser was held at Newcastle University Gallery who supplied this image.

physically shovelled up to 15 cwt of coal down tubes 7-10 feet in length in the face of searing heat from the fires beneath the retort settings. In 1820 plant was being constructed of firebrick which later enabled operating temperatures to be increased from 760°C to 1200°C which resulted in a rise of gas production from 9,500 to 10,500 cubic feet per ton of coal. During the nineteenth centaury many attempts were made to mechanise the charging of retorts and some were very successful but from 1905

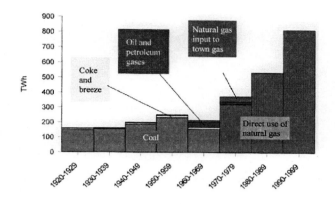

an increasing share of gas was made in vertical retorts, especially those designed and built by Woodall /Duckham and Young /Glover. Their invention saw gas output increase to 13,400 cubic feet per ton of coal. The advantage of this type of plant was that coal tipped into the elevated hoppers of the retort house slipped down by gravity and the resultant coke ready quenched extracted from the bottom. Gas making became a continuous process.

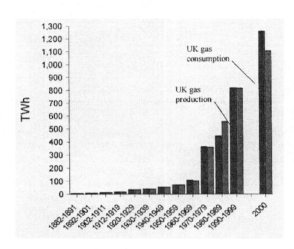

By 1948 the Gas Industry was employing 125,000 men with a further 75,000 men mining gas making coal and a further 20,000-30,000 men engaged in making gas manufacturing plant and appliances, ranking the industry as the seventh largest employer in the country. The Gas Industry became the greatest industrial enterprise of the 19th century. Gas manufacture increased greatly in efficiency, so much so, that by the 1950's, 25% of the heat value of coal was recovered as gas and a further 50% as coke, as compared with electricity which when generated from coal barely achieved a 20% recovery of energy. The industry probably employed in the early 20th Century as many people as do the financial service industries in the 21st Century.

Further Government legislation saw the nationalisation of the Coal Industry in 1947, nationalisation of the Electricity Industry in 1948 and of the Gas Industry in 1949. During the 1950's much oil and gas exploration took place, Canvey Island was developed as a gas terminal for the import of natural gas from Algeria. 1965 saw the first strike of gas from the UK North Sea and in 1966 the decision was made to cease manufacture of town gas from coal and switch production exclusively to natural gas. Between 1967-1977 forty million gas appliances owned by fourteen million consumers were modified to burn the new fuel at no cost to the consumer or replaced with a new appliance which would burn natural gas. As natural gas had no distinctive smell like town gas to warn consumers of leaks and un-light appliances, it was decided to intro-

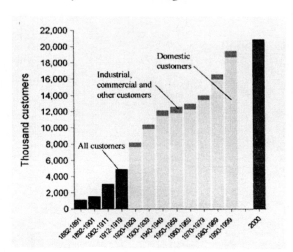

duce an odorant to forewarn users of leaks so as to avert explosions and human fatalities. Several odorants including Tetrahydrothiaphene (THT) were used.

Today the components of the former British Gas PLC trading under a plethora of names world-wide, is an international conglomerate of immense capital wealth with investments in gas fields and distribution networks world-wide. The generating of electricity by gas fired power stations as distinct from coal fired generators now supplies 35% of the country's power. Gas output in the UK has risen from 2,660 million therms in 1950 to 19,062 million therms by 1990. The customer base has risen from 1,971 million in 1882, to 17.717 million in 1990 and 20 million by the year 2004. The revenue generated per therm of gas sold has jumped from 5.5 pence in 1951 to 36.7 pence in 1990. The number of employees has fallen from 142.5 thousand in 1951 to 79.2 thousand in 1990 and is now a fraction of this. The days of the humble gas undertaking in Ely, which are beyond the memory of most, are but a distant blip in the evolution of the Industry.

Following the passing of the 1948 Gas Act the name Ely Gas ceased in 1949, to be superseded by The Eastern Gas Board, a State owned monopoly. The 1972 Gas Act resulted in the centralisation of the industry and the creation of The British Gas Corporation the largest privatisation of the Thatcher Government.

History was to repeat itself following the passing of the 1986 Gas Act which saw the return of the industry to the private sector and the trading name changed to British Gas PLC. Shareholders once again eagerly sought shares in a fast expanding industry. In 1997 British Gas de-merged, the pipeline and exploration business trading as BG whilst the supply business together with the More-cambe gas field was given a new name - Centrica. The latter in turn marketed a credit card under the name 'Goldfish'. Meanwhile the pipelines which supply the nation's gas are owned by Transco - a subsidiary of British Gas. Now BG has re badge itself 'Lattice Group plc' and B G Group plc. In 2002 the National Grid merged with Lattice and four years later four gas distribution networks were sold. Oh for the days of the local gas company run by real people with real names, people who live in the community.

Town Gas manufacture still continues in some parts of the world and gas plants are still operational in Chile, Pakistan, China and South Africa but almost everywhere natural gas has superseded it and remains the ideal fuel.

Older generations often speak of the decline of Britain's manufacturing base citing the closure of the shipyards, steel-works, car making plant, the coal industry and town gas manufacture. The gas industry, dependent on home mined coal, found itself a captive customer locked into the National Coal Board who progressively introduced crippling cost increases in the price of coal. The gas industry was on its knees and as a result initiated large scale research and Development Programmes with the intention of making gas from reformed oils and refinery tail gas and so as to diversify sources of raw materials. Liquefied natural gas was imported from the Sahara to Canvey Island and then on to reforming stations where it was 'converted' to town gas. After years of abortive exploration natural gas was discovered in the North Sea and so great were the deposits that it was decided to convert all gas burning appliances in the country to burn the new fuel. By 1970 the gas industry was using no coal at all. The decline of the Coal Industry followed.

One Ton of Coal carbonised in a gas works, produced approximately

	Sold to consumers
75 therms of Gas 15,000 cu ft or 7,500,000 B.Th.U.	
10- 14.5cwt Coke	Part of which was used for heating the retorts via a process which made Producer Gas , but the greater part sold for domestic use for burning on fires and in stoves. It was harder to light but burnt at a much higher temperature. A gas poker was ideal for lighting a coke fire.
Ammoniacal Liquor	Removed in condensers and by washing with copious quantities of water (15.3 galls) to become ammoniacal liquor. Mostly disposed of by spraying on agricultural land as a fertilizer or dumped in ponds on agricultural land. Too toxic to be put in council sewers as it contained cyanide, isocyanide and phenols which kill fish. Much liquor was converted to sulphate of ammonia, a popular fertiliser
9-12 lbs Sulphur as Hydrogen Sulphide	Hydrogen Sulphide characterised by its smell of rotten eggs is very poisonous and carcinogenic. Largely removed in the Purifiers using iron oxide powder The spent oxide (ferric sulphide) was returned to manufacturers to extract the sulphur and make sulphuric acid.
3 gallons of Benzol	In some works benzol was extracted and sent to specialist refiners to make petrol sold under the brand name National Benzol Mixture. The 3 gallons of benzol also included 3 lbs of toluene which was extracted on some works for munitions (TNT) in World War 2. If not extracted benzol remained in the gas stream as a fuel.
10 gallons of Tar	Largely removed in the Condenser but also in the Electro-Detarrer. Most was sent away for refining into a wide range of chemicals but in the early days in Ely most was sold as a road surfacing binding material. Occasionally in Ely it was put in landfill. Highly toxic to wildlife and major contaminant to ground water aquifers.

Chapter 15
Company Finance

No records so far have come to light as to who financed the building of the gas works and the investment made. My father relates that in 1839, five years after its founding, the rental income was a mere £250 and that the owners decided to sell out to the County and General Gas Consumer Co Ltd.

The next reference to finances occurs in 1850 when John Bacon signed an Indenture to purchase land south of Back Lane to extend the Gas Works property for which the County and General Gas Consumer Company paid the sum of £500.

An Indenture dated 1864 refers to a John Butcher mortgaging the works for a sum of £4,525 and the following year he re-mortgaged his investment presumably to spread the financial risks and provide working capital for a sum of £3,016-13-4d. Clearly it had dropped in value by 33% in the space of one year!

By 1868 some prominent Ely citizens lead by Mr Muriel negotiated with The County and General Gas Consumer Co Ltd hoping to buy the Ely Works for £6,000. The offer was rejected. (A Dr Muriel is known to have lived at The Chantry on the Palace Green at this time).

By 1871 The Holding Company were declared bankrupt, the works taken over by liquidators and some were sold to Stephenson Clarke the Coal Factor, who incidentally had bought out several ailing gas works before selling them on at a profit. This occurred at Ely where the works was sold to the new Ely Gas Company Ltd for a sum of £11,500.

The Provisional Orders Act of 1881, some 46 years after the gas works was built, do shed some light on its capital. The Order says that the Original Share Capital amounted to £12,000 of which £10,500 had been issued as shares to investors lending weight to the demand for a buy out at £9,000. What market value these might have had either when founded or in 1881 is again not known. The same Act authorised Directors to issue Additional Shares up to but not exceeding a total of £12,000, but subject to the total of ordinary and additional shares not exceeding £24,000. Further capital if needed required either a Provincial Order under the Gas and Water Works Facilities Act of 1870 or an Act of Parliament. The same bill goes into detail as to the trading and auctioning of shares and limited the company to borrow no more than £6,000 at an interest rate not to exceed 5%. Finally the legislation, as a price control measure limited directors to paying a dividend no greater than 10%. In practice the company were by 1949 doing so well that my father told me the company could have paid a dividend of 30%, an amazing investment even by today's standards, had the company been allowed to pay it.

In the absence of a Deed of Settlement establishing the company or a company stock register which appears lost, it is impossible to trace early investors. Minutes from 1886 do make clear a slow but steady trading of shares, naming in full the buyers and sellers, largely but not exclusively people living in the Ely area. The Directors had their own shares and played an even more active role in the company finances as they would from time to time lend money either short term or for a set number of years to the concern to keep the books in balance. In 1898 a new £100 Mortgage Bond was offered to investors at 4% interest and Directors Arthur Loss, Col Ambrose and Arthur Hall loaned a total of £500 to the company whilst the chairman Alfred Kitts made a loan of £5,000, a very wealthy man! In 1899 £5,000 of debenture stock was issued at 4% interest and a further £2,000 of stock raised. In 1901 Mr Cathey an auctioneer sold £3,000 of stock at 1.5% commission making £3,599 so an average £10 share sold at £11-19-11 a premium of almost 20% so they must have been popular and seen as a good investment.

The company deeds were originally kept in the company safe before being entrusted to its bankers Fosters Bank. Fosters amalgamated with Capital and Counties Bank on 1st April 1903. Sometime later the company switched to Barclays Bank who financed a substantial loan for the installation of the vertical retort. A few years later interest rates on this loan became unfairly weighted against the Gas Undertaking and as Barclays refused to lower their interest charges the loan was transferred in 1932 to Lloyds Bank.

In March of 1885 a Mr Lase, was appointed auditor and was instructed to 'supervise, prepare books, papers and statements for shareholders for the year ending December 31st 1885'. The minutes are written in such a way as to imply that this procedure had not been followed earlier or possibly legislation had tightened up on the preparation of year end accounts. A dividend of 8% was recommended at the time.

By 1915 it is recorded the company profit was £791-9-5d but by 1917 the dividend had fallen to 3.5%. By 1922 the dividend had dived to 2.5% and 1.75% interest on the additional shares and by 1928 this had dropped again to 2%.even though the company had made a profit of £1,829.

In 1940 Mr Bunney presented his accounts for the half year in which reported a decline in gas made (11.3% or 2,784,800 cu ft) attributable to the loss of the street lighting contract but an increase in gas sold recorded on consumers meters (352,500 cu ft). Un– accounted gas had fallen from 9.2% to 6.8%. Directors were very satisfied with these results in view of the conditions imposed by the war and the heavy decrease in gas production. A dividend of 4% was paid on Ordinary Shares and £2.16s on additional Shares. Whilst Messrs Wood Drew were paid an additional £20 tin dealing with the companies Excess Profits Tax. The tables had at last turned in the companies fortunes for by 1942 dividends had risen to 6.7% and £4.4s for additional shares and by 1944 they reached the maximum levels set by Government of 10% for Ordinary shares and 7% for additional shares. Directors took an increase in fees of £300 per annum between them and War Damage Payments payable by the Government of 0.75d per therm produced during an average year between 1941 and 1944. By '46 the works was expanding fast that 600 Preference Shares carrying 5% interest were sold at a price of £12 10s each to enable the retorts to be increased to six in number. Directors bought most of the shares. By '48. Mindful of impending nationalisation The Ministry of Fuel agreed to raise £17,000 to finance the heightening of the gas holder by two lifts, the building of a CWG plant and associated plant.

The Ely gas works was from all accounts a failing industry in 1933. Its shares had dropped appreciably in value, the gas manufacturing plant was in disrepair and only the brave would have bought its shares or managed the undertaking. By the time it was nationalised share values had rocketed. During the last war Government restrictions had limited the maximum dividend that any private company could pay to its shareholders at 10%. My father is on record as having stated the company could have paid a dividend of 30%, a spectacular financial return in those days. A brave speculator would therefore have made a good selection if they bought shares, had they been available in 1939, when they yielded 4%, just before they made a steep ascent in value in 1944 and hit the jackpot. Records show that my father held Ordinary shares (2,000) as did my mother Beryl and Grandfather. There would have been many shareholders. The company was a Public Limited Company but was not listed on the London Stock Exchange probably because it was relatively small.

The spectacular rise in the financial fortunes of the company was in the main attributable to my fathers introduction of a two part gas tariff in 1945 to which 50% of consumers subscribed. Because of the halving the sale price of gas, sales rocketed by 250% and the Annual revenue account rose by 1,800% so payment of a 30% dividend was technically possible.

The redundant site of the Old Gas works was valued in 1959 by the surveyor to Eastern Gas at £5,250 for the northern yard containing No. 1 Potters Lane the foreman's 3 bedroom cottage, scullery and external WC, an office block and retort house plus £1,000 for part of the southern yard. An area of this yard was retained as it was the site of the two gas holders and relatively new governor house. The contract of sale for the two sites was not signed until 1985 when the Eastern Gas Board insisted on sealed bids owing to purported irregular practices on the part of one bidder. The northern site was sold for £27,050 and the southern one for £22,100, way above their market value.

Sale of both sites had been made on the written understanding that both areas were contaminated with the medium level residues expected of a gas works and responsibility for de-contamination left to the new owners. Gravens Garage who acquired the northern site sold on to the Trigon Motor Company who when installing a below ground level petrol fuel tank discovered a gas tank still full of liquor. Samples were taken by British Gas and laboratory analysis confirmed cyanide and thiocyanide levels at 12.2 ppm as well as phenols. There were strict instructions the material should not enter a public drain. Where the 33,000 gallons of spent ammoniacal liquor and water gas tar from within the tanks was disposed of is unknown. The ghosts of the former gas works had it seemed decided to make one last stand.

Nothing now remains above ground level of the old manufacturing plant. A solitary gas holder still stands on the southern yard and a smart residential block fronting onto Station Road has replaced the Trigon Garage.

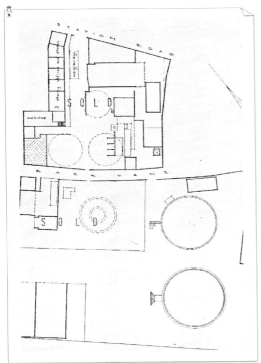

Part of the Conveyance Document showing the 'Sold' north and south sites The land retained by Eastern Gas comprised about two thirds of the land south of Back Lane with an access on to Potters Lane and of course the two prominent gas holders.

National Gas Archive

Chapter 16
Company History

The first documented records concerning a gas works in Ely appear in the Cambridge Chronicle dated 24th April 1835 in which William Marshall, Solicitor and Clerk to the Inspectors, invited tenders from Builders, Contractors and Gas Factors to build a gas works in Ely for the purpose of lighting certain streets in Trinity Parish with coal gas.

There appears no record as to which persons responded to the invitation but an entry in the minutes of the vestry of St Marys dated 23rd September records that a motion was put to rate payers that parts of the provisions contained in an Act of the third and fourth year of the Reign

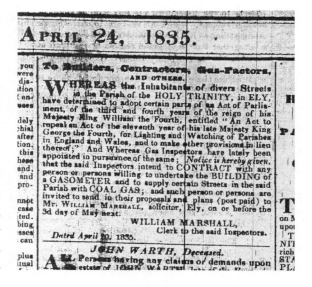

of his present Majesty William the Fourth instituted an 'Act to repeal an Act of the eleventh year of the late Majesty King George the Fourth for the Lighting and Watching of Parishes in England and Wales and to make other provisions in lieu thereof.' Parishioners voted to adopt the motion.

A mere four days later the Cambridge Chronicle carried a report that the principal streets of Ely Trinity were lighted with coal gas. There then followed extensions to the street lighting system recorded elsewhere in this book and for the first time credit was given to the proprietor of the works, a Mr George Malam of Lynn.

The Malam family are well documented in the history of the gas industry and it is worth expanding on the information about them.

George Malam was one of nine children, offspring of John and Rebecca Malam of Lincoln. His brothers and sisters were Abraham, Benjamin, James, John, Rebecca, Sarah, William and it is believed Aaron. John, James and George went on to become inventors and entrepreneurs and highly skilled engineers who made a significant impact on the fast developing gas industry and who rightly deserve credit in the history books of Britain's Industrial Revolution. Other members of the Malam family are also documented as having connections with the Gas Industry including George Malam's son.

George Malam senior 1796-1870 is believed to have acquired his technical training either on a London Gas works or perhaps at Newton Chambers iron works. He focused most of his building programmes in East Anglia as well as building and operating the Enniskillen Gas works. He died in that town. He is credited with building works in the following locations.

Baldock	Ely	Horncastle	St Ives
Chatteris	Enniskillen (Ireland)	Kings Lynn	Sudbury
Dereham	Holbeach	Spalding	Swaffham

Robinson's Commercial Directory of 1839 documents George Malam as proprietor of the Ely Gas Works and gives his address as Anersdale, Ely.

His brother John Malam 1792-1844 is believed to have been associated with Clegg, one of the famous gas engineers, during the construction of the Peter Street Gas works in London. John was awarded the Society of Arts ISIS medal for development work associated with a gas measuring device upon which the entire industry was later to become dependent, as well as the design of a centrally guided gas holder. He is credited with gas works constructions at: -

Barnsley	Howden	Knaresborough	St Peter Westminster
Beverley	Otley	Kingston upon Hull	Horseferry Road London
Bungay	Keighley		

Lastly, the third brother James Malam of Bridlington 1797-1850, is credited as having made significant contributions to the development of gas supplies in the UK and was the pioneer of public gas lighting in Scandinavia. He died aged 48 in Frederikshald (Halden) Norway where he is buried. His portrait is in the archives of the Technical Museum of Norway. He is credited with the building of gas works at: -

Beccles	Kendal	Penrith	Thorne
Bedale	Maryport	Pocklington	Whitby
Cockermouth	Northallerton	Retford	Whitehaven
Driffield	North Walsham	Tadcaster	Winslow (Bucks)
Hamburg (Germany)	Oslo (Norway)	Thirsk	Worksop

Also in conjunction with his brother John: -

Bridlington	Otley
Malton	

At the time the gas works was founded life expectancy was much lower than today; thirty five for country dwellers and just twenty nine for those people living in larger townships where disease particularly cholera were rife.

James Malam 1797-1850
Portrait from Fred'k Schreiner's Oslo Gasworks
1848-1978 Original in Oslo gasworks archives

I have found no definitive evidence as to who financed and built the Ely works but the circumstantial evidence that George Malam did both is compelling. He, in turn, left the running of the plant to lessees.

The next we read of the Ely gas works is an advertisement carried in the Cambridgeshire Chronicle dated 21st November 1840 in which John Cross 'had been instructed to sell by auction (unless previously disposed of by a private contract of which immediate notice would be given) on Wednesday 16th December next, at the Lamb Inn, in Ely at 7 o'clock in the evening, and subject to such conditions of sale as will then be produced, the following' : -

> Very valuable Property viz
> The Gas Works
> And entire apparatus (constructed on the most approved patient principles) situated in the City of Ely, including lamp posts, lamps, pipes etc and a convenient detached residence for the superintendent of the premises.
> The above property is freehold, and affords an unusual opportunity for the advantageous investment of capital.
> The works etc, were built only in 1835, and are consequently in excellent repair. The premises lie within 200 yards of the River Ouze, presenting great facilities for the taking in coals and lime. The concern is now let on lease for an unexpired term of five years, at a net rental of £3,250, and commands a prosperous and still increasing business.
> For further particulars apply to Messrs Marshall and Son Solicitors Ely, or to the proprietor Mr George Malam, Gas Works, Spalding Lincolnshire. Messrs Bacon and Son, the present lessees, will shew the premises.

The Cambridge Chronicle then reports on November 25th 1848 that 'an offer having been made to the Gas Inspectors of Ely for the sale of the above works, and the same being deemed by them worthy of public attention'. Notice was given of a meeting of the inhabitants 'for the purpose of taking into consideration the proprietary of purchasing the same, and of the best means of raising the capital. - By Order of the Inspector W. M. Marshall clerk 21/11/1848.

The meeting at the Shire Hall was reported in a subsequent edition of that newspaper as follows. 'On Monday night last a meeting of the inhabitants was held at the Shire Hall, for the purpose of considering the proprietary of purchasing the gas works by the formation of a company. There were present Geo Hall, J Muriel. H Rayner, T Archer, and W. Marshall, Esqs', amongst others Messrs Scott, Haylock, Careless, Portington, and Ingram. The proprietor had furnished certain information which could be given to the public but before doing so it was appropriate to determine whether this was the communities wish. Mr Scott thought it would be wise to 'see the effect electric light', which he was informed would come about one twelfth of the present price of gas. (The present street lighting contract had three years left to run.) Mr Muriel concurred with Mr Scott. Mr

Gasworks in the early days fell into one of three categories. Firstly there were those registered as Public companies. Secondly those in private ownership and lastly those in Municipal Control. Ely it appears was in private ownership from the outset to be sold on as a subsidiary and later still to have become a Public Company with a Board of Directors and financed by shareholders. It is believed it was one of the few private companies in 1835. An incomplete listing of the gas undertakings in the country in February 1849 lists 115 as Statutory, 380 Non-Statutory and 23 in Private ownership. (The first two categories were both Municipal undertakings varying in size and technical skill to run the plants)

Archer considered they should first ascertain if they could raise the necessary funds -£5,000. Mr Bacon explained that the price of gas had fallen from 15s to 7/6 per thousand cubic feet in eight years and the importance of obtaining the best supply of pure gas for a fair price. He suggested that if a company were formed, the shareholders might be content with 5% per annum and the entire factory could become the property of the town in a few years. The Chairman Mr Hall took a vote on the proposals and only one member of the public voted in favour.'

My father then recounts that a 'London Gas Company' bought the business and strong circumstantial evidence suggests this must have been the County and General Gas Consumer Company whose name appears in subsequent deed documents. On 11th November 1848 a reconveyance document was signed between J Cudden plus A. N. Other and the County and General Gas Consumer Company. This new gas company's name does not appear on most gas works lists because it was what today we would call a business conglomerate or holding company. It bought several works in East Anglia but did not construct any plant itself.

An indenture dated 14 February 1853 was signed concerning the purchase of land to the south of Back Lane to enable the works to expand. The indenture was between the Very Reverend George Peacock DD, Dean of the Cathedral Church of the Holy and Undivided Trinity in Ely plus The Chapter of the same Church Lords of The Manor of Ely plus others and John Bacon. The County and General Gas Company agreed with the sale and paid £500 for the land.

> The County and General Gas Consumer Company was founded to exploit and develop small undertakings in various places. In 1859 it purchased the South Essex Light and Coke Company through which it acquired the Lea Bridge Works. The following year it bought the Abbey Mead works in Chertsey but succumbed to local opposition and then closed down the works. The company went bankrupt in 1868 and both Ely and Lea Bridge Works were sold to Stephenson Clark as was Pembroke gas works. They also owned a gas works in Plymouth.

On third of June 1854 the Cambridgeshire Chronicle carried a Letter to the Editor by a J. N. Cross stating 'he had been solicited to join a movement towards establishing a new gas company in the city and that he wished to obtain the best information from a mercantile point of view. He asked the Board of Health to make public a report by their officer a Mr Burns upon the present gas works in the hope that the great body of the rate payers and consumers would have an opportunity of discussing the merits of the case. A large amount of money had doubtless been spent on the old works and it would appear that more extensive alterations are in contemplation which will take two months to complete. Should the old works be capable and the manufacturers willing to give a full supply of pure gas, at a fair price, then the idea of a new works must in his opinion be abandoned.'

The proposed improvements to the old works did occur and an article in the paper of 31 June 1854 stated that "The works are now superseded for a short time, for the purpose of making extensive alterations and improvements. The entire apparatus will be new, and all the mains much enlarged, new shafts, etc. (retorts?). The proprietors and

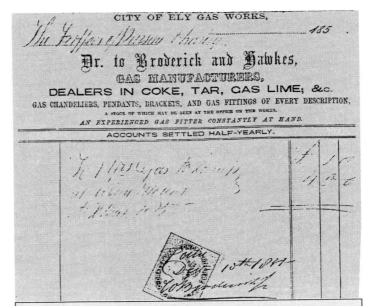

> One of the features which marked out a progressive gas company was a showroom, something which was not available in many of the larger towns. This billhead above is quite remarkable in that it shows that the Ely Company was well advanced for its time offering 'gas fitting of every description' and 'experienced gas fitters constantly on hand'.

> Information contained in local directories and even census returns can be misleading. It was not unknown for resident gas makers/stokers to inform a compiler that they were the Manager. This appears to be the case of Broderick and Hawkes. The 1941 June Census returns is also unreliable as a proportion of gas workers were laid off sometime between March/April when they did seasonal work often in Agriculture.

the present lessees, Messrs Broderick and Hawkes, are determined that every reasonable want, and gas of good quality, shall be supplied to the public. The works altogether are under the supervision of an imminent and practical man, of longstanding and experience in managing gas works. (His name is not disclosed). Hawkes' connection with the gas works continued for many years.

Bidwell's map of 1851 shows very clearly the location of the works with buildings and gas holders on Potters Lane, fronting what was later to be called Station Road ,for there were no trains in those days, plus the newly acquired land south of Back Lane. From about this time until 1st July 1863 John Butcher was known to have been a tenant who sub-let the works to William Broderick and John Hawkes to operate the plant. The two sub tenants occupied three of the small cottages in Bentons Yard which adjoined the works or indeed may have been within the works curtilage. By 1863 The County and General Gas Company took the business 'in hand' meaning ceased letting it to tenants but there are grounds for believing that Messrs Broderwick and Hawkes were still on the scene possibly as contractors or employees. Broderick and Hawkes were coal and timber merchants known to have had trading premises on Station Road in 1883. Meanwhile the County and General Gas Consumer's Company were to remain owners of the site from 1863 to 1868 when they went bankrupt.

There seems little doubt that Hawkes and Son had roots that went back long before the 'Gas Company'. Operating the gas undertaking was not the initial business. The 1881 census lists John Hawkes aged 63 as a Coal Dealer and Slate Merchant employing five men. He lived in Station Road. William Hawkes is listed in the same census as a Coal and Timber Merchant living in Railway Terrace.

Kelly's directory of 1916 lists Hawkes and Son who claimed to have been established in 1800. Even though they no longer operated the works they were still dealing in its products as Coal and Coke Merchants, firewood, slates, pitch and tar.

John Hawkes, son of John Hawkes seniour lived at Northwold, Egremont Street. William Hawkes lived at Brithnoth House, Station Road.

The oldest surviving document concerning the freehold of the site is an Indenture dated 30th June 1864 between firstly John Bacon, a draper, who lived at Minster Place located at the bottom of Ely Park, secondly, Robert Monro Christie of 74, King William Street City of London (acting as Company Agent) and thirdly, The County and General Gas Consumers' Company (Department of Trade Number 725). Christie acting as agent to the Gas Co paid £8,525 for the freehold of the site. This included all the mains and services belonging to Mr Butcher, in addition to pipes he had laid to extend the network of mains during his tenure. The First schedule documents there being 16 retorts, the usual range of gas manufacturing plant together with street lamp posts and lanterns. The second schedule identifies the buildings erected in an Orchard or Garden Ground adjacent to the Black Swan Public House which is clearly identified in Bidwells map of 1851.

John Butchers name re appears on 1st July 1864 when The County and General Gas Consumers' Co mortgaged the works to him for a sum of £4,525 and interest at 5%. Exactly a year later 1st July 1865 John Butcher with the agreement of The Country and General Gas Consumer's Co, transferred the financial security to James Cudden Barrister of The Middle Temple and Frances Thomas Cudden of 5, Grays Inn Square at a cost of £3,016-13-4d.

Edward Hills is documented in 1865 as being the local Agent to the National General Gas Consumer's Company Ltd and by 1881 he is known to have had offices in Minster Place, Ely, where he ran a business as a bookseller and printer. He was married to Jane and had a daughter Jennie Gertrude.

The Cambridge Chronicle carried the following report from Ely in their weekly edition of fourth January 1868:-

> On Saturday last, handbills announced that a sale by auction would take place, "under a distress" of the coke, coals, tar, and other property belonging to our Light Company; and no one regretted the fact. For our gas we pay six shillings per thousand feet, and generally speaking it is of a very inferior quality. It must not be supposed that this company has sustained any pecuniary loss by Ely; on the contrary, the gas works here are very profitable; but other places we understand have brought our Light Company into a "distressing" condition. The news flew about Ely last week "like wild fire" that our gas was seized by "fits" meaning, we suppose, that Mr Fitzjohn, a sheriff's officer, was "in possession of the Gas Works". It is not a generous feeling to triumph over anybody in distress, but it must be admitted that Mr Fitzjohns visit to Ely, under the circumstances, made him "a welcome guest". On Monday night the town crier publicly announced that the sale at the gas works would not take place; so we presume that something has transpired to relieve the distress of the London "gents" connected with the Ely Light Company.

Discontentment continued, for on the twenty first of March 1868 the following appeared in the Cambridge Chronicle:-

> A meeting of the Gas Committee met at the Shire-Hall on Saturday night last for the purpose of appointing an engineer to confer with the London Gas Company with the view of purchasing the Ely gas works. Of course, as reporters are not present the proceedings are somewhat difficult to obtain. We understand that Mr James Cropley presided, and there were thirteen other gentlemen present. The candidates for the office were Mr G Muriel (whose father is a native of Ely and who has great family connections here), Mr Childs and Mr Bower. After a first voting Mr Bower's name was withdrawn and the contest was between the "Elymite" and the veteran Childs. The voting on this occasion proved to be equal, there being five for each candidate; and the not very pleasant task of giving a casting vote devolved upon the chairman, whose choice fell upon Mr Muriel, who, we hear, was proposed and seconded by two relations. We congratulate the younger engineer upon his victory and hope that his efforts to please both buyers and sellers will be crowned with success, which, however, it is only fair to say, can hardly be anticipated. From what we hear, we shall not be surprised if the purchase of the Gas Works at Ely by the citizens do not fall to the ground. We did not think so a week or two back; but "circumstances alter cases".

My father records the local people offered the Holding Company £6,000 (25/4/1868) for the entire business but on rejection of the offer threatened to build a rival works at a cost of £7,500 (9/5/1868). The 'London' Company' meaning the Country and General Gas Consumer Co, demanded £9,000. The sale never occurred for financial misfortunes befell the County and General Gas Consumer Company when later that year they were 'in Chancery' meaning the Chancery Division of the High Court in London.

Mr Bower was a gas engineer from St Neots who built many hundreds of small gas works and operted a few himself.

Edward Henry Crawford, a member, and Stephenson Clarke, a creditor, and Coal supplier, of 4, St Dunstans Alley, succeeded in their case against County and General. The judge ordered the company to be wound up and liquidators were appointed. These were Henry Palfrey Stephenson, a Civil and Consulting Gas Engineer of St Mary Axe, City of London and William Joseph White, an accountant, of King Street, Cheapside, City of London.

The following year 1869 a conveyance presumably of the mortgage was entered into between The County and General Gas Consumers Co Ltd and John Bacon a gentleman of Ely. It is presumed that it took several years to resolve the financial matters of the liquidation for it was not until 10th January 1871 that The City of Ely Gas Company was founded by which time John Bacon had died.

In 1870 Parliament wishing to help place Gas Undertakings on a Statutory footing passed a series of provisional Consolidating Acts (which was an Enabling Act having no force in law) pertaining to a number of gas undertakings in order to put them on a statutory footing. This was ratified under the Gas Act of 1881 and specifically mentions the Ely Company.

A conveyance dated 1st May 1871 between The County and General Consumers Co and Stephenson Clarke transferred the assets of the Gas works valued at £9,750 to Stephenson Clarke. It seems the original owners had reasonable expectations to demand £9,000 Not slow to make a quick profit Stephenson Clarke then sold the works to The City of Ely Gas Company on 7th August 1871 for £11,500. (Department of Trade Number 5,284). The difference in value might have been to redress debts to Stephenson Clarke. However, the Ely gas company failed in its attempts to buy the works for £6,000 three years earlier. It is worth noting that the firm Stephenson Clarke was to continue as one of the principal suppliers of coal to the works until its closure in 1959. Three Directors to the new Ely company were Charles T (Fred). Robinson, William Neal or Heal, Chairman and Thomas Allpress, Secretary as well as clerk to Edwin Cross.

The following day 8th August, but confirmed on 29th August at a meeting convened at The Lamb Hotel, Ely, the new Directors resolved to 'borrow £3,000 at 5% on Mortgage of the Companies Property and works at (Ely?) Cambridge and additionally, to borrow a further £300 on Mortgage at 5% interest for the purposes of buying and installing a purifier, scrubber, boiler and engine when required by the lessee', who was a Mr Alfred Williams.

> Mr Williams was a well known Ga Engineer and plant dealer who also operated several small works on his own account.

On 22nd October 1880 at an Extraordinary meeting of Members of the Company held at Minster Place, Ely, a resolution was passed and confirmed on 11th November to 'issue the remaining 300 Ten Pound shares of the capital of The Company the shares carrying a premium of One Pound per share and a sum of Five Pounds to be paid on each share at the time of allotment'. These shares were bought by three gentlemen all from Cambridge but in business as co-partners as Bankers in Ely. They were Ebenezer Bird Foster, George Edward Foster and Charles Finch Foster. The Ely Gas Companies Bankers were Fosters Bank, later to merge with the Capital and Counties Bank.

The Gas Orders Confirmation Act of 1881 validated in law the Gas Act of 1870 and incorporated eleven undertakings of which Ely was one. The schedule of orders attached to the Act gave Ely Gas "Orders empowering the City of Ely Gas Company [Limited] to maintain and continue Gasworks, and to make and supply Gas in the parishes of Holy Trinity, hamlet of Stuntney St Mary, hamlet of Chettisham, and the parish of the College of Ely". It was cited the Ely Gas Order 1881. An important side effect was that the Gas Company now had powers to open public highways no longer having to rely on permission from the Local Authority.

The full detail of the schedule attached to the Order refers to such matters as capital, shares, the sale and auctioning of shares, premiums on shares, and limits on dividends and indeed the different types of shares. There are limits on the undertakers borrowing powers, purchase of land, maintenance and continuance of gas making plant, the quality of gas, its pressure, its price and means of testing. Finally, there is a description of the works location and a scaled drawing of the site prepared by Alfred Williams an engineer from Bankside, London, copies of which were lodged at the Board of Trade, Whitehall Gardens London, the Clerk to the Peace of the Isle of Ely at his offices in Wisbech, the Clerk to the Peace for the County of Cambridge at his office in Royston and finally in the Private Bill Office of the House of Commons. Williams was of course the new Lessee.

The site is described as being on two separate pieces of land lying both north and south of Little Back Lane. The northern site adjoins Little Back Lane, Potters Lane and the premises of a public house and yard belonging to Henry Hall, by Station Road to the north and to the east, by houses reputed to belong to Thomas Appleyard. The southern site was bounded by Little Back lane to the north, Potters Lane to the west, by the waterworks under the jurisdiction of the Ely Local Board of Health to the east, and to the south, by an orchard belonging to James Button. The 1881 census documents a Fredrick J. Sweet Secretary and Manager, as living at Railway Terrace later to be known as Casllehythe or Castelhythe as it was sometimes spelt. This was on the opposite side of the road to the gas works in what today is Station Road.

Of the few shareholders meetings now traceable, one of particular significance is an Extraordinary Meeting convened in the Company Offices in Station Road on 16th July 1913 under the Chairmanship of Alfred Kitt. Here the Special Resolution put to members was to alter the memorandum of Association of the Company by deleting Clause 3 and adding - 'To carry on in the City of Ely and elsewhere in the County of Cambridge the business of an Electric Light Company and to construct, lay down, establish and fix all necessary cables, wires, lines, accumulators, lamps and works to generate and distribute and supply electricity to light buildings both public and private. Also to carry on the business of electricians, mechanical engineers of electricity for the purpose of light, heat, motive power and to manufacture all apparatus, fittings, appliances for generation, distribution and employment of electricity. Additionally, to arrange with authorities, supreme, municipal, and local to obtain rights, privileges and concessions which the Company may think it desirable to obtain. To obtain any provisional order or Act of Parliament for enabling the Company to carry any of its objects into effect and oppose any proceedings or applications, which may seem calculated to prejudice the interests of the company. Finally, the name of the Company be changed and be hereafter the 'City of Ely Gas and Electricity Company Ltd' countersigned by Thomas A. Guyatt Secretary. Later the same year, the Ely District Council considered an application from the Ely Gas Company to the Board of Trade for a Provisional Order under the Electric Lighting Regulations authorising them to produce and distribute electricity in the City. By a majority of 7 votes to 5 consent was refused (Gas World 27/122/1913)

Little more is known of early history as the first Minute Book 1871-1885 seems to have been lost. The subsequent history of the Company between 1886 and 1959, drawn largely from the five remaining Minute Books, is recounted in the following chapters of this book.

Image from National Gas Archive

Chapter 17
Gas Works Site, buildings and gas making plant

Maps and Plans

In the absence of documented records when the works was founded, as to the type and extent of plant on the works, then early maps and the occasional site plan are the best means of establishing the extent of the business. Bidwells map of 1851 produced, it is believed, for rating purposes, is the first map to explore. The Gas works is easily picked out by the circular structures, although the extent of the site can only be guessed at as it nestles alongside what appear to be small houses. Bentons Square, referred to in the minutes, adjoins the works but again it is not clear whether this and the surroundings buildings were owned by the works at this time. Not far away are to be found five public houses, one or more of which might have been patronised by stokers whose heavy manual work charging and emptying the retorts was very hot and exhausting.

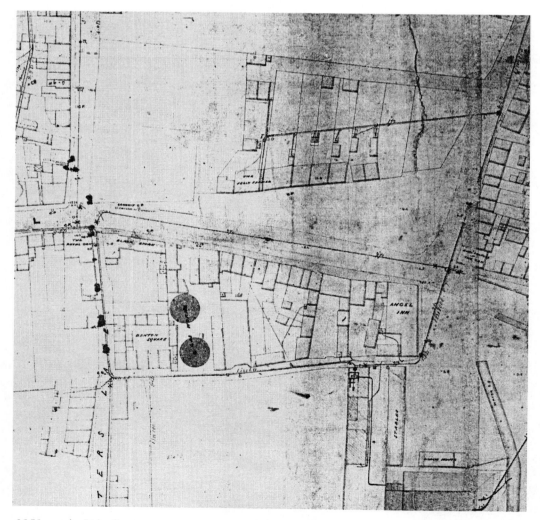

1851 map by Bidwells.   Courtesy of Cambridgeshire County Council Archives

110

1881 - Scale Plan of Works

This shows the location of the retort house, (containing what would have been the horizontal retorts) adjacent coal stores, tar tank and gas holders. An exhauster house containing an engine (certainly steam) and exhauster and boiler. A condenser, scrubber, four purifier boxes 9 feet square, a meter house and governor are easily spotted. There were three gas holders of 30 and 34 and 42 feet diameter, the later of which was south of Little Back Lane. The 34 and 42 foot diameter holders have been constructed since Bidwell's map of 1851. Finally, a 30ft diameter tar tank, the base tank of an earlier gas holder, a smithy [with chimney], shed, store, stove house and two stables are all contained in the main, northerly yard. The small office abutted Station Road and the foreman's house fronted onto Potters Lane. Coal deliveries to the works almost certainly were made via an entrance in Little Back Lane. The deed records document the area of the two sites. The land parcel north of Back Lane was 0.43 acres and that south of Back Lane 1.07 acres.

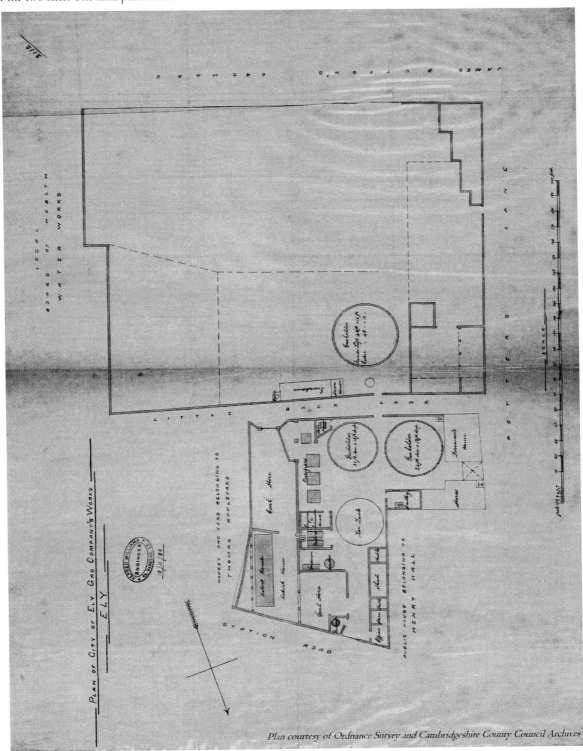

Plan courtesy of Ordnance Survey and Cambridgeshire County Council Archives

An Ordnance Survey Map 1886 Scale 1:2,500

Map courtesy of Ordnance Survey and Cambridgeshire County Council Archives

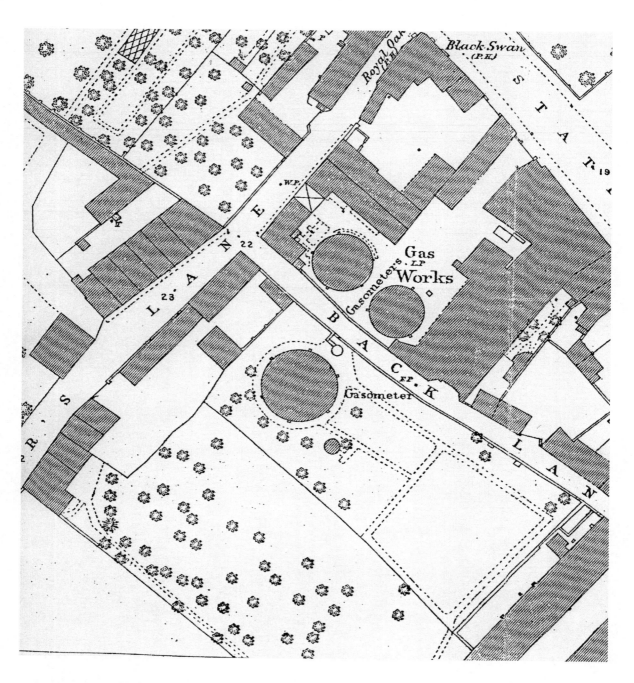

This map shows the expansion of the works and most strikingly the vertical guide pillars of the gas holders or gasometers as they are shown on the map. The trees in the south site clearly show its former use as an orchard. The new entrance onto Station Road has superseded the former access from Back Lane.

1900 Ordnance Survey map from District Valuer's Office. Original Scale 1: 5,000

Map courtesy of Ordnance Survey and Cambridgeshire County Council Archives

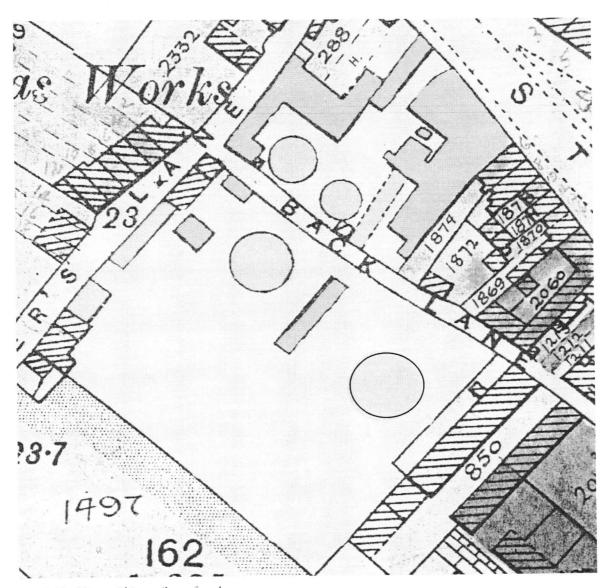

Shaded buildings within cartilage of works

The 5,000 scale Ordnance Survey map of 1900/1911 from the Ely Land Valuer's office, not only shows the works, but amazingly numbers the individual buildings under the company's control. It is believed this is the same map used when the Ely Gas Company lodged an appeal on its ratings in 1933 when there was a need to identify the works curtilage and all the structures in it. Whilst the works has not been ascribed a land parcel number it has been annotated at a later date with the number 279 which is believed to refer to its Valuation Reference.

The Ordnance Survey map of 1925 original scale 1:2,500

Map courtesy of Ordnance Survey and Cambridgeshire County Council Archives

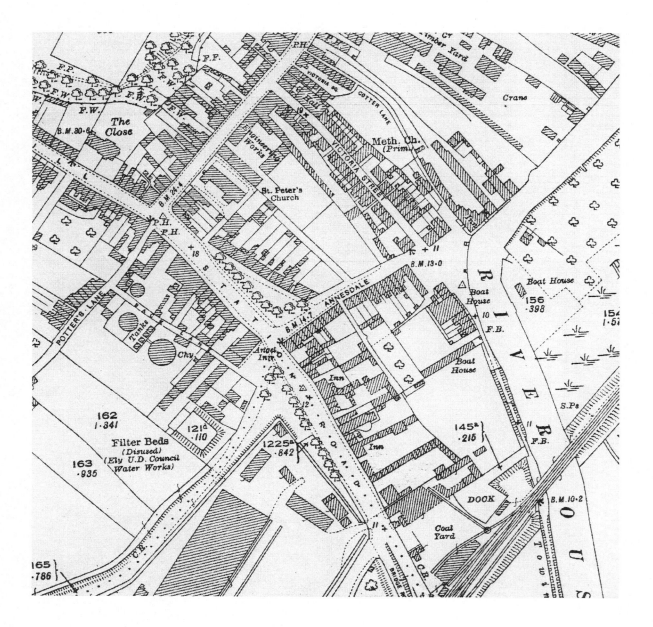

This shows no further expansion of the site but for a set of purifier boxes of which there is a photograph on page 112.

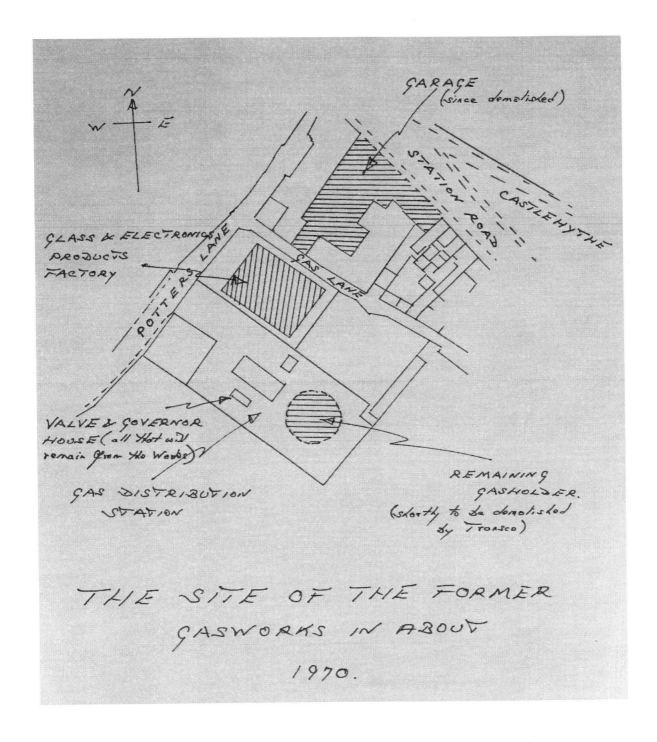

GARAGE
(since demolished)

N
W — E

STATION ROAD.
CASTLEHYTHE

GLASS & ELECTRONICS
PRODUCTS
FACTORY

POTTERS LANE
GAS LANE

VALVE & GOVERNOR
HOUSE (all that will
remain from the Works)?

GAS DISTRIBUTION
STATION

REMAINING
GASHOLDER.
(shortly to be demolished
by Transco)

THE SITE OF THE FORMER
GASWORKS IN ABOUT
1970.

The manufacturing plant north of Gas Lane has been demolished and a Trigon Garage built in its place, subsequently replaced by a residential building complex. On the southern site the new premises of the Glass and Electronics Products (Cambridge) Ltd. The Gas distribution centre is confined to one gas holder, the last to be built and a selection of outbuildings probably containing valves and a pressure reducing governor.

British Gas Property Plan

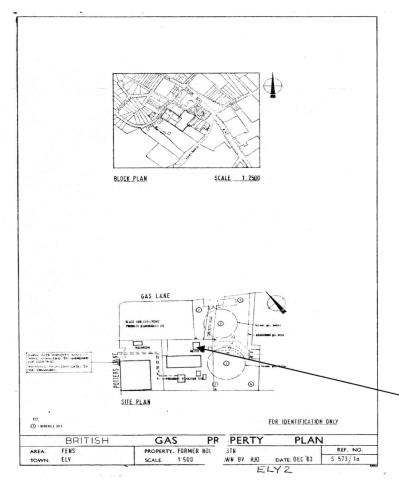

A Property Plan dated 1983 identifies the land sold off south of Back Lane for the purposes of building a Glass and Electrical Industrial Unit. What was left of the former gas works comprises a gas meter and pressure reduction valve gear for the medium pressure main from Cambridge which fed the lower pressure network in the Ely District as well as the two gas holders.

Below- he Governor house built in the south yard, with its meter and valves survived the sale of the works and served the community for many years. Note the lamp shades and curtains, my mothers touch I am sure!

The Gas Holders

Old maps and site plans are the most useful source of information as to the early structures, particularly as these give a good indication of their plan size from which can be approximated their capacity.

Bidwell's map, the earliest record in 1851, reveals two gas holders built in the north yard, close to the gas making plant. These would have been of the single lift type, for multi-sectional holders had not been invented at this time. I believe that the works when first built probably had only one holder and as gas usage increased, additional storage was needed. Gas was manufactured over a twenty four hour period but in those days used exclusively for lighting and was consumed in a few hours after sunset. From scaling these drawings it is possible to guestimate that they held 11,300 cu ft each.

There is an approximate ratio between the diameter and height of a single lift holder, necessary to ensure its stability especially in high winds and this enables a rough calculation as to their gas storage capacity. It seems appropriate to briefly describe a gas holder as an inverted glass floating in a pan of water. As gas storage diminishes, so the glass submerges and as it fills it rises higher and where it is a multi-lift holder a second or third glass telescopes upwards. A water seal prevents gas leakage and surplus steam from the works was blown into the seal in winter to stop ice forming.

The Map of 1880 shows two additional holders, the first of thirty four feet diameter and the second, a more modern two lift holder, of forty four feet diameter. At some time one of the earlier holders had gone and its base below ground level used it is believed for a tar and gas liquor store. Gas storage in this holder would have risen to about 16,000 cu ft by this date.

By 1901 plans were afoot amongst directors to expand the gas storage capacity and the manager at the time, a Mr Guyatt, had been sent to Leeds to negotiate on the Companies behalf. Directors later that year closed a contract with Messrs Clayton for a 60 foot diameter holder with two lifts each 24 ft high at a cost of £2,416. Five foot diameter trial excavations were made on the planned

site to ascertain the soil type and then a 64 feet diameter concrete foundation 12 inches thick was constructed. The gas holder stored 45,000 cu feet of gas. By 1925 a second holder had been demolished and the fifth holder erected of 114,000 cu ft capacity.

Plant failure on the works occurred from time to time and this applied equally to gas holders. In 1931 a leak was found in the crown of one holder and repaired by a Lincoln Company. Directors agreed in future they should make regular checks. A year later, water was found in the syphon outlet of a second holder. Two holders were dismantled in 1937 and months later a gas leak was found in the crown of a another holder which was repaired at a cost of £140. Much more serious was the partial collapse of the central pillar of a holder due to settlement and the sides of the 'dumpling' on which it stood. Repairs were effected by pouring fifteen inches of concrete into the base.

The potential dangers of gas holders were very shortly enshrined in legislation later that year, by the passing of the 1937 Factories Act. Clause 33 required all gas holders to be inspected by a competent person once every two years. At Ely this work was entrusted to the British Engine, Boiler and Electrical Insurance Co who made the inspections and provided the insurance at £16-15 -0d less 10%agents fee per year for cover of £3,400. Whilst most works insured their holders which necessitated their regular inspections by an outside specialist this legislation forced the lax companies like Ely to fall in line.

In 1940 the manager presented a case to directors that the existing holder capacity was insufficient, there being only fourteen hours storage at times of peak demand and using the very inflexible three vertical retort system left the company at risk of damaging the plant or running out of gas in an attempt to meet fluctuating demand. These conditions had prevailed for three years. The existing holder would in a few years need major refurbishment which meant deflating it to undertake the work. That in turn would necessitate building another holder alongside to keep the plant working and the town supplied with gas. Meanwhile the cost of new gas holders had risen 33% in seven months largely because of the war. The manager reported that the works was particularly vulnerable to 'new enemy bombing', with just the one gas holder and the works could be put out of action

The photograph shows the four purifiers with gas holder no 4 in the background and number 3 to the right in Benson Yard. Number 4 gas holder is really very old as it has cast iron columns wear as later ones used steel. For some reason the wheels, chains and weights which counterbalance the crown have been removed. The photographer is standing on an elevated site looking west towards Potters Lane. It seems quite possible that he was standing on the concrete base of holder no 5.

Nine people are caught on camera, probably all of the works staff, the same number as appear in the photo of works staff later on in this book. The man with the moustache standing next to the travelling gantry might be the manager and the character to the left of the photograph the foreman.

The travelling gantry with its suspended pulley block was used to lift off the top covers of the purifiers. A thatched cottage is visible to the left. The foreman's house is visible in Benton's Yard to the right. It is estimated this photograph was taken sometime between 1898 when the purifier boxes were bought from the Corporation of Newcastle under Tyne and 1933.   Image courtesy of CCC Local history collection very easily. The new RAF hospital was by now the company's largest consumer and the manager advised directors that the company had a duty of care vested in it, to take every possible measure to ensure continuity of supply. Should directors prevaricate the gas works risked ordering a new holder when prices were at their highest. A holder of 150,000 cu ft was suggested. The national steel shortage was now so great that only the strongest case could be made to secure a licence and the Manager considered Ely had such a case.

To finance the venture estimated at £8,000 he suggested the 'Excess Profits Tax', which the company looked set to have to pay to the tax authorities, could, in part, be offset by this capital expenditure. Additionally, the remaining 600 £10 shares could be issued, but this was likely to meet with disapproval as this would lower the share dividend paid to shareholders, which included all the Directors. Alternatively, £6,000 of Preference Shares could be issued but this would require Treasury approval which was not easily obtained. A bank loan could be explored on the personal guarantee of the Directors. Finally the holders could be bought on a ten year HP agreement, the payments for which could come from revenue. Directors decided to consult the company auditor, assess the likelihood of obtaining a steel licence and consult the British Engine and Electrical Insurers as to the expected life of the existing holder.

Minutes in 1941 record that on February 1st and 2nd gas stocks fell to 1½ sheets at eleven pm.

(Sheets meaning the steel panels on the sides of the holder), a dangerously low level. A stoppage had occurred in the retorts reducing the amount of gas made. This merely reinforced the need for more gas storage.

Months of shuttle diplomacy ensued with the auditor, Wood Drew, who advised directors not to pursue an HP agreement, the banks who refused a loan and the Board of Trade initially had refused a steel licence. Mr Whaley, the consulting engineer, then recommended a modified design incorporating a concrete rather than a steel tank at the base to save steel and the contractors prepared revised estimates. Messrs George Lock and Son had meanwhile completed trial excavations. By February 1942 the Board of Trade gave permission for a single lift spirally guided holder designed to take three lifts at an estimated cost of £2,500 for the concrete base, (which from memory was above ground level) £2,650 for the above ground level steelwork and £210 for the pipe-work connections. F C Construction were engaged to build the concrete base. A second lift was considered but abandoned on cost grounds. By 1943 the holder was tested and brought into use having been financed by the company from its mushrooming profits. It was finally painted by J H Kenyon with red lead based undercoat and finished in 'foliage green' all paints being supplied by the Torbay Paint Co. At the same time the old holder next door was chipped, cleaned and repainted in a similar way.

Gas usage was shortly to rise by over 25% year on year for a number of years and at one stage Directors and the manager struggled with ways to meet the consumer boom. One option was to build a completely new gas works on land currently part of the railway sidings, a second choice was purchase existing properties adjacent to the works, demolish and expand the gas making plant. The third option, the one selected, was to install additional gas making plant on the present site and increase the storage of the recent holder by two further lifts giving it a capacity of 500,00 cu ft. I just remember this being done, so believe it occurred in about 1949.

This twelvefold increase in gas storage between 1835 and 1885 must accurately reflect the increase in gas manufacture and usage in the City over a period of about fifty years. Bearing in mind that the census return of 1831 showed a population of 5,079 inhabitants (6,257 according to Robinsons Directory) and by 1925 there were slightly less, namely 5,025 then increased gas consumption has to be attributable to more people being 'connected up' to the gas supply, rather than an increase in the local population. After that date there was a considerable influx of refugees into Ely, anxious to avoid the blitz, and they certainly boosted gas sales as is borne out by the company minutes.

In 1891 the works is documented as having an annual usage of 1,300 tons of coal [3tons 11 cwt. per day] but seasonal demand between summer and winter probably resulted in 1 ton of coal per day in summer, and up to 7 tons of coal per day in winter. In those times using a horizontal retort 1 ton of coal would produce roughly 8,000 cu ft of gas or about 28,000,000 B.Th.U {British Thermal Units} equivalent to 280 therms per day. With a declared c.v. {calorific value} of 500 B.Th.U. per cu ft, which was the richness of the gas, then the average volume of gas produced daily would have been approximately 50,000 cu.ft. or 18 million cu.ft. per year. By 1940 vertical retorts had been constructed and these combined with refinements in manufacture increased gas output per ton of coal to 80 therms. My father recorded the plant had a 82.2% efficiency which was high.

By conclusion one can surmise that daily gas production in 1851 was in the order of 8.5 million cubic feet per year, 23,000 per day, just over half the calculated volume of the gas holders in that year. I calculate about 12 hundred weights of coal would have been needed to run the works each day and allowing for higher winter demand 225 plus tons per year.

Gradual expansion of the works over time
showing increasing gas holder capacity, make of gas and coal usage

Year	Holder	Location of holder	Capacity in cubic feet *Estimated	Total capacity of holders cu.ft.	Make of Gas per year in million cubic feet *Estimated	Coal used per year tons *Estimated
1835 Opening	Guess No 1	Main Yard	*11,300	*11,300	*Between 1-2	*90-175
1850 Bidwells Map 1851	No 1 +2	Main Yard Main Yard	*11,300 *11,300	*22,600	*Between 2-4	*175-350
Site Plan 1880	No 2 +3 +4	Main Yard Benton Yard Orchard	*11,300 *16,000 *45,000	*72,300	*Between 4-8	*350-700
1886 OS Map	No 2 +3 +4	Main Yard Benton Yard Orchard	*11,300 *16,300 *45,000	*72,300	*12	1,100
1901 Holders 3 & 4 probably redundant	No 3 +4 +5	Benton Yard Orchard Orchard	*16,000 *45,000 114,000	*175,000	*Between 13-26	1,702+ 1,040 gall spirit
1915	No 5	Orchard	114,000	114,000	28	2,487
1937	No 5	Orchard	114,000	114,000	42	2,924
By 1948 to 1959 closure	No5 +6	Orchard Orchard	114,000 500,000	614,000	91 102 (1951)	5,777

120

40 therms per ton of coal is about average for a 1890 country works.

I therm = 100,000B.Th.U
= 200 cu.ft. @500c.v.

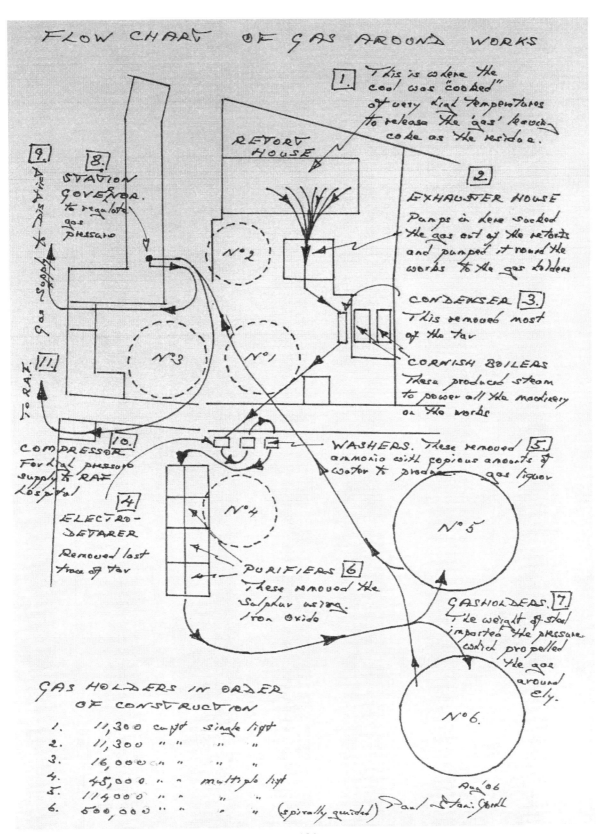

FLOW CHART OF GAS AROUND WORKS

1. This is where the coal was "cooked" at very high temperatures to release the 'gas' leaving coke as the residue.

RETORT HOUSE

9. To RAF | Gas Supply & Distribution

8. STATION GOVENOR. to regulate gas pressure

2. EXHAUSTER HOUSE Pumps in here sucked the gas out of the retorts and pumped it round the works to the gas holders

CONDENSER 3. This removed most of the tar

CORNISH BOILERS These produced steam to power all the machinery on the works

No 2

No 3

No 1

11. To R.A.F.

10. COMPRESSOR. For high pressure supply to RAF hospital

4. ELECTRO-DETARER Removed last trace of tar

No 4

WASHERS. These removed 5. ammonia with copious amounts of water to produce gas liquor

No 5

PURIFIERS 6. These removed the sulphur using Iron Oxide

GASHOLDERS. 7. The weight of steel imported the pressure which propelled the gas around ely.

No 6.

GAS HOLDERS IN ORDER OF CONSTRUCTION

1. 11,300 cu ft single lift
2. 11,300 " " " "
3. 16,000 " " " "
4. 45,000 " " multiple lift
5. 114,000 " " " "
6. 500,000 " " " " (spirally guided)

Aug '06 Paul Stani Gould

121

The Retorts

There is scant detail as to the type of gas making plant in use in the early days. All retorts would have been of the horizontal type used throughout the industry. An indenture dated 1864 states that there were sixteen retorts in the works. Very early retorts were made of cast iron, but were superseded by retorts constructed of firebrick or fireclay which certainly were constructed in Ely. These were built and rebuilt at regular intervals owing to their rapid disintegration when operating at temperatures of 750C°, (2,190 ° -2,370°F) as well as to expand to meet ever increasing demand for gas.

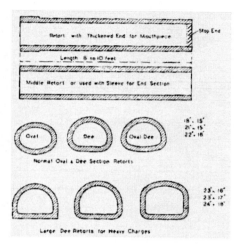

Drawings of 'stop ended' fireclay retorts showing 'end on' and horizontal profiles of a selection of differing designs. The 'Mouthpiece' was a door made of cast iron which attached to one end of the lozenge shaped retort. Upwards of 2 cwt of coal was thrown into the retort through the door and coke later extracted.

In 1885 we read that the manager was instructed to acquire tenders for a new set of retorts from Messrs Cliff, Corvein, Moberly and Percy, to which telescopic 'Mouthpieces' were fitted bought from Williamson and Son at 10/- each. During the period 1886 to 1900 there was not only regular maintenance of retort settings but expansion too and it is believed there could have been up to twenty seven stop ended retorts available for use comprising two settings of 'sixes', two beds of 'fours' and a setting of 'sevenses'. In 1895 a consignment of used railway lines was purchased for use as 'bulkstaves' for incorporation in a bed of retorts. For most of the year only some of the retorts would have been in use leaving spare retort capacity for the winter months when gas usage increased. A further eight horizontal retorts were commissioned in 1905 designed to the Waddle Patent and erected by Messrs Dempster at a cost of £130. Their cost rose to £270 and the retorts

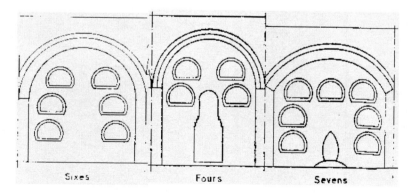

Illustration of three 'Beds'. The first of 6 retorts, the second of 4 retorts and the third of 7 retorts all found at the Ely Works at some stage in its history. All were probably 'direct fired', with a coal fire immediately beneath each bench of retorts. Together the three beds made a bench of retorts.

proved unsuccessful. They were totally rebuilt twelve years later and at the same time the two beds of fours demolished.

In 1888 tenders were again sought for retorts and one accepted from Mr Alfred Williams. He quoted 3s/10d per foot run of retort, (they were each about 10 feet long) and bricks at 62s.6d per

1,000. The same year directors resolved to accept a tender from Messrs Harper for more retorts priced at 3s.5d per foot and for fire bricks 59s.0d per thousand delivered to Ely Station. Mr Kitt, the recently appointed Director, supervised the work as he was a qualified gas engineer, more experienced, we assume, than the works manager.

The Company minutes of 1891 are a little more explicit in that they detail tenders being secured to build two beds of sixes, meaning twelve retorts in two blocks or beds as they were known, the work to be done by Messrs Cliff and Gibbons and Alfred Williamson at 4s.0d per foot, 68s.6d per thousand for fire bricks, 19s.9d per ton for fire clay, 80s. for Eville [a silicatious clay] and 30s for yellow brick loam. In 1893 the directors instructed the manager to 'let down,' meaning shut down the two beds of 'four' for them to be 'reset' meaning rebuilt which was undertaken by Alfred Williams and Co in February 1894. By February 1896 a further setting of seven retorts had been commissioned to the design of Messrs Gibbons at a cost of £25-5s-0d.

At this time in the Company's growth, the need for higher gas production was very much in the Directors sights. They instructed the manager to acquire tenders for a charger, a piece of equipment for mechanically filling the retorts instead of stokers having to manually throw coal on to each retort. The cost turned out to be prohibitively expensive £1,000-£1,200, so the idea was dropped. However, this marked a turning point in the way gas would be produced in the future to meet increased demand in Ely. In 1925 the manager reported to Directors that gas production had risen from 23 million cu ft per year in 1918 to 41 million cu ft seven years later, that the works had a capacity for 60 million cubic feet and based on anticipated City usage the works would be overloaded in four to five years time.

The following year Directors were making provisional enquiries about Vertical Retorts, a new design, which was much more efficient than the existing horizontal retorts and they wished to ascertain the success of one they knew about recently erected at Newbury. Woodall-Duckham from , one of the two best known firms making this type of plant, submitted drawings containing three retorts at a cost of £7,500. Directors deferred an immediate decision, sought some modifications and looked to means of financing the venture. By November 1926, a contract was signed for £8,793 to build the plant, finance being advanced by Barclays Bank with whom directors tried unsuccessfully to negotiate better terms for the loan than they were originally offered. Only after the contract was signed did the gas company apply to the local council for permission to erect the structure.

By March 1927 it was almost complete. A year later the manager reported the new gas making plant had saved 400 tons of coal and that Barrow Coal was not suitable in this type of retort- although records show the works continued to buy it, maybe to be blended with other coals. The three retorts were about twenty five feet top to bottom and fifty four inches maximum width and were "downwardly heated".

As with all retorts, they had to be relined with fire bricks from time to time, the new manager as soon as he

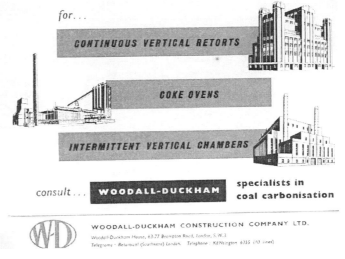

for...

CONTINUOUS VERTICAL RETORTS

COKE OVENS

INTERMITTENT VERTICAL CHAMBERS

consult... **WOODALL-DUCKHAM**   specialists in coal carbonisation

WOODALL-DUCKHAM CONSTRUCTION COMPANY LTD.
Woodall-Duckham House, 63-77 Brompton Road, London, S.W.3
Telegrams : Retortical (Southerns) London.   Telephone : KENsington 6355 (10 lines)

123

joined the firm in 1933 arranged for the two old beds 6 horizontal retorts which had been mothballed, to be rebuilt. By 1935 these were brought back to use so the Vertical Retort could be let down to enable Woodall Duckham to re-build the top 10 feet at a cost of £430. The re-built retort is documented as having saved 2,000 tons of coal as a result of improved efficiency in its first year of use.

Two years later as an experiment the manager discovered he could supply 110,000-120,000 cu ft of gas per day from one retort alone ,enough for the entire City, but it was not financially efficient to run the plant in this way. Barely four years after re-building the retorts, the Manager was advising Directors as to how inflexible the system was, as the entire Vertical Retort should have been designed around four smaller retorts, which would have proved easier to manage than three slightly larger ones. One retort had been let down cold whilst the others were still in use and workmen climbing inside discovered it was badly 'spalled'. Fire cement was used to fill the cracks. In an adjacent retort coal had 'hung up', meaning, become stuck, and carbonising suspended for 2½ days. This all reinforced the manager's opinion that the existing system produced poor results, had high repair costs, that the retorts were too large

Woodall-Duckham was founded in 1903 by Harold Woodall Manager and Engineer to the Bournemouth Gas and Water Co and his assistant (Sir Arthur Duckham) to exploit their patents in gas manufacture.

The continuous Vertical Retort was soon in production and by 1914, 64 plant had been erected and manufacturing licences let in France and Germany. By 1918, 100 plant had been sold, Ely's CVR being built in 1927. By 1939, 700 plant had been constructed and a rush of orders occurred following Nationalisation and rationalisation of the Industry up to 1952.

The company was taken over by Babcock and Wilcox Ltd in 1973.

and the system inflexible such that it was necessary to always keep a bed of horizontal retorts on standby because the verticals could not be repaired when under fire. After acquiring quotes for repairs to the vertical retort and costs to build three beds of horizontal retorts, directors could find little to choose between horizontal retorts and the newer type of vertical retorts and turned wisely to their consulting engineer, Mr Whaley, for a second opinion. After much discussion, directors agreed to accept a quote from Woodall Duckham for £5,300 to repair the vertical retort in part because the contractor reduced their quotation by £1,000 out of what appears good will and to spread payment over three years. The existing three retort system was adapted to become four slightly smaller retorts.

Because of the National steel shortage it was essential to apply to the Board of Trade well in advance for a licence to buy what little steel was available. This the Manager did only to be told that he could only have a licence for 12 tons of the 36 necessary for the task. It was left to him and the contractor to look for second hand steel as best they could.

In order to commence the new building work in 1941, the horizontal retorts were fired up after first fitting a second hand Hydraulic Main acquired from the East Dereham Gas Co. It was most unusual for a gas company whose staff had become accustomed to the labour saving and less arduous work of a vertical retort, to switch manufacture back to the old fashioned manually charges horizontal retorts. The brickwork to the Woodall Duckham retorts was completed in 1942 and after some delays acquiring specialised castings the retort was under fire by January 1943 and was tested by Mr Waggs for forty eight hours. My father reported it was delivering the guaranteed results promised and was proving satisfactory in every way. Mr Whatley tested the plant after which

Woodall Duckham sent a Mr Grasby to Ely for a month to fine tune the plant and train the foreman as to how to operate it.

By 1944 the manager was reporting existing carbonising capacity of 250,000 cu ft and gas demand for the winter ahead of 285,000 cu ft, more in the event of a severe winter. Directors therefore agreed to commission Woodall Duckham to extend the plant from the existing four vertical retorts to six. At a cost of £8,000, with a payment of £2,000 on completion and the balance spread over four years.

Meanwhile the lift, essential for conveying coal to the feed hoppers at the top of the retort had been overhauled, five extra large locking lift gates having already been fitted by the Preston Lift Company to comply with the Factory Regulations. (there must have been four levels at which the lift could be stopped). New steel ropes had been fitted in 1939 at the insistence of the National Insurance Co, insurers for the lift.

A piece of equipment which my father was particularly pleased to have purchased was a patent portable electric airborne retort sealing system for £100. It enabled powered silica to be blown into an empty but still very hot retort where it fused with the silica brickwork in all the cracks and crevices through which gas would otherwise leak out. It improved the efficiency of the works.

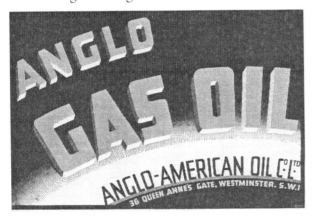

Consumer demand continued long after the war, much to the relief of directors, who somewhat hesitantly had invested heavily in the new retorts. In fact demand was such that by 1948 Directors were considering installing a 10,000 cu ft per day gas Carburetted Water Gas Plant which 'gassified' coke to make water gas and carburetted it by cracking 'gas oil' on hot brickwork. It was a cyclic process. After referral to the Ministry of Fuel the go ahead was given and a contract closed with Messrs Humphrey of Glasgow. Cost £10,000. This in turn necessitated increasing the steam raising ability of the works which at the time delivered only 50 psi. The carburetted water gas plant demanded 300,000 cu ft of steam at a greater pressure. Two new steam boilers were proposed by Economic Boiler with stoker and grate from Edwin Danks at a cost of £6,500 and a Cochrane Vertical Boiler from Cochrane's. The case was put to the Ministry of Fuel for approval.

The development of the works especially the building of the last gas holder was quite remarkable for wartime Britain when the nation was desperately short of steel most being used for armaments. Equally the acquiring of the electro detarrer was a minor miracle. They were as rare as gold dust.

My father seemed to do the opposite of what the politicians wanted and went out of his way to make and sell more gas when other gas works were looking to economise and eek out their supplies of coal.

Expansion of the works hastened apace stopping only when gas supplies from the Cambridge works were piped to Ely. The Cambridge works was then closed as supplies of 'Grid Gas' became available to all. Only later was North Sea gas exploited and distributed nationally.

Other Buildings and Machinery on the works

Directors instructed the manager in 1901 to acquire maps and plans of the old water works building nearby. Three years later an adjoining piece of freehold land and buildings of approximately 276 square yards was acquired from A and B Hall. Whether this was the same piece of land is open to question, but the Gas Company were clearly planning for future growth and expansion. In 1940 the company were again trying to purchase land behind the old water works chimney belonging to the Urban District Council.

The office block was built in 1903 by Messrs Brotherton Bros at a cost of £500 and this building survived until the works was demolished. The workshop, which also survived until the plant closure, was built by Messrs Tindall in 1908 at a cost of £392-16-7d. Other plant changes that had occurred were the heightening of the works chimney in 1900 and installation of a Blakeley Regulating Condenser for £220 in 1903.

Whilst all these developments were in progress other improvements went on at the works. The yard was resurfaced with blue bricks laid on edge and cemented together at a cost of £12-4s-0d. [Blue bricks are usually engineering bricks which were extremely hard and impermeable to frost damage so they would have been a sensible choice.] By 1898 two Cornish Boilers, used for raising steam, were installed measuring 15 ft long and 4ft 6 inches diameter at a cost of £192 from Davey Paxman who offered a twelve month guarantee. G. Waller of 165, Queen Street, Ely fitted a compensating governor which may have been fitted to them or an associated piece of equipment. Also four second hand 10 ft square purifier boxes were installed, acquired from The Newcastle upon Tyne Gas Co.

A new station meter of 1,000 cu ft per hour capacity was acquired from the Gas Meter Company in 1907 and a Cockeys Washer installed in 1912 at a cost of £68. A replacement exhauster was advised by the manager Mr Guyatt in 1922 and directors agreed to purchase a second hand one which the manager had traced, from the Wellington Gas Co for £75, with overhaul costs estimated at £40-£50. It proved so successful that instead of refurbishing the second existing smaller exhauster that directors agreed to buy another second hand one which they sourced from the Torbay Gas Co for £50. Father always used to remind me that a works must always have two exhausters, to cater for the eventuality that if one broke down there was always a standby without which gas production would cease immediately. [These sucked the gas out of the foul main of the retort and pumped it round the works to the holders]. One of these had worn out by 1940 and was replaced by 10,000 cu ft per hour exhauster made by George Waller and Son at a cost of £86 delivered. By 1949 the Governor on the retort house was struggling and was replaced by a Revall Askania

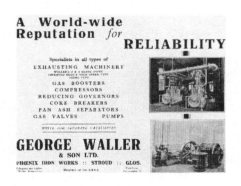

A new 10 ton per day tar dehydration plant was erected in 1928 provided by Messrs Clayton Sons at a cost of £375. This appeared to function effectively until the still corroded in 1936 and a new one made. Further repairs were undertaken in 1940 by Messrs Graven. By 1942 it must have been well and truly worn out for a brand new gas condenser was ordered from Firth Blakely at a cost of £440.

Improving energy efficiency was the goal of any forward-thinking manager and at Ely a tar burner was fitted in 1931 (presumably within one of the Cornish Boilers), to raise steam as distinct from running the boiler on coke. I am quite sure what environmental health officer today would have say as to its risk of creating atmospheric pollution.

A Vertical Gas Condenser believed to have been in Ely which removed most of the tar located behind the coke screen, 1950

The new manager recommended to directors in 1937 installation of a second hand Spencer-Bonecourt Waste Heat Boiler from Messrs Firth Blakely at a cost of £720. A Revall Asknia Governor was fitted. Together they recovered much of the waste heat which was lost from the works chimney, but not for long, for a water leak was found in the new installation which lost the company half a million gallons of water costing £30. Once repaired, it was possible to shut down one of the two trustee Cornish boilers, the second being left on a low heat as a standby. Cornish Boilers, were used for steam raising usually to power other equipment. The waste heat boiler made a saving of 25% of the works production of coke, which was now sold to the public to generate more income.

To keep down costs the company explored ways of obtaining its water independently of the water undertaker. I presume this to mean drilling a borehole or water pumped from the river. Whether this was implemented is not clear but a second hand Permutit Water softener was connected into the steam raising system a few years later.

Transport for the works staff improved with the passage of time. A hand cart was used in early days to barrow appliances up Backhill and bicycles by employees who were paid an annual allowance to use their own bicycles providing they had robust and reliable lights. Rates in 1938 were 20/- for a gas fitter, 30/- for a lamp lighter. By 1943 the existing 30 cwt Ford Lorry was fast wearing out and directors approached the Board of Trade for permission to buy a 5 ton Bedford truck from F H Nice and Co at a cost of £438. By 1946 the manager expressed a need for a 10 HP motor van costing £380 for conveying gas appliances around the district. A 10cwt Ford van was acquired for the purpose to which was attached, pipe cleaning equipment for emptying gas main siphons, made by Allan Taylor Ltd. Later still increases in coke production necessitated acquiring a further small lorry.

During the war Dr Nash, of the National Benzol Committee of the Board of Trade, asked the directors in 1943 to install a benzol recovery plant from which petrol and other products could be refined, but they refused on the grounds that the efficiency of the plant would fall and there was inadequate labour in the city to cope with yet more equipment on the works.

In 1942 many smaller pieces of equipment were acquired including a Wararsop Road breaker to replace the Pegson Road Ripper which had broken, a control board for exhauster house £100 and in 1944 an oxide crusher for £160. A Whessoe electro-detarrer

was installed to upgrade the inadequate facility at a cost of £1,200 and four second hand purifier boxes measuring 16ft by 16ft by 5ft tall were assembled in 1947 from the Coalville Gas Co in Leicestershire at a cost of £1,750. It is also possible after nationalisation, when there are no company minutes, the company acquired in about 1950, two new steam boilers one from Edwin Danks 'Economical Boiler' equipped with an Oldbury stoker and grate and a second boiler a Cochrane Vertical Boiler all costing £6,500.

Attempted False Pretences

Lived at Home—
Charged for Board

a slip of paper, purporting to be a receipt for £2 10s. for full board, given by a Mrs. Franklin, of 35, Cambridge-rd. Knowing the gentleman who lived at that address, witness

"I tried to get lodgings at Ely, but could not afford to pay the prices charged. Then I hit upon the idea of living at home and travelling between Cambridge and Ely,

Basil Horace Miller was charged with attempting to defraud the Gas Company at Ely between 16th and 19th November 1951 of a sum of £2.10s by falsely claiming a lodging allowance in Ely when he was in fact living with his parents in Cambridge and travelling daily by bus and train.

Miller presented to the Board a false receipt in the name of a fictitious person in the hope of being reimbursed by his employer. The first receipt was written out in the name of a Mrs Franklin of 35, Cambridge Road and when questioned Franklin said he had got the wrong address and later presented a second receipt this time in the name of Mrs Frankey. Mr Secker at the Ely Gas Company became suspicious. Interviewed later by Detective Constable J. Cox at the railway station, (Ely or Cambridge?) Miller replied "I made the receipts out myself. I thought with a bit of luck and keeping quiet I could get away with it".

Miller in mitigation said he had two children aged five and one, that his wages were £6 3s. Superintendent F.G. Wells reported that Miller was already on probation for two years for larceny of a pedal cycle and stealing a postal packet.

Magistrates Ald F. Everitt, Mr A. Barker and Miss J. Tebbutt fined the defendant £2.

The works yard as I remember as a young man of twelve

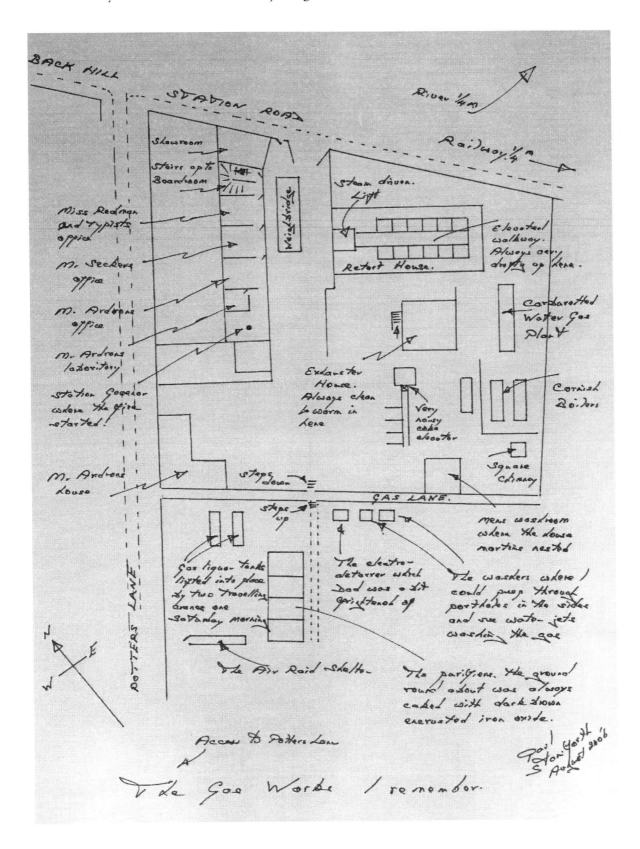

The Gas Works I remember.

Chapter 18

Coal – its sources, transport, contracts, costs, coke sales and the disposal of gas water.

Miners in about 1920
Note the moustache

Institute of Gas Engineers
leaflet

The Ely gas works was founded at a time of immense poverty and deprivation particularly in the mining communities of north England. Mine owners ruled their workers with a rod of iron, keen to win coal as cheaply as possible for export to the prosperous towns and their new gas works. There were no pit inspectors to keep an eye on safety, no pit props to hold up the roof, ventilation was at best poor, miners worked half naked and before the invention of the Davey lamp in 1815, miners relied on candles to see the coal face. Explosions of fire damp, flooding, roof falls and asphyxiation were common. Although miners received twice the pay of agricultural workers, poverty was so widespread that young women and children, as young as five years, also worked in the coal pits. The seams had tunnels as low as 32 inches in places. Coal mined in 1839 sold for 2/6d per ton of which the miner earned 7d before stoppages. Transporting it cost 6d per mile. It was in this setting of poverty and deprivation that hardy souls in the north risked their lives to earn enough to eat and in so doing provided the City of Ely with its source of coal with which to light the streets of the smart City.

Beamish Open Air Museum Northumbreland

Early pits were of the bell type where coal was won from holes in the ground. Coal was hauled to the surface in wicker baskets called 'corbes' often using a horse gin to wind it to the surface.

No early gas works, excepting those which operated using whale oil as their source material, could function without coal from which to make Town Gas, as it was known. This inevitably caused undertakings to have to decide right at the beginning, from where to buy their coal and how to transport it from the pit-head to the works.

Horse drawn chaldrons being used to fill the holds of colliers. The gantries were the common means of filling in Northumberland.

Beamish Open Air
Museum Northumberland

Images below from the National
Gas Archive Warrington

In the case of the Ely works, early supplies of coal were transported by sea and river. Whilst there is no documentary evidence to validate this there could have been no other way. What is known with certainty is that Kings Lynn was a thriving port with an extensive trade in coal from Newcastle, with a recorded 40,000 tons of coal passing through the port as far back as 1682. Little of this was used in the town, most being conveyed inland by river barges.

Additionally there was a thriving commercial trade on the river between Kings Lynn and Cambridge passing Ely on the way. Several gangs of watermen with horse drawn lighters were based in Ely and were known to moor up at Grassyards, Waterside Quay, Castle Hithe and alongside the Cutter Inn and Annesdale Wharf. The latter extended almost up to the gas works, with I am told, a bridge over the cutting, carrying what was to become Station Road when the railways came to the City. The Cutter Inn had stabling for fourteen horses.

Consignments carried included wine, sugar, spice, beer, hay, barley, beans, peas, malt, timber, turf, sand, gravel and coal. Early records state that it took twenty four hours for horse drawn lighters to travel from Lynn to Cambridge. At a distance of twenty eight miles from Kings Lynn to Ely and forty four to Cambridge. Norfolk County Archives documents five known coal buyers in Ely in 1835 who traded with Biggs a Coal Importer at Lynn. (Hall, Harlock, Crofts/Bell, Duck/Clarke and Marsh/Swanson). Pigots Directory in 1823 lists six watermen plying from Ely to Lynn. John Cross snr, Richard Hawkes (a name that recurs frequently in the Ely Gas Companies history), Abra-

ham Johnson, William Laws, John Lee and Thomas Smith. Might one of these have 'sold on' to the owners of the Ely Gas company? Shipments into Lynn and poor deliveries were frequently thwarted by unfavourable winds, lack of water in the rivers and ice to allow berthing of laden ships and quarantine restrictions on ships in the Humber when the cholera epidemics were rife. Coal types were known as 'Ducks'-25/6d per chaldron, 'Tanfield' 23/6d, 'Blyth' 22/6d, 'Hebburn', 'Hillingworth', 'Medomsley' and 'Welch'.

A screw driven steam powered tug of a type which probably plied the canal system in Yorkshire before the introduction of the tom puddingd
Yorkshire Waterways Museum

Whilst most of Ely's coal was sourced from the Yorkshire coal fields, the port of Goole did not open up until 1826, so it is certain very early coal deliveries to Lynn came from the well-established coal fields in the River Tyne and on the Durham coast. Some of this coal may have made its way to Ely. An act of Parliament of 1830 withdrew the tax on all coal shipped by sea and this would have been a great encouragement for the building of all gas works.

The Cambridge Chronicle Feb 11th 1837

NOTICE OF SALE OF LIGHTERS AND HORSES

The property of Mr William Laws , late of Ely, deceased and long known as the best and most competent Gang navigating the stream between Lynn, Ely, Cambridge, Bury etc.

Composing

Great Fore Lighter	20tons
Decked House Lighter	20 tons
Third Decked Lighter	20 tons
Little Fore Lighter	18tons
Little Decked House Lighter	18 tons
Sixth decked	20tons
Seventh decked	18 tons
Eighth decked	18 tons
Ninths decked	17 tons
Tenth decked	15 tons

Also four powerful young Water Horses. Likewise a very large and complete assortment of materials, necessary for navigating so large a Gang all of the very best quality, consisting of sails. Masts and rigging, anchors, lines, gears, steering and jambing poles, fests, corn, victual and sail barrels, corn and coal, shovels, sprits, tarpaulins, horse gear, beef kits etc. Twelve months credit will be given on approved joint security for all bargains amounting to £5 and upwards. The sale will commence punctually at ten o'clock and a cold collation will be provided for the company at the Ship Inn.

Minutes of the London Gas Light and Coke company record that there was a thriving trade of chartered sailing brigs plying along the eastern seaboard carrying coal from mines in Durham and Newcastle to consumers and businesses along the coast but particularly to the large London Gas Companies. The crews on these ships had often been displaced from whaling ships, the future of which was threatened by the increased use of coal rather than whale oil for making gas. Life on board was harsh and the crews were often later recruited into the Navy. By 1853 screw driven steam propelled colliers of larger capacity, 500 tons upwards, started to supersede the sailing brigs of 50-100 tons. Many colliers were lost in storms along the coast and other vessels were commandeered by the Admiralty for use during both the Crimea and later the great World Wars, during which many were lost to enemy action.

As the demand for coal increased to meet the mushrooming boom of Victorian Industrial revolution so too did the means of conveying greater and greater quantities. A canal system was built to link the Yorkshire collieries with the port of Goole. This, in turn, brought the invention of the 'tom puddings, rather ungainly floating coal tubs which were towed by tug in crocodile fashion. Once at the port, they were individually lifted fully laden out of the water on one of several giant hoists and tipped into the holds of colliers moored up alongside. By this time sailing vessels had given way to coal fired screw driven colliers of even greater capacity.

The early Cog sailing ships were superseded by the smaller but faster ketches and brigs and these vessels sailed into Kings Lynn carrying their cargoes. Once at Lynn they were unloaded manually with gangs of what were called 'whippers' who lifted the coal from the ships holds with a series of hoists using wicker baskets with hoisting ropes slung over sheaves attached to the rigging.

Tom puddings
An accident at Goole port resulted in a fully laden duck being sunk. Because the string
of ducks were close coupled the sinking duck pulled the adjacent ducks under water so
eventually the entire chain of ducks were under water all within one dock.
Yorkshire Waterways Museum

Left - The Collier Brig Mary by John Scott off Newcastle (about 1885)

Above - A coal fired screw driven collier of the 1920's

South Shields Museum and Art Gallery (Tyne and Wear Museums

Gas Council publication

The routes along which coal was conveyed from the mines of northern England to the Ely works.

Hatched areas- coal reserves
Darkened areas- coal fields

National Gas Archive

Legend

———	Likely route of shipping from Northumberland / Durham pits to Kings Lynn 1835
••••••••	River conveyance of Coal from King Lynn to Ely 1835 onwards
- - - - -	Likely route of shipped coal from Goole to Kings Lynn
– – – –	Probable route of coal by rail from Yorkshire coal fields to Ely starting between 1846 /1855 until closure

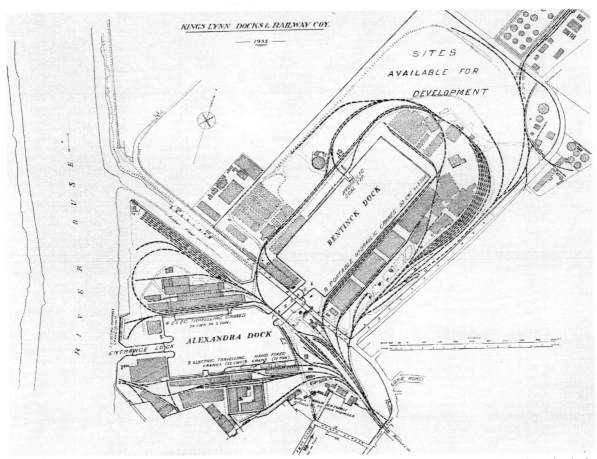

Kings Lynn Port 1933 - Alexandria dock is clearly shown together with the widened mouth to the dock
Taken from the Kings Lynn Docks and Railway Co. Commemorative Issue 1865

Left - Alexandra Dock Kings Lynn on the River Great Ouse some time between C1860. One or more sailing Brigs or Keel in the photo might have carried coal destined for use in the Ely Gas Works. Coal stocks, horse drawn and railway wagons are clearly visible.

Photo courtesy of Norfolk County Council Millennium Library

Boat traffic was certainly used to convey some of the most bulky waste 'gas water ', as it was called, in the early days, 'gas liquor' in my father's time, from the works to Kings Lynn to the fertiliser factory for re-processing. No company records detail which watermen were engaged but it is known that Cambridge works used the services of two skippers and it seems a reasonable assump-

Steam tug Olga in the distance and tank barges Lizzie and Enid loading gas liquor at Cambridge Gas Works. The buildings in the background are part of the gas driven sewage pumping station located adjacent to the Gas works.

Image taken from Eastern Gas Board publication

tion that the same two people handled Ely's liquor. Two steam tugs were used for the purpose Olga helmed by Edwards towed tank barges Enid and Lizzie whilst Nellie skippered by Jack Lee worked with barge Eric. The round trip Cambridge to Lynn and back took a week. In 1905 4,600 tons of gas water and 335 tons of gas lime were carried but it is not known whether this was exclusively for the Cambridge works. Trade ceased y 1932.Tar sold on long term contract to the Prince Regent Tar Company may have been conveyed in a similar way. Originally liquor was poured from barrels into the barge hold but later a pipeline was laid. It is believed that the railway came to Ely from Bishop Stortford on 30th July 1845 and from Kings Lynn, (it had a branch line to the harbour), from 27th October 1846. The rail route from Ely North junction to Peterborough East was

Steam Tug Olga
From Fenland Barge
Traffic by John Wilson and Alan Faulkner

authorised under ECR Act of 4th June 1844 and opened on 14th January 1847. The case as to when the means of coal haulage changed from river to rail has to be some time between 1847 when the Ely - Peterborough link was completed and 1885 when the second minute books document that railways haulage was used.

The Gas company minute books record that coal was conveyed, presumably from the railhead to the works by a contractor, for the minutes of June 1885 record the existing worker had died and one, John Pope, was contracted to carry on the work. By 1929 the Directors decided to buy four railway wagons of two tons capacity each on a seven year hire purchase agreements.

Between the years 1872 and 1874 there was a coal famine which resulted in an increase in price. This necessitated the industry to applying to the Board of Trade for a revision in gas prices and brought about the Metropolitan Gas Bill of 1875, which was dropped, but the principle of a sliding scale for gas pricing was accepted.

The type of coal as well as its quality used in gas manufacture was crucial for an economically viable company and the Ely works was continually trying alternative coals and complaining to suppliers as to the quality that was delivered. Generally speaking, a gas works requires high grade bitumous coal with a high volatile content but low inert content with good caking qualities to form a hard coke.

The quality of coal used in gas manufacture was crucial in order to achieve a high gas output in relation to the weight of coal used and the quality of the residual coke. We read in the minutes that the manager was instructed to write to Stephenson Clarke, coal contractor, in December 1888 complaining of the poor quality of coal on account of pyrites, slate matter and dust. Similar complaints were raised in 1891when the manager reported poor gas conversion on account of the inferior coal quality. It is believed that vertical retorts demanded more stringent coal types than the early horizontal retorts for it is known that in 1929 coal from Barrow was found to be unsuitable for that sort of plant.

The minute books of 1890 document that tenders for the supply of coal were sought from Stephenson Clarke who could deliver "Real Old South Yorkshire Silkstone Gas Coal" at 16/9, screened at 17/6 and nuts at 15/9 all per 20 cwt. John Browne Ltd could supply "Aldwarcke Main Gas Coal" at 18/9 per 21 cwt. Eveson of Birmingham tendered "South Yorkshire Best screened Silkstone" at 17/1 per 20 cwt, John Harokes and Son could supply "Newton Chambers Best Thorncliffe Silkstone Gas Coal" screened at 18/7 per 21 cwt and the Nunnery Colliery Company offered "Screened Bright Gas Coal" at 18/1 for 21 cwt. Finally, The Midland Coal and Cannel Company offered "Hatherly Screened large Gas Coal at 18/2 for 21 cwt. Only 5 years earlier coal had been delivered to the works at twelve shillings and six pence a ton.

Over the years most of these coal Merchants tendered annual or two year contracts and directors usually spread their purchases between several merchants. Stephenson Clarke and Foster appear to have been the two most consistently successful companies to be awarded contracts.

Company minutes of June 1891 record 1,300 tons of coal orders being placed and references to the manager being instructed by Directors to hold 460 tons of coal over the winter period. By 1955 coal usage had grown enormously with 5,800 tons brought in by rail each year.

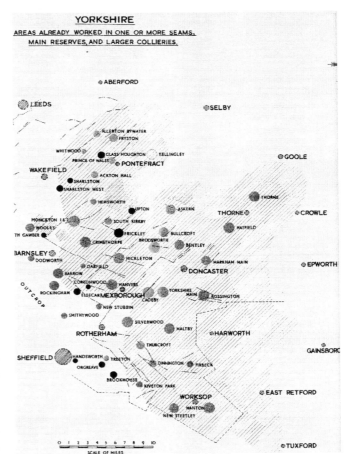

YORKSHIRE
AREAS ALREADY WORKED IN ONE OR MORE SEAMS, MAIN RESERVES, AND LARGER COLLIERIES.

Some of the Yorkshire Coal Pits between Doncaster, Sheffield, Barnsley and Pontefract a selection of which sold coal to the Ely Gas Company. Goole the port of shipment is to be seen to the right.

Print courtesy of National Gas Archive

Silkstone was the name of a coal seam south east of Barnsley which was first worked in 1823. Early excavations were Bell pits sometimes with addits and these were worked until they collapsed. Coal was hoisted to ground level in baskets. Silkstone coal was known as 'Peacocks' on account of it's beautiful colours. The area is particularly well remembered following a flash flood in on 4th July 1838 when 15 boys aged 7-12 and 11 girls aged 8-17 drowned in the mine.

Initially, it seems that coal tonnages were measured at the pit head, for it was not until 1912 that the manager was instructed to buy a weighing machine for coal. It was a five ton cart weighbridge which had been acquired second-hand. Not until 1938 did directors instruct the manager to put all coal deliveries over the weighbridge which lasted until 1942 when it failed checks by the Inspector of Weights and Measures on more than one occasion. The seals were struck out making it illegal to use. It was replaced in 1942 by a thirty ton weigh bridge of 32ft by 9ft installed by Messrs Pooley and Son at a cost of £490.

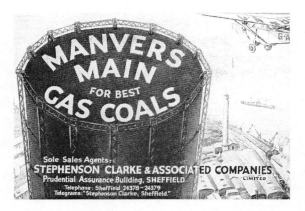

Supplies of coal were contracted annually to the large national supply companies or factors as they were called but even they were not immune to shortages caused by wars and strikes. In 1920 they were unable to undertake their annual contracts pleading they would do their best for existing customers. The national coal strike of 1920/21, brought acute shortages and the manager was able to source coal from Belgium to keep Ely supplied with gas. The coal was grossly inferior to that from the Yorkshire pits producing far less gas per ton and a coke of very poor quality. The cost to the company of this imported coal is recorded as £1,075 and precipitated the Gas Regulations Act authorising all companies to increase the price of gas. By 1922 it was all over, coal prices fell and gas prices too and coal stocks were restored sufficiently so that when the Rail Strike occurred in 1924 the Ely stockpile enabled the works to continue unaffected. By June 1926 the nation was in the grip of yet a further coal strike and the Ely works was down to only three weeks supply. In desperation the enterprising manager was able to buy 200 tons of Silesian coal at 47/6 per ton and by November the same year the company was granted, presumably by the Board of Trade, 1,184 tons of emergency coal costing some £1,537 more than the normal contract price. Acute traffic delays on the railways in 1927 resulted in thirty wagons of coal not being delivered. In order to maintain supplies over the winter the Directors of the Cambridge and Newmarket Gas Companies kindly sent emergency supplies to Ely.

Coal haulage by the railways and hire of their trucks was an overhead the Directors were keen to reduce so they contracted to buy their first four 12 ton coal wagons, in 1925 two from Coote and Warren on a five year hire purchase agreement of £33-18-2d each, payable quarterly and two from Messrs Rigley and Son Ltd at £22-7-6d acquired on a seven year HP agreement in 1927. All wagons were fitted with 2.25 inch steel wheels and an annual maintenance and painting contract was an extra. By 1932 the wagons were making 249 journeys per year from the pithead to Ely and were temporarily withdrawn from traffic to enable them to be repainted. [249 round trips by four rail wagons each containing 12 tons was equal to 3,000 tons per year, half the works annual consumption]. Two trucks were hired from the Littleport Gas Undertaking for two months, presumably to allow the painting to be undertaken. By 1935 we read that five coal wagons Nos. 1,2,5,6 and 7 required repainting and there is reference to an eighth wagon on the books, so further trucks must have been purchased although not fully documented. A further 12 ton wagon was acquired from Coote and Warren in 1938 making nine.

In May 1934 the company placed its annual coal contracts and as usual divided its coal sources as follows. 750 tons Maltby Main at 26/8 per ton, 250 tons Wombwell at 27/- per ton both from Foster. 1,000 tons Birley at 26/6 per ton, 250 tons Newton Chambers at 27/- per ton both from Stephenson Clarke. 750 tons Dalton Main at 27/3 per ton from Rotherham and District Colliery

and finally 300 tons Handsworth at 27/3 per ton from Jonathan Longbottom and Sons. Months later the Company was in trouble with Rotherham and District Colliery who impounded three of the company's coal wagons pending settlement of an overdue account.

By 1935 the country was astir with the threat of another coal strike and Directors are recorded as having discussed the impact on the Ely Works and the actions they should take. Coal prices were rising so they decided to order a further truck of coal per week to be delivered in a colliery wagon and by January 1936 when 500 tons of coal had been stocked in the yard they cancelled the extra truck of coal. In March 80% of the Industry voluntarily agreed to an increase of 1/- per ton for coal.

Minutes of July 1936 record Directors relief that the Government had announced that 'The interests of Public Utilities would be safeguarded by the Coal Mines Bill'. New Coal contracts were agreed with the collieries in March 1937 as follows.

In 1936 directors in an attempt to limit costs for coal, the price of which was steadily advancing, approached Messrs Bowgen and Peachley who hauled the coal from the railway sidings to the works in the hope that they would reduce their cartage costs but they declined. Two years later Directors instructed the manager to explore the possibilities of reverting back to coal haulage by river as had been done when the works was first founded in 1835. Stephenson Clarke, the preferred coal factors, were approached to make the necessary enquiries. Their findings revealed that the maximum saving that could be achieved would be 1/6 per ton as compared with rail transport, and that there were practical difficulties of bringing a sea-going vessel from Keadby to Ely and that such transport would be unavailable in the winter months.

Having abandoned that idea directors then agreed that the manager should approach the London and North Eastern Railway in the hope of bargaining down their freight charges. Needless to say their Minerals Manager would hear no such pleas. Ely Directors were amazingly tenacious, for they then instructed the manager to enquire of the Beet Factory in the hope that their barges could be used for coal transport. "Not a word of it" was the response from Major Fowler, their transport manager, who considered such a proposal impractical. There upon directors told the manager to buy another 12 ton capacity rail wagon from Messers Coote and Warren, number nine in the company's fleet, for £150, as coal delivered in customers own rolling stock worked out cheaper than delivery by the railway company trucks.

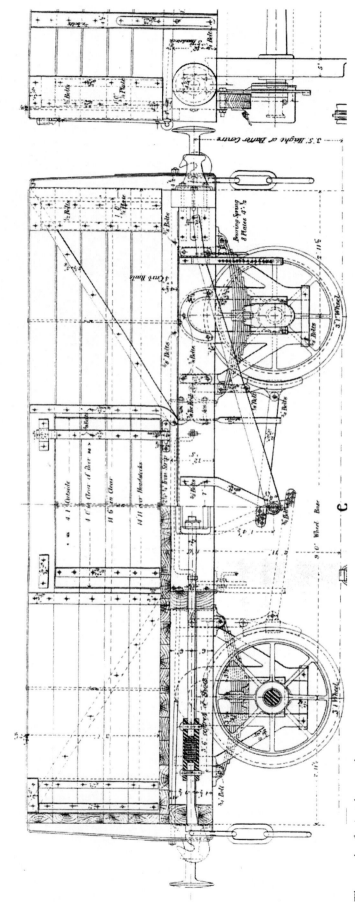

Coal Wagon Side profile taken from the The Modeller's Sketchbook of Private Owners Wagons by A. G. Thomas 'Owners Wagons. book two.

Published by Model Railway (Mfg) Co Ltd.

Thousands of privately owned wagons were run on the tracks of the railway companies. This as a Drawing of A Private Owners Standard 8 ton Railway Wagon with timber under frame Sept 1889. Scaled at ¾ in = 1 foot. More modern wagons holding 12 tons which the Ely gas company bought had unloading doors at the end and instead of grease lubricated bearings had instead oil lubricated axle boxes. I do remember timber sided wagons with a hinged down flap each side through which all coal was shovelled standing at sidings in Ely.

Drawing courtesy of Transco National Gas Archive

142

In October 1939 the Manager reported to Directors the first of many price rises in the cost of coal as a result of the outbreak of war and very shortly afterwards all the companies coal wagons were commandeered by the Government and coal was now delivered in colliery wagons. Compensation was first paid for this in 1940 :-

When Built	Compensation	No of Wagons	Compensation per annum
1933-1939	5/9 per week	1	£14/19/0
1926-1932	5/-per week	6	£78/0/0
1919-1925	4/6per week	2	£23/8/0

By May 1940 coal had advanced by 4/2 per ton which with an earlier rise of 3/- amounted to 7/2 since the outbreak of war which had an immediate effect on production cost and the gas price to consumers. Bowden and Peachey haulier of coal from the station then asked for a rise to 2/6 per

1,150 tons Brierly at 28/4 per ton		300 tons Barrow at 29/6 per ton	
300 tons Newton Chambers at 29/- per ton		350 tons Brierly at 28/10 per ton	
400 tons Maltby Main at 29/2		200 tons Maltby at 29/2 per ton	
400 tons Wombwell at 29/- per ton		3,100 tons in Total.	

ton to which directors had to concede. A little later shortages in tonnages delivered were noted, the matter reported to the railway authorities and later these were narrowed down to shortfalls from Maltby Main Colliery. The same year the Cambridge Divisional Coal Office nominated Ely as a coal store to supply Soham, Littleport, Brandon and Mildenhall with coal in the event of enemy bombardment knocking out the rail network.

In April 1942 supplies of Yorkshire coal became unobtainable and the manager was advised to order Durham coal, Ryhope singles, which was available and could be used in the horizontal retorts, which had been brought back into commission, as the vertical retorts were being rebuilt. By August 2,000 tons had arrived in Ely and extra railway siding space was hired for storage. It had cost between 43/2 to 44/0 per ton 6/- a ton more than Yorkshire coal. By November 1943 coal stocks were down to eleven days usage a situation common thought-out the eastern counties. The Manager visited Mr Anderson, of Stephenson Clark, in London, phoned Fosters several times, consulted The Divisional Coal Officer, as well as the Regional Gas spokesman and the secretary to the Midland Coal Selling Scheme. The situation was becoming serious.

The nations coal mines provided the Ely Works at its peak with 5,777 tons of coal per year all of which was hand shovelled from the pit face. That same 5,777 tons after delivery to the railway sidings in Ely was again shovelled manually into lorries which tipped the fuel onto a coal stack in the works yard with the help of a bit more shovelling. From there, the stokers shovelled the same 5,777 tons of coal into the coal buggy for transport to the top of the retort house. If that wasn't enough the residue of coke, of which the works produced 2,170 tons, was shovelled into sacks for conveyance to customers' homes. A team of say six stokers and under-stokers must each have shovelled a minimum 3.6 tons per day (in an 8 hour shift) and almost 1,300 tons of coal and coke per year and when perhaps they were short staffed or their numbers reduced to four, then very briefly, up to 5.4 tons per man per day!

Coke was the major by-product of all gas works. It was the residue of the coal after it had passed through the retort and was a light brittle irregularly shaped fuel which could be burnt smokelessly on domestic grates to heat rooms. Indeed, in some areas of the country it was used by large industrial undertakings, such as steel works, to heat blast furnaces for smelting iron, but Ely's production quantities were not on that scale and coke was sold largely for domestic burning. The sale of coke was crucial to the financial viability of any gas works, so not only did a manager have to have a ready market for the gas produced but equally for the coke left over. A ton of coke sold for a higher price than a ton of coal. The sale of coke resulted in recouping two thirds of the cost of the coal used in the gas manufacturing process. Much coke was sold to private householders who collected the material in whatever conveyance they had available. Larger quantities were latterly sold to Coal and Coke Merchants for deliveries to consumers homes. Excessive stockpiles were sold for industrial use or latterly sold to another gas district which had a shortage. Sedge Fen Farm owned by Chivers used Ely coke, as did Papworth Village Settlement and the Ely Brewery, but the Gas company failed to interest the Cathedral authorities to use coke.

The company minutes of April 1893 refer to there being a surplus of 100 chaldrons of coke which the manager was instructed to sell at about 8 shillings per chaldron and a little later 50 tons having been sold at 15 shillings per ton.

| 3 bushels = 1 sack | 84-88 lbs coal per bushel | 1 chaldron of coke = 12-15 cwt |
| 12 sacks = 1 chaldron | | 1 chaldron of coal = 25.5 cwt |

A Chaldron was a volumetric measure as follows: -

| 1 ton of coal = 0.78 chaldrons | 1 ton of coke = 1.66 to 1.33 chaldrons |

A sack therefore held 2.125 cwt of coal or 1 to 1.25 cwt of coke.

It is worth recording that some early gas works refined whale oil as a source for gas as distinct from coal. This means of manufacture fell into disuse in about 1826 when whale oil advanced in cost from £18 to £30 per ton. Records reveal that between 75-100 cu ft of gas could be made from one gallon of the oil. The Whitby Repository records that comparative costs of lighting were-

Gas from whale oil burnt in an Argand burner 1/6,
Tallow Candles 3/6
Whale Oil burnt in an oil lamp 2/6.

The introduction of the incandescent gas mantle would have made gas lighting very much cheaper and one begins to appreciate how expensive candles were to buy and burn. By way of comparison a Hull gas engineer studying, in 1890 the properties of coal mined from Wombwell, the same pit that supplied Ely established :-

Gas made per ton of coal	10,296 cu ft
Coke made from one ton of coal	13.75 cwt
Illuminating power of gas from coal with little storage	15.17 candles
Illuminating power of gas from coal stored for 18 days	14.33 candles
Illuminating power of gas from coal stored for 20 days	10.36 candles

These figures serve to illustrate that coal stored on a gas works deteriorated over time.

Chapter 19
Gas- its smell, purification, quality and gas liquor

The smell of town gas was revolting, so much so, that there was never any doubt as to whether there was a gas leak in the house or from the main in the road. The smell was pervasive and an appropriate warning of the danger of explosion if it escaped in a confined space such as in a house where, ignited by a flame or cigarette, it would explode and destroy the home. The old adage 'never look for a gas leak with a naked flame', was wise advice, but one my grandmother always interpreted as meaning 'use a lighted flame to find a gas leak'! Fortunately she was never put to the test. I should add that gas when burnt in a cooker or fire loses the unpleasant smell, although the resultant flue gases do have another odour all of their own.

Town Gas was a generic name for gases produced by one or more processes for domestic purposes. Some very early gas works produced gas from whale oil but the first type of gas manufacture in Ely was Coal Gas, but later refinements in plant lead to a gas generated from coke and light fuel oils which came to be known as Carburetted Water Gas. The composition of gas varied from day to day and from one coal to another. Like petrol it was not a precise combination of chemical constituents but a blend of mostly flammable gases plus impurities, the latter of which impart the appalling smell.

Every effort was made to remove as much of the impurities as possible at the gas works and for that very reason the worst smells always arose at the works. This is borne out in the company minutes of August 1885, when John Toombs wrote complaining of 'the inconvenience arising from the noxious smells and steam'. Again in May 1883, shortly after a new gas making retort had been erected, George Conius, an agent complained about 'the nuisance from the fumes from the retort house' and asked for the height of the wall to be raised by two feet six inches. The whole area

Left Ely High Bridge (the railway bridge) in flood. Following complaints by residents of Annersdale concerning the smell of loading gas liquor at the quay, subsequent loading took place near Ely High bridge. 1937

Right The Cutter Inn - in Flood 1937

around the works smelt, for in 1893, a petition was raised together with numerous letters of complaint from residents in the Annesdale area close to the works, regarding the smell of ammoniacal liquor which was loaded into barges on the river nearby and shipped to Kings Lynn. The liquor was a by-product of gas manufacture, and was sold to Fison and Son. Directors instructed the manager that in future all loading should take place at Ely High Bridge and not on The Quay.

Town Gas extracted at high temperatures from coal contained about 8% Carbon Monoxide, 3% Ethylene, 28% Methane, 48% Hydrogen, 10% Nitrogen, 2% Carbon Dioxide, 0.5% Oxygen, plus Ammonia, Aqueous Vapour (Water), Hydrogen Sulphide, Carbon Disulphide, Benzole, (which in the two World Wars was extracted on some works for munitions), and Tar from which pitch and many chemicals were derived. It can give off about 20.5 kJ /l (400-500 BThU per cu. ft), of heat as compared to natural gas at 38.3 kJ/litre, (about 1,000 BThU per cu. ft).

To enable the gas to be extracted from the coal it was necessary to have a source of heat to raise the temperature of the retorts. Originally, this was simply by burning a small proportion of the coal brought into the works in a fire under the retort. This was greatly improved by burning some of the coke which had been scraped out of the retort again under the retort and Ely certainly used this method as is borne out by the photograph of the works staff with the type of coke hood used for the purpose. This technique produced a hotter retort and was more economical.

This eventually gave way to the manufacture of Producer Gas under the retorts, where coke straight from the retort was subjected to a stream of air to generate a gas, which was piped to the outside of the retorts where it was burned all around the retort furnace. To the chemists amongst my readers its composition is expressed as $O_2+4N_2+2C=2CO+4N_2$. The Nitrogen is inert but the Carbon Monoxide burns to Carbon Dioxide and heat. It had a calorific value of about 300 B.Th.U. per cu.ft.

Another process was the manufacture of Water Gas where a jet of steam was introduced over white-hot coal to produce a gas as expressed in the equation $H_2O+C=CO+H_2$. When burnt heat is produced leaving carbon dioxide and water vapour as shown by the formula $CO+H_2+O_2=CO_2+H_2O$. 11.2kJ/l. Because the jet of steam gradually cooled the coke, it was necessary to blast air or oxygen into the producer to heat it up again in an alternating cycle. Water gas or Blue Water Gas as it was called burnt with a distinctive blue flame. This gas was unsuitable for direct sale without enrichment because its heating power was too low.

To supplement the town gas in times of high demand Carburetted Water Gas was made by injecting an oil into a furnace of incandescent coke instead of steam. This generated a very 'rich' gas which was mixed with the water gas and town gas to arrive at the correct calorific value for the consumer. Carburetted Water Gas had a calorific value of about 1,700 B.Th.U. per cu.ft, depending on the amount of oil used in the carburettor, before dilution. These comparatively small plants could be brought on stream very quickly compared to a coal retort to meet sudden surges in consumer demand.

As part of the manufacturing process, all the town gas was purified and as much of the toxic and odorous material as possible was removed. The only contaminant gas undertakings had to remove by law was hydrogen sulphide, a highly toxic gas which had a pungent 'bad eggs' smell.

The minutes of October 1887 show tar was sold at 3d per gallon or 6/- per barrel (36 gallons) and 5/-per barrel for quantities in excess of 360 gallons. Customers for the larger quantities of tar would have been the Ely District Council for Road repairs, and the Great Eastern Railway where it was delivered to the railway station at 1½d per gallon. It is believed it was used for road surfacing and for weather proofing building walls. It was also advertised for sale in The Gas Journal.

Tar was removed in the condensers and stored in tanks usually below ground level for later disposal. It contained between 500 and 3,000 differing compounds which became the foundation of the chemical industry for many years. Some of those chemicals are toxic to mammals and plant life and some carcinogenic. This didn't restrict its use in those days, but it is said this was a major contributory factor in the demise of the gas industry in North America in the 1960's. I read that tar products, are not susceptible to natural degradation, and American scientists have found it to have leaked into ground water aquifers and into the atmosphere as Polycyclic Aromatic Hydrocarbons - said to be a major environmental concern.

After the tar was taken out the gas was passed through a washer where water was sprayed onto the gas as it passed through, removing a large proportion of ammonia to produce an evil looking, tarry smelling black syrup, the disposal of which became the bane of all gas works across the land. Originally, a proportion of this was allowed to drain into the public sewers, where it was mixed with sewage, but in Ely the manager was able to sell most of the liquor, which contained about 3% ammonia to the West Norfolk Farm Manure Company for ½d per gallon for use as a farm fertiliser. It was conveyed by barge to their factory, a practice that lasted for many years but which was eventually withdrawn.

The final cleaning to remove the highly toxic and evil smelling hydrogen sulphide was undertaken in the purifiers, where the gas was allowed to pass through a series of enclosed cast iron boxes. Initially lime was used as the purifying agent but after about 1880 this was substituted with iron oxide powder which was stored on slatted wooden shelves. The dark brown iron oxide turned to a lighter coloured brown ferrous sulphide before losing its power. After a while the purifier would be opened and the old powder removed and spread out, probably under cover, to be exposed to the air. After some while, revivification of the old oxide took place and it could be re-used once more, at which point it became a very black ferric sulphide. New bog ore had constantly to be purchased to replenish supplies. In the early days about 90%-95% of the hydrogen sulphide in the gas was removed leaving the consumer to breathe in and purify the rest, but not of course unless they breathed the un-burnt gas! Latterly works introduced stringent tests for detecting small traces of the gas. The minute books make regular reference to the purchase of supplies of iron oxide from The Gas Purification Company and in 1880 a price of 40/- per ton is quoted for the purchase of new oxide and 7/6 per ton for the disposal of the old material from which sulphuric acid was made. The material was hauled by rail.

The quality of domestic gas and the means of measuring quantities were clearly highly dubious in the early days of the industry. The Government introduced the Metropolitan Gas Act in 1861 to lay down the need for undertakings to maintain a constant light value to their product, together with accurate means of measuring consumer's consumption. It was not until the Gas Works Clauses Act of 1871 that works were obliged to undertake regular testing. The Ely Gas of 1881 stipulated that the quality of gas supplied by the Ely Undertaking " shall, with respect to its illuminating power, be such as to produce a light equal in intensity to the light produced by fourteen

During the first half of the eighteenth century it was discovered that candles could be made from an oil present in the head cavities of sperm whales. One entire whale could yield nearly one ton of a substance called spermanceti in its crude state. It was refined by first placing in a cloth and compressing to remove the oil. The residue was broken into pieces and dropped in boiling water to separate impurities. It was then placed in fresh water to which potash had been added and boiled again. The solidified material was a hard white mass with a fine flaky crystalline appearance. Spermanteceti candles burned with a bright white flame and in 1887 Parliament made the spermanteceti candle the standard unit of light in photometry. One candle power was achieved by burning 1/6 lb weight of spermaceti candle at a rate of 120 grains per hour. In practice an early standard gas lamp produced light equal to 12 candles.

sperm candles, and shall in all respects be in accordance with the provision of the Gas Works clauses Act, 1871".

A letter from Arthur Bidwell in about 1885 complained to the Directors of the 'bad quality of the gas as well as the impurity with deficient illuminating power, also several people had complained to him during the back month'. The directors responded saying that they wished to inspect the gas lights and their settings before passing comment. In Nov 1888 Directors did instruct the manager to test the gas weekly for its illuminating power and record the results. In December 1895 Mr W. J. Evans, Chapter Clerk to the Dean and Chapter wrote to the board of Directors complaining about the quality of gas and the following year Charles Bidwell also complained as to the quality and price of gas. By 1921 Directors conceded they would have to fall in line with the Industry and adopt the 'Therm' as the measure of gas quality and the following year ratified that the City's supply would be set at a calorific value [c.v.] of 500 B.Th.U [British Thermal Units]. Other works adopted different standards. A gas examiner was appointed by the Board of Trade to test gas quality, an early form of consumer protection. He used a Sugg London Argand No1 burner, with 1 ¾ inch glass chimney or if the gas flame tailed over the top, then a 6 inch by 2 inch diameter glass chimney. In 1926, he reported 'the City's supply to have a deficiency in the calorific value of the gas last Michaelmas' and this incurred a penalty of £40 9s 7d to be deducted from shareholders dividends.

The questionable quality of the City's gas supply appears to have rumbled on for years for in 1896 a letter of complaint was received from the District Council. Members had voted on a resolution that "this Council is of the opinion that the lighting power of the gas supplied to the city is unsatisfactory to ourselves and hope that the gas company will suffect some means of considerable improvement". Directors are recorded as having said to the Manager 'use a little more Cannel [a type of coal mined largely in Scotland but also in some parts of Yorkshire], and to arrange for the illuminating power to 17 candles' meaning the richness of the gas to be increased. A jet Photometer was ordered for testing the illuminating power. Gas from a good Yorkshire coal when burnt at 5 cu ft per hour would give a light intensity of ten to thirteen candles whilst a Cannel coal would produce a light intensity of 20-28 candlepower

Thirty five years later, the Urban District Council were pursuing the Gas Company again, this time complaining about the smell of Hydrogen Sulphide in the gas. It was very noticeable, so much so, that nobody needed special testing equipment to know the sulphur level exceeded the maximum permitted level of 1%. The Gas Company made their own tests, realised they were at fault and rectified matters immediately, but Directors played their cards close to their chest as they feared being taken to court. By good fortune for Ely Gas, the UDC solicitors failed to initiate legal proceedings within the time frame specified in the legislation and lost any chance of pursuing their case in court even though the gas undertaking was technically in breach of the law.

For the technically minded, I should explain that H_2S is an acidic and highly toxic gas, so consequently there was stringent legislation to 'try' and ensure it was removed. The gas industry saw

Above An Argand Burner No 1. The street lights in Ely were of this type in 1914 before the introduction of gas mantles.

A simple water gauge used for measuring gas pressure.

John Doran Gas Museum Leicester

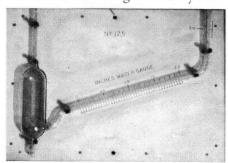

things slightly differently and emphasised they removed the gas as it corroded pipes and appliances. Additionally, that removal allowed consumers to operate small room heaters without fear of the Hydrogen Sulphide gas entering their room, which burnt to produce a sulphurous acid. The fact that customers were breathing Carbon Monoxide fumes seemed to be 'by the way' and would be prohibited today.

Early gas meters were of the 'wet' pattern. They had one over riding design fault. In very cold weather the water contained in the bottom of the meter would freeze and the supply was cut off. Over time the water gradually evaporated and it was necessary it be topped up by consumers to ensure accurate recording. Consumers soon discovered that by failing to replenish the water the meter recorded less gas passing through than was the case, there-by reducing their annual gas bill. Gas companies overcame this problem with the invention of the 'dry' meter.

The gas pressure at which the City's supply should be delivered to consumers was determined by the 1871 Act "at six tenths of an inch water gauge from midnight to sunset and slightly higher, eight tenths of an inch between sunset and midnight when gas usage was higher, at a point where a service pipe connected to the mains". Such a pressure was sufficient for lighting purposes only, for by the 1950's, it had been increased to a minimum of four inches at midnight and a maximum of seven inches water pressure to keep up with the demand for gas for heating appliances, a rise of almost eight times the original gas pressure. It is interesting to read that in 1943, men whilst working on the plant, accidentally cut a 12 inch live gas main. In the course of six minutes 12,000 cu ft of gas was lost to the atmosphere and from the companies coffers and the district pressure plummeted from 6 inches to $^3/_{10}$ of an inch.

This was not the last of the gas pressure misfortunes for on 30th October 1946 the gas pressure fell to one inch water gauge. Demand for gas was rising year on year and as fast as new plant was commissioned consumer demand rose to match it. One of the four vertical retorts was being scurfed at the time and the horizontal retorts which were also in use just couldn't

keep up. The gas holders were empty and for a short time gas was being used as fast as the plant operated. The situation prevailed for only six minutes before pressure rose to three inches. Again, the works risked peoples' lives and property but there is no record that the gas examiner even noticed for I am sure he would have fined the company heavily had he inspected the pressure charts thoroughly!

Gas meter showing dials and most important slot for inserting a shilling. Photo courtesy of Fakenham Gas Museum

In order for a private company to set up in business it was necessary for the venture to seek permission from the local vestries. The easiest way to do this was to offer gas for public lighting at a preferential rate to that of private consumers. In Ely demand for public lighting opened the doors to an entrepreneur willing to build a gas works and within a year of opening gas lights were installed in the parishes of St. Mary and elsewhere. Gas at this time was used in Ely exclusively for lighting as early gas cookers and heaters were rare outside London. Gas meters had not been invented. Consumers were charged a fee depending on the number of lights they burnt, for how many hours per day they could use them, and I have read, by the length of the gas flame. Only later were gas meters used to record gas sold by volume rather than 'hours of burning'.

149

In the early part of the eighteenth century gas for consumers in the larger towns had been very costly at 16 shillings per 1,000 cubic feet, making it the preserve of only the very wealthy. By 1881 the price had fallen substantially for the Ely Gas Act stipulated the maximum price at which gas should be sold to consumers as being no greater than five shillings per one thousand cubic feet and in proportion to lesser quantities supplied. This is substantiated by minutes of 1887 which talk of a price reduction of 2d per year for three years until 1894 when it came down to 4s 6d per 1,000 cu.ft. Thereafter, the price fluctuated, but during the latter part of the First World War coal stocks diminished and prices rose, the manager arranged with Wood Drew and Co solicitors and accountants to apply to the Board of Trade to draw up necessary particulars under the Statutory Undertakings Temporary Increase in Charges Act of 1918 for an increase of 6d per 1,000 cu.ft. By 1921 coal supplies had reverted to normal and gas was being sold at 1s7d per therm only to drop further to 1s 2d per therm by 1923.

Frequent references appear in directors' meetings to the supply and refurbishment of gas meters. Because of the number of customers with gas rental arrears directors were keen to investigate the adoption of prepayment meters, with the guarded threat that consumers who did not pay accounts on time would be put on slot meters or 'cut-off'. The passing of the 1900 Metropolis Gas {Prepayment Meter Act] regularised the use of gas meters which had been introduced eight years earlier. The manager acquired some slot meters in October 1894 designed to deliver 16 cubic feet of gas per hour for one penny, equivalent to 5s. 2½d per 1000 cu ft. (the 'change wheel' could be adjusted to a wide range of prices). By the end, of the year 50 gas meters in the Bishop's Palace were discovered not to have been working at all for the last quarter! By the following June thirty three slot meters were in use and surprisingly four individuals had been issued with a County Court summons, for not settling their accounts which in total amounted to £11 13s 9d. Slot meter popularity rose dramatically in the subsequent years with seventy six in use in 1896, one hundred and two in 1897, one hundred and sixty three in 1900 and eight hundred and one plus five hundred and thirty two ordinary meters by 1923, making a total of 1,333 consumers. By 1955 there were a total of 2,121 consumers of which 1,703 were on slot meters. Unlike today, Ely meters were not then checked or replaced at regular intervals and could be recording incorrectly for years. For this reason Directors agreed to replace all meters over twenty years old and by 1935 agreed to scrap a further one hundred meters and adopt a meter replacement policy.

Domestic Meters were not the only sources of meter inaccuracy for the Station Meter installed second-hand in 1907 by The Gas Meter Co was in 1935 found to be 0.32% fast, meaning it was recording more gas made by the works than was actually the case. What was done about that is not recorded.

In those days it was not unknown for a town to have two or more rival gas works with pipes from each undertaker in the same road. The more unscrupulous companies would on signing up a new client proceed to connect the new client to their competitor's pipe and then charge the client for gas supplied by their rival.

Chapter 20
By products of the gas manufacturing process.

In order to understand the operation of a gas works, I feel a little time explaining the simple chemistry of gas making, will help readers understand the operation of the works.

Manufacturing town gas from coal, is in many ways, similar to an oil refinery producing oils, and petro-chemicals for both processes are concerned with chemical cracking of the raw material. The destructive distillation of the coal resulted in a range of by products which included coke, tar, ammoniacal liquor and sulphur. From the tar alone 300-400 chemical products can be synthesised, some of which are in every day use, including such things as motor benzene with particularly good "anti knocking" properties for vehicles, aspirin, dyestuffs, carbolic acid [disinfectant], toluene for munitions, nitrogenous fertilizers, aniline dyes and so on. Gas works did not refine the specific chemicals for public use but instead sold on their by-products to chemical plants and tar distillers for further processing.

An engineer, in order to run his plant, had to understand the chemistry of what was going on and be able to regulate the process so as to extract the most gas possible and at the same time produce a coke which was saleable as a commercial product. The quality of the coal and its size was all important, as was the speed at which it went through the retort, and the temperature of the furnace. The temperature had to be adjusted from hour to hour to maintain the optimum gas extraction, for there were no automated systems in the early days. Producer gas

'How do you do, Mr. Therm — we haven't met since we both left the gas works'

National Benzole is produced from British coal at gas works and coke oven plants throughout the country. Support your own Industry.

NATIONAL BENZOLE MIXTURE

NATIONAL BENZOLE CO., LTD., WELLINGTON HOUSE, BUCKINGHAM GATE, S.W.1.
(The distributing organisation owned and entirely controlled by the producers of British Benzole.)

made in a separate furnace from white hot coke and was used to heat the main retorts. If the retorts become too hot, very serious damage could arise, as the silica linings would start to melt, resulting in a retort having to be shut down and re built with either firebricks or silica, a costly process taking months to rectify. Gas plants producing Producer Gas, Blue Water Gas and Carburetted Water Gas, had all to be regulated with great precision, which in practical terms was more of a 'black art' than a science. Technology did not arrive until the 1960s with instruments and technical controls.

If the normal coal used on a particular works was unavailable and a different coal from another colliery was used or if the blend of differing coals used regularly was changed, then the engineer had to adjust the retort temperature or coal feed to the plant. One problem that could occur was when the coal 'hung up' This terminology referred to a charge of coal sticking in the vertical retort and not slipping through by gravity as it was supposed to do. The retorts were tapered being narrower at the top than the bottom but in spite of that some coals would swell excessively as they dropped through, jam half way down and block their own exit. When this did happen long steel rods were thrust into the retort through 'rodding eyes' in the top to dislodge the blockage.

Another process that had to be undertaken regularly was 'scurfing the retorts'. After a period of several weeks, a thick layer of pure carbon would build up on the inner surface of the firebricks and if not removed it too would prevent the passage of coal and reduce heat transference. This was removed or scurfed by emptying the retort of coke in the normal way, keeping it on full heat and by introducing some air, the carbon could be burnt off as carbon dioxide and the free passage way for coal restored. Again great care had to be exercised doing this, for there was even more likelihood of overheating and damaging the retort. The whole operation was a continual juggling act and kept everyone, engineer, foreman and stokers on constant alert. My father refers to an occasion when the coal in the feed hopper to a retort caught fire. One never knew from day to day what scenario would arise.

The bi-products produced during gas manufacture from one ton of coal were approximately 14.4 cwt of coke, 10 gallons of tar, 15.3 gallons of gas liquor and finally 12 pounds of spent oxide which had removed the sulphuretted hydrogen.

By far the easiest by-product to handle was the coke and provided it was of a saleable quality and a ready market to hand, it brought in a sizable and necessary income for the company. The red hot material was extracted from the horizontal retorts, quenched with water to stop it igniting and then once cool passed through a coke breaker and grader for separating the material into different sizes or grades. Vertical retorts produced a cool coke so there was no need to quench. The quality of coke was in the first place determined by the source of the coal. Some coals produced little useable coke and were avoided, whereas others were high in ash or they would not 'cake' to produce a hard brittle fuel and instead disintegrated to dust. Additionally nothing upset buyers more than when the quality of the coke varied from one delivery to another, so consistency was essential. The type of coke produced was in part determined by the temperature of the retort. First call on coke supplies was the works itself because this was used as the fuel to make producer gas, which was burnt to heat the retorts and additionally in the case of Ely, Carburetted water gas which was blended with the town gas. At its peak the Ely works would have produced about 3,200 tons of coke per year.

The tar produced from the Ely works was separated out by the condenser and the electro de-tarrer. It was largely sold to the Urban District Council for road making. Some went the Great Eastern Railway Company and a little to the Regent Tar Company, who refined it for some of its constituents. The Ely works at its zenith would have produced 60,000 gallons per year. To help with its disposal the company laid a pipe from the works to the river wharf, (believed to be Old Kiln Lane Wharf) so tar tanks could be pumped out directly into a river barge for transport to Kings Lynn.

The chemical content of the tar also varied from day to day depending on the operating of the retort. The main constituents it contained included benzol, toluene, creosote, naphtha, heavy naphtha, tar acids, crude pyridine, creosote, pitch, [from which black varnish was made], crude naphthalene, crude anthracene, and heavy oil. From creosote oil, disinfectants and naphthalene could be refined and from these crude carbolic, creosote, phenol and acesalicylic acid, better known as aspirin.

The ammoniacal liquor or gas liquor, as it was often called, was extracted in the scrubbers and its disposal was a constant source of concern for the manager. About 5.6 gallons were produced per ton of coal but diluted with the water used for its extraction bulked its volume up to 15.3 gallons per ton, making Ely's production in the order of 92,000 gallon per year. It contains a high proportion of ammonia and was a potential source of ammonia for making into a fertilizer, but it did have an extremely noxious odour. When companies like the West Norfolk Farmers dropped their buying in favour of other sources, then disposal of Ely gas liquor was either by spraying it on farmland or pumping it into a hole in the ground. An environmental practice which today would be swiftly followed by a high court injunction, prosecution and heavy fine.

Hydrogen sulphide and other impurities were removed from the gas by passing it through the purifiers where wooden trays filled with iron oxide would absorb the hydrogen sulphide and cyanide compounds and the spent oxide would be returned for processing from which was derived sulphur, sulphuric acid, a dye and Prussian blue. Benzol was derived from tar and from it pure toluene, motor benzene, solvent naphtha and xylol could be refined. It is worth mentioning that spent oxide is carcinogenic, but in days of old this powder was manually shovelled by the Ely gas workers out of the purifiers, the men having in the early days no protective clothing whatsoever. The resultant testicular cancer was an prevalent illness within the gas industry and manual staff were eventually to receive mandatory annual health checks to detect the disease in its early stages.

The gas produced by the retort also changed in consistency from hour to hour and this was a factor of the coals in use at the time, retort temperature, the speed with which a charge of coal would pass through the retort and finally whether any other gas enrichment plants were running alongside the main retort. The most important aspect was to ensure the mix of gasses constituting Town Gas had

EASTERN GAS BOARD

DIVISIONS

1. CAMBRIDGE.
2. IPSWICH.
3. NORWICH.
4. TOTTENHAM.
5. WATFORD.

the minimum calorific value, in the case of the Ely District 500 British Thermal Units [B.Th.U.] To infringe this was asking to be caught by the inspector and for a fine to be imposed.

The commercial incentive of the company was to make as much gas as possible per ton of coal at the highest efficiency. The horizontal retorts were less efficient at extracting gas than the vertical retorts. To complicate things coal gas could be blended with producer gas and carburetted water gas. In the early days a horizontal retort would produce about 17,400 cu ft of gas per ton or 87 therms and using both a vertical retort and a carburetted water gas plant and much new automatic control equipment, the Ely works achieved an efficiency of 85.8% the most efficient in the Cambridge Division and from time to time the most efficient in the Eastern Region, in which there were about 90 gas making works.

Image John Doran Gas Museum

Chapter 21
Street lighting and Gas Pipes

The street lighting contract was in the 1830's an important source of revenue to the gas companyies and a very public advertisement to the 'up and coming' new industry. The Vestry minutes of St Marys record that on 21 November 1838 members met to decide if they should adopt the provisions of the 1833 Lighting and Watching Act which would enable them to levy a rate for the lighting of the streets of St Marys with gas. Eighteen people voted in favour, three opposed, and the motion carried, (all the individuals voting are named on the minutes). Six people Mr William Asprey, Thomas Page Esq, Mr Thomas Haylock, Mr George William Careless, Mr John Luddington and Mr Luke Dench were elected 'Inspectors'. They were empowered to spend up to forty five pounds in the execution of their duties. Some time later there were celebrations in the City to commemorate the introduction of street lighting, a common occurrence in those days and a party was convened in the White Lion. In St Mary's Parish there are recorded eleven lamps, Trinity parish fifty two lights and in the college eleven lights, whilst some areas of the town remained unlit.

Parish of Ely Saint Mary
At a Meeting of the Rate payers in the
Street from the Lamb Inn to the Old Workhouse
called "Saint Marys Street" in this parish held
in Vestry this twenty first day of November 1838
pursuant to Notice duly given for the purpose
of determining whether the provisions of an Act
of the 3rd and 4th Year of the Reign of his late
to repeal an act of the eleventh year of his late Majesty King George the fourth
Majesty entitled "An Act for the Lighting and
"Watching of Parishes in England and Wales
"and to make other provisions in lieu thereof
so far as the same relates to the Lighting
of the said Street with Gas and raising
the necessary funds for that purpose, be
adopted and carried into Execution -

On 26th February 1836 the Cambridge Chronicle reported the principal street of Ely Trinity were lighted up with coal gas, and on Sunday evening, and since that time. The lamps have been most effective. The contractor (George Malam engineer of Lynn) has furnished the works in the most satisfying manner. The lamps are well made and full sized, placed on elegant painted cast iron pillars. These and the brilliancy of the lights have much improved the appearance of this ancient city. Several private burners already ornament the shops and inns and fresh orders are given daily. The inhabitants are much pleased and satisfied; and it is hoped Mr Malam's acknowledged liberality in the performance of the works will be rewarded by general support.

As time went by, the revenue from the gas street lighting contract diminished in financial importance and was eventually superseded by the electricity undertakings but much later than most towns and cities in the country. Originally street lighting was the responsibility of the Parish Vestries, then Ely Board of Health followed by the Urban District Council. Initially yearly and then three yearly contracts were negotiated after which the Gas Companies 'Seal of Approval' was attached to the document. Considerable effort was made to renew the contract and to ward off the electricity company which was keen to secure a slice of the cake when power came to the city .

Minutes of 1885 record one of many extensions to the street lighting with five new lights in Littleport Road the Ely Board of Health having to pay both for the excavation and main-laying as their side of the bargain. Directors in 1887 agreed to two 'Star lights' being erected and illuminated on the works to celebrate the jubilee of Queen Victoria. The following year they agreed as a favour to the citizens of Ely to light without charge a public clock recently erected in the New Public Rooms in the Market Place. Mr Johnson, an agent, and Murdock Bank complained that the street light outside their premises had not been lit for some time. The manager apologised but pointed out the difficulty of 'opening up the ground' [meaning digging the pipe up in probably frozen ground], during such severe weather.

"NICO-FLEXIBLE" TYPE
Flexible after burning off. Absolutely Shockproof.
Especially suited for Street Lighting and Maintenance Purposes.
Made for all standard burners.

For complete range of "Nico" Specialities see current "Nico" Catalogue. Post Free on application.

Schoolboys' pranks do not change over the centuries, for in 1893, the manager reported breakages to public lamps particularly in the college grounds. He was instructed to write to the headmaster of the Grammar School to ask 'his kind influence to abate the damage which was at some measure imputed to pellets from catapults and stone throwing'. In 1945 Mr Thrower, headmaster of Silver Street School reported one of his pupils, Derek Price, who had damaged a gas lantern. Directors decided to send the boy's father a letter demanding payment for the damage with the implied threat that in the event of non payment a summons would be issued against him in the County Court as a deterrent to others.

1 Standard Candle Power = One Sperm Candle 1/6 pound in weight burnt at a rate of 120 grains of wax per hour.

Gas lights in the early days must have been of the batswing or fishtail burner for it was not until 1897 that Directors agreed to erect twelve experimental incandescent burners i.e. gas mantles, of the latest improved pattern to be fixed to the Ely Gas Companies premises in the hope that Council Members would inspect the lamps and adopt such a system though out the city subject to their paying 16/6d for burner and accessories. The Urban District Council, who had by then superseded the Board of

The incandescent mantle was made of cotton, ramie or artificial silk knitted into a stocking or hose about 2 inches diameter which once made was washed and dried. Once dry, it was saturated with a solution of nitrate of thorium and a 1% solution of nitrate of cerium. After washing and drying again it was cut to size and sewn at one end with asbestos thread. The mantle suspended by a bit of surplus thread was then held in a Bunsen flame to burn away the thread to leave the mantle consisting now of just the ashes of thorium.[Thorium oxide]. The mantle was finally shaped in a flame with great care and hardened before being dipped in a stiffening solution comprising gun cotton, good alcohol and acetone to which castor oil and shellac had been added.
Early mantles were rigid and as a result extremely fragile and shattered but later types some of which were flexible before their first firing were much more robust. A single mantle could provide 60 candle power and burn for 3,000 hours providing the appliance was regularly serviced.

Health on public lighting, bargained down the price to 5 shillings per light. By November 1898, sixty two Welbach burner lights had been added with Clumbury lights and governors and by 1900 there were one hundred and forty six public lights in the City. The lamps were cleaned weekly and

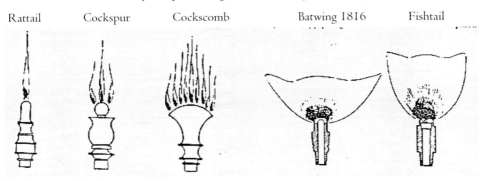

Rattail   Cockspur   Cockscomb   Batwing 1816   Fishtail

annual lighting contracts worked out at about £3 per light per year, a price which gradually increased over the passage of time. The annual lighting contract extended from 18th August to the 14th May, the lights being illuminated between half an hour after sunset to midnight. A tender document dated 1914 sealed with the companies seal and signed by Alfred Kitts, Director, for the company and G. M. Halls, solicitor, for the Urban District Council lists one hundred and seventy nine street lights. Each lamp consumed five cubic feet of gas per hour and required a minimum of $1^1/_2$ inch water gauge pressure to emit the light which would be emitted sixteen sperm candles of six to the pound, burning 120 grains per hour. The tender price agreed was five pound per annum for the lights to be lit from one hour after sunset to one o'clock in the morning. The total price of the contract was £563 17s 9d.

A Rochester light used extensively in Ely made by Sugg.

The early batswing burners consumed 5 to 10 cubic feet of gas per hour producing at most three candles of light per cubic foot. The incandescent gas mantles produced five times as much light per cubic foot of gas burned.

By 1924 experiments were being made with twin mantle burners which were more effective and by 1930 a three burner light was on trial. By 1932 the lighting contract had been extended from April to September but the 'all night' lamp on Lamb Corner was withdrawn from 'all night' use in 1930.

The real breakthrough with the Street Lighting contract occurred in 1934 when the Gas Company offered to upgrade all the City lights if the Ely Urban District Council would agree to a five year contract. This they did and as a result all the lights were raised to a minimum of 13 feet above pavement level, each was fitted with a clock controller of the catalytic type made by Horstmann with a compensatory dial and finally, each had a Parkinson stainless steel reflector fitted. The compensatory dial automatically adjusted for the advance or decline of sunrise and in so doing spelt the demise of the lamplighters, who had manually lit and turned off all the lights each night. However, a lamp attendant was needed to rewind the clocks each week and attend to maintenance. Additionally, in the centre of the city twenty six three light Bijou lights were removed and replaced with thirty much more powerful six light Rochester lamps plus one eight light Rochester and three , light Bijou each with Morlite reflectors. According to the minute books Ely became the first town in the country to have fully automated ignition by clock controllers to its public lighting. Mean-

Coinage in front includes a Victorian half Crown and florin, 12 sided Elizabeth 3d, a silver three penny bit, sixpence, a penny and a ship halfpenny, farthing and half farthing.

Chris Sugg, director, of Sugg Lighting compiled this explanation.

A selection of gas mantles, some most unusual, bought by the author in an antiques and bygone shop, 'Cobwebs' in Holt, North Norfolk in 2006 and gifted to the National Gas Museum Leicester.

The open boxed mantle to the right of the display is a Number 1 'Bijou' used in many domestic lights. In the centre is a 'Number 2' also used for more powerful domestic lights. Both were used in street lights often as multiple burners. To the left is a very large 'Number 4' mantle known as the 'Graetzin' more suited to a powerful outdoor yard light. These are what are called hard inverted mantles.

The elongated Kaybee mantle is a high pressure mantle capable of emitting an even brighter light and represented the panicle of gas lighting technology. Again it is an inverted but soft mantle. It was reliant on a high pressure gas supply, which was essential especially on first lighting, to get a good shape to the mantle. The larger volume of this type of mantle enabled more gas to burn inside the envelope as gas burning outside would not add to the incandescence of the fabric. Characteristically, these and all soft ceramic mantles shrank by about 1/3 after lighting for the first time. The reference 'made under plaissetty licence' refers either to the original manufacturer or maybe the method of knitting the fabric. Unusually, in this case the hard ceramic ring is threaded enabling attachment to the light.

The Helix mantle in the centre is also a soft inverted mantle marked as size A, which is thought to be similar to a Number 1 or Bijou mantle. Early mantles were extremely delicate and the invention of soft fabrics greatly helped their safe distribution before use.

158

while some districts of London where the council owned the electricity works, had converted to electric street lighting. The lighting upgrade cost the company £850. By 1939 there were 227 street lamps and the Urban District Council was committed to a five year contract.

A few months later war was declared on Germany, Parliament imposed the 'Black Out' and street lighting ceased. The gas company were quick to remind the Council that the outbreak of war did not terminate the contract for the Directors had specifically instructed the Manager to add a clause to the contract, protecting the company in the event of war. The Council were trapped ! Many District Councils were caught in a similar way, because they had signed contracts earlier before the likelihood of war became reality. The Gas Company offered the UDC a maintenance contract of the lights and services provided the Council agreed to a five year contract at the end of the war. They had little choice, and it left the gas undertaker in the strong position of being able to charge as much as they could get away with, 20/- per light per annum in fact. The authority did experiment with wartime street lighting but the UDC decided later not to erect any ARP lamps. At the termination of hostilities there was a frantic effort to get the lighting system up and running again. All street lights were removed for repair and the columns re-painted whilst fifty new lights ordered from Sugg and Co.

Gas usage, equivalent electricity consumption and light output approximately of differing mantles and public street lights in Ely

Size	B.Th.U	Cu Ft of gas/ hr	Light output watts	1 Light Bijou Cu Ft/hr (watts)	3 Light lamp Cu Ft/hr (watts)	8 Light Rochester Cu Ft/hr (kW)
Bijou No1	875	1.75	25	1.75 (25)		
No 2	1375	2.75	40		8.25 (120)	22.0 (3.2)
No 3	2250	4.50	160			

One of Ely's Streets lit by gas taken 1937. Can you identify the street?

A Standard Gas light was said by 1935 to be equal in light intensity to 12 candles

The first photograph has a wrapped telegraph pole in the pavement to the right beyond which is a gable end building fronting the road with a porch and hanging shield shaped sign over the door. A similarly shaped shop sign appears on the left hand side of the street.

The three elevated gas lights are considerably higher than the standard cast iron lamp stand to be seen to the right of the picture half way down the street.

The second photo may be the same street. Was this, I wonder, part of the trial of new gas street lighting to which my father alluded? Broad Street, February 1939, using Maxwell 10 light No2 lamps with Superline Mantles mounted 13 feet above road level giving 3,100 lumen per 100ft of road-surface.

Before the advent of automated ignition, street lamps in the city were lit and extinguished by a lamplighter, who would walk the streets equipped with a lamp-lighting pole. It is not documented how these worked but common methods used elsewhere were by means of a small hand held oil lamp, or I suspect more likely in Ely, by a small carbide lamp attached to the end of a long pole which was inserted through a port hole in the bottom of each street lamp which ignited the gas when the supply of gas was turned on using the same pole.

The annual tariff charged in 1939 under a 5 year contract per light was : -

12th August to 12th May half an hour after sunset to 11pm

Winter Lights

3 light	Bijou	£4-19-0
5 light	bijou	££6-9-6
6 light	Rochester No 2 upright	£8-2-6
8 light	Rochester No 2 upright	£10-5-0

Summer Lights

6 light	Rochester No 2 upright	£8-2-6
8 light	Rochester No 2 upright	£10-5-0

Although not in Ely, the very earliest gas pipes were made from musket barrels following the Napoleonic Wars. Other reports refer to wood, earthenware, concrete, lead, cast iron, and copper pipes all having been tried before wrought iron became the preferred choice. By the eighteenth century mains distribution network was gradually replaced in the nineteenth century from two inch wrought iron pipes to four; six inch or even eight inch diameter cast and spun iron pipes in the 1920's and ductile iron in the 1950s and 1960s. The former cast and pipes were prone to fracture and when replaced the larger pipes were chosen to provide for greater consumer demand and better pressure. Wrought iron pipes were heavy, with even a 2 inch pipe, having a wall thickness of ½ inch (4lbs 6½ oz per linear foot) and above ground level collars for bolting sections together would have used B.S.P. taper threaded spigots and sockets.

Underground mains were of a spigot and socket type which were sealed with lead run joints. These were made by wrapping a hank of yarn around the pipe spigot which was then inserted into the adjoining pipe socket where the yarn was caulked meaning driven home with blunt chisel and hammer. Behind this was inserted either a temporary clay faced metal clip or a loop of asbestos rope. Molten lead was then poured into the small gap between the caulked yarn and the asbestos rope. In spite of these measures a considerable gas leakage occurred over time.

The Broad Street main was replaced with an 8" pipe in 1898 and a 10 inch main was installed coming out of the gas works. Directors asked the manager in 1906 to acquire a map of Ely and mark on it all the street gas pipes and hang it on the Board Room wall. By 1915 there was six miles of main which expanded to eight miles by 1939. The last of the two inch cast iron pipes were replaced by 1930. A new main in St Marys Street in the 1930's cost £150 for 300 yards of piping. Heavy traffic fractured the main in Forehill but the UDC declined the Directors request to divert heavy traffic down Backhill. Minutes record that a further significant fracture occurred in 1942, when a pipe in Broad Street cracked at the junction with Back Lane. Escaping gas probably got into the sewers and then into the home of Mr and Mrs Charles at No 16 Broad Street. They were gassed but rescued and taken to Addenbrooks Hospital,

Cambridge where they recovered. Other people in the house were less severely affected. Main laying continued over the years primarily to meet increasing gas consumption as well as improvements to pressure. In November 1945 the UDC advised to the gas works of plans to relay the highway in High Street and advised the company to effect any maintenance before their work commenced but in practice, the road work was much delayed as was the main relaying. Cast iron and steel were 'controlled' and were in very short supply in post war years.

'Un-accounted-for' gas was a constant headache for managers. It was gas produced and measured on the station meter but lost in the mains distribution system under the roads and consequently not recorded on consumers' meters. It represented a significant loss of revenue and in Ely strenuous measures were taken to cut this wastage. In 1933 the quantity of gas leaking from the pipe network was 12% and this was reduced to 4% by 1945. The principal cause was leakage in the 'run lead' joints between sections of pipe which were generally 9-12 feet in length, but records from other works state that leakage actually occurred through the walls of the old cast pipes, which were later coated with tar to effect a seal. It is likely that most of the Ely underground mains in the 1950 were joined with spigot and socket joints and molten lead. Gas from the works was wet and si-phons to collect the water were built into pipe runs, the pipes being laid to gradients flowing to the siphons and these in turn would be emptied periodically. However, from a comment made by the manager in 1940, who was endeavouring to make a new map of the city's gas mains, they did not know where all the siphons were, so they clearly did not go round emptying all of them. They were opening up the roads to find them.

The Government's ban on street lighting was lifted on 15th July, VJ Day. Directors asked the UDC whether the city's lights should be prepared for the event, although lack of labour would re-sult in some lights not being brought into commission. The Council replied that Summer lights, the ones which had been prepared, would not be needed and instead asked for the winter lights to be brought into use. In 1947 the Manager reported the UDC had made a request to light all the streets, in spite of the Government ban and they would accept liability.

A John Malam gas lamp in North Bar Without, Bever-ley. The lantern at the top is a modern electrified re-production but the original cast iron pillar was made at Thorncliffe Iron foundry. It clearly shows J. Malam and on the reverse the date 1824. Might some of Ely's lamp columns have been to this design? The leopard face was not part of the standard range of images used by Thorncliffe ironworks and is believed to have been unique to J. Malam.

Thanks to Ken Golisti who spotted the find.

The Lamplighter
By Robert Louis Stevenson

My tea is nearly ready and the sun has left the sky;
It's time to take the window seat to see Leerie going by;
For every night at tea time and before you take your seat,
With lantern and with ladder he comes posting up the street,
Now Tom would be a driver and Maria go to sea,
And my Papa's a banker and as rich as he can be;
But I, when I am stronger and can choose what I'm to do,
O Leerie, I'll go round at night and light the lamps with you!
For we are very lucky, with a lamp before the door,
And Leerie stops to light it as he lights so many more;
And O! before you hurry by with ladder and with light,
O Leerie, see a little child and nod to him tonight!

A cartoon making fun of the fumes and
smells associated with 'gas'.
Illustration sourced from the John Doran Gas Museum

Chapter 22
The People

The Ely works touched on the lives of many, be they the Shareholders, Directors, the employees, the sub-contractors, or most of all, the gas consumers. At the time of the works closure there were 2,100 registered household consumers and over the duration of gas manufacture it must have lit the homes of several generations and supplied the needs of perhaps as many as 5,000 households and may be as many as 15,000 Ely citizens. Many firms, some local, were engaged to construct buildings, erect gas holders, install gas making plant and supply cast iron pipe and of course domestic gas appliances. Additionally, there were the seamen who sailed colliers down the east coast, as well as bargees from Kings Lynn and railway engine drivers, signalmen and other railway staff who took over coal transport. Finally, I should not omit mention of the many miners, particularly around Barnsley in Yorkshire, who won coal from the pit face to supply the retorts but who themselves never set foot in Ely. There were 3,268 collieries in 1864. I calculate that at least 17,000 peoples' fortunes were in some way affected by the Ely Gas Company during it's 135 year history.

The shareholders, the owners of the undertaking who risked their capital in the hope of good investment returns were very much the silent, indeed almost anonymous individuals. The directors, of whom there were usually three in office at a time, guided the company through its turbulent history and latterly its meteoric growth and they played a slightly more visible role. The company secretary, manager and foreman would have been those public figures best known to the people of the City. The works employees who grafted so hard to fuel the retorts and keep the supply going with great physical effort were barely mentioned, at least in the first 100 years. Thankfully, that all changed in the last thirty five years when their names did appear from time to time in the Ely Standard, Eastern Gas news and other gas news sheets.

The first reference to shareholders appears apart from the official register on 22nd October 1880 when Charles T Robinson chaired an extraordinary meeting of shareholders at the offices of the Company Secretary, Mr Edward Hill in Minster Place for the purposes of issuing three hundred £10 shares. Was he I wonder a notary in the City? By 1885 Chairmanship had changed to Mr Arthur Clarke with fellow directors J A Bailey, A Williamson and Colonel Ambrose. In March of the same year a Mr Alfred Kitts was elected to the Board on account of his being a "qualified gas engineer" which by inference suggests that no one else, not least the manager was 'qualified'. He was Chairman by 1900.

The company secretary at the time was a Mr E Hills, who was responsible both for preparing the books for the auditor, a Mr Lass, and the issue of Gas Company shares and dividends to investors. Shares were not traded on the Stock Exchange. The manager then was a Mr Yarston, who had overall responsibility for the plant and a salary of £75 per year. The individual responsible for the day to day running of the works and the stokers was the foreman, Mr Jones, who left in 1890 to be replaced by a Mr Richards on a weekly wage of 30/- (£78 per year).

In 1893 we read that Mr Foster, manager, tendered his resignation on account of financial difficulties. Investigations by the auditor and directors revealed Mr Foster had been negligent and sloppy in his documenting of the company accounts to the tune of £94/13/4d, which Mr Foster later admitted in writing. The directors when choosing a successor agreed that a new manager "shall be appointed who is to give ample guarantee of faithful service". A few months later Mr Thomas A. Guyatt was appointed to replace Mr Foster at a salary of £160/-/- per year, providing he found an assurance of fidelity from the Guarantee Society of 19, Buckyard Lane, London for £300. This practice of managers having to put up a surety or bond as a condition of employment was a common practice in the Industry. He was granted the privilege of using the company's house as a residence, an offer he declined weeks later. It is interesting to discover that Mr Guyatt also managed the Littleport Gas Company in 1914, a post which he may have taken after his appointment to Ely, or conversely held before joining the Ely Gas Works.

Mr Guyatt remained manager and by 1914, 'Engineer, Manager/Secretary', until 1933 when he died in harness after thirty seven years service to the company. History was to repeat itself as his successor, Claude Bertram Staniforth, my dad, found on his appointment that the company's finances were in dire straits with many debtors and equally many unpaid bills.

We read in the minutes of 1898 that two directors died. Mr Alfred Williamson and George Tukiss and were replaced by Mr Arthur Hall of Forehill House, Ely and the Rev. G.W Cooper also of Forehill who resigned on health grounds four months later. Col Ambrose, the senior director, died in 1821 and directors expressed their appreciation for his long and valuable service. He was succeeded by his son Mr Owen Ambrose. At the same time Mr Charles Trimmer was appointed to fill the vacancy left by Rev Turkin. James Bailey died in 1891. Mr Kitt was superseded as Chairman by Horace Martin in 1923. Mr Goodwin Archer resigned in 1927 as did Mr Arthur Luddington Hall. Mr Ambrose junior, Mr Martin and Mr Archer were to remain Directors until the Company was nationalised in 1949.

The lot of the labouring man on the works is hard to imagine for they worked a twelve hour shift probably seven days a week, with no paid holiday entitlement but Sunday work was probably minimised. The beer allowance was withdrawn in 1885, so stokers sweating hard shovelling coal in front of very hot retorts would have had to quench their thirst probably with barley water or cold tea. Not until the National Amalgamated Union of Labour approached Directors in 1917 concerning wages to staff did their lot improve and Directors instructed the Manager to make the best arrangements he was able to do, obviously in the Companies and not the employees favour although by 1914-18 there was statutory control of wages and labour. This was a significant turning point in the remuneration of employees who previously had to negotiate their own contractual terms but who now enjoyed standardised conditions of both wages and terms of employment with others in the industry. In time wage rates were negotiated according to the gas output of the works and the Ministry of Labour Cost of Living Index. Probably to discourage pilfering men were given an allowance of one sack of coke per week, recorded in the books as coke sold at 1/- per bag. During the First World War employees were paid a 5/- per month war bonus which was enhanced to 5/- per week by 1917. The bonus was a temporary measure and wages were reduced in 1923. Another perk given to men from 1943 was 2/6 worth of gas per week and above that quantity, half price provided they lived in the companies area but this was withdrawn as wages advanced.

In 1905 William Cross, a lamplighter for twenty five years was allowed 5/- per week during his illness. In 1915 Thomas Lucan, an old employee, was granted a pension of 5/- per week. Thomas Cross aged seventy four with thirty years service with the company, was in 1923, granted a pension again at the pleasure of the directors of 5/- per week. The Minutes record that in 1928 Thomas

Browne now in receipt of his old age pension be given notice that being unable to perform the same amount of work as a younger man his wages would be reduced to 30/- per week or alternatively the Directors would offer him a 10/- per week compassionate allowance, at their pleasure. Mr Rickwood died in hospital in 1905 and his widow given a £5 donation. G. Gardner an ex employee died in 1935.

Photograph courtesy of Mike Rouse. Possibly taken by Tom Boulton

A photograph from 'Ely Cathedral Market Town 1900-1953' by Mike Rouse and Reg Holmes 1975 of the Ely Gas Works. The building to the left is the office complex I remember, which was to remain until the works was demolished. It was built in 1903 and was clearly fairly modern for its time The Board Room was on the first floor. The door to the left lead to the laboratory and station governor. The building to the right with the arched opening is probably the entrance to the horizontal retort house but it is impossible to reconcile this with the plan of 1881. The picture must have been taken after 1903 when the office building behind was erected. Mike and Reg suggest a date of 1915. This ties in with the period when gas stoves first started to become available in Ely.

The picture depicts either the manager or more likely foreman sporting his pocket watch on chain, holding a coke fork which was wide and would have had a distinct curve to help hold the coke. In the front row the two lamp lighters hold their tall poles for lamp lighting and the stokers are distinguishable with their robust pokers with circular handles for cleaning ash from the bars of the furnaces below the retorts. The stokers are dressed in waistcoats which would have been more practical than jackets for their hot and physically arduous job. They appear to be all young men. The two wheeled hand chute would have been used when 'drawing a retort' to re-direct some of the spent coal, now hot coke into the producer furnace below which heated the bench of retorts. The gas stove is one of the early models of gas cooker which were hired to townsfolk. They were made of cast iron, coloured black and relied on a heavy door latch much like a gate. A small stack of coal is to be seen on the left.

It is not clear which type of lamp lighting poles were in use at the time. The early ones relied on a three sectioned carbide lamp, one containing the water, the second the carbide and the third the carbide gas reaction chamber. The later lamplighter comprised a perforated cylinders which contained burning coltsfoot oil connected to a benzene receptacle in the lower handle. Depression of a rubber bulb squirted the benzene gas into the burning oil to produce a flash of flame which was used to ignite the gas mantle in the street lamp. The stick turned on the gas tap just a moment before.

An annual summer holiday was first granted to workmen in 1898 when they were allowed three days plus a 5/- allowance instead of double pay but the manager had enjoyed an annual holiday usually two weeks from 1886 or earlier. By 1921 the stokers twelve hour shift was reduced to an eight hour shift. This may have been prompted by four men resigning to take up work at the beet factory, which offered more attractive working conditions than the gas company. By March 1947 the annual holiday was extended to two weeks and the forty four hour week was brought in quickly after that, these matters no longer being local decisions.

Minutes record that in 1885 the company gave its staff a Christmas gratuity. The foreman received 7/6, all men on the works 5/- and a present of game and poultry was presented to the manager and to the surveyor of the Ely Board of Health. The latter gentleman was the key to the continuing lighting contracts secured by Ely Gas to light the public street of the City. By 1942 the value of these gifts had risen to 21/- for stokers and to 42/- for the foreman. The practice of Christmas gratuities continued until Nationalisation in 1949 when the Eastern Gas Board ceased to follow the annual time served practice of thanking its staff in this way.

> The wages of staff employed in the industry reflected the rapidly expanding enterprises. Stokers were the most highly paid manual workers but their work was arduous. It was not uncommon for them to shovel 8 cwt of coal per hour and an equal quantity of coke. They worked seven days a week with only two paid holidays per year, Christmas day and Good Friday, although this changed over time and the work was for some seasonal.
> General wages were on a sliding scale with managerial staff, as well as manual workers receiving an income commensurate with the size and wealth of the undertaking. Large London works paid very much more than the rural

In 1888 there was a significant accident on the works for which a worker was temporarily suspended. The severity of the accident was sufficient to justify a special report to shareholders but no mention was made in the minutes as to whether anybody was injured or indeed the nature of the incident. By 1898 as a result of the Workmen's Compensation Act, the company took out insurance with the Ocean Accident and Guarantee Corporation at 8/6% of the company wage bill. Such insurance was very timely for in 1900 a stoker, called A N Lovell, reported personal injury to his eye whilst drawing a retort, meaning removing the red hot residual coke in preparation

for a new charge of coal. His case was referred to the insurers. It seems likely that a red hot piece of coke might have lodged in his eye possibly causing blindness. A further accident befell Walter Peak a labourer whilst erecting a new roof to the coal house. It is believed he recovered from his injuries. Later the insurance was transferred to the Norwich and London Accident Assurance Association at 17/6% for works staff, 12/6% for outdoor men and 3/-% for clerical staff who were at a much lower risk of accident. On 16th November 1933 there was a gas explosion at 23, West Fen Road, and loss adjusters Messrs Ellis and Buckler and later Robert Crawford and Co Insurers were engaged to help come to the' best possible term's with the parties involved, the inference being it was probably the company's fault. W G Lester went sick due to an accident in 1946.

One vital role of the company secretary was to maintain the company register of shareholders and to effect share transfers between investors. Clearly it was a public company for investors came from the length and breadth of the land, but most shareholders were local people. The minutes record each share transaction in detail together with details of lost certificates, transfers following the death of a shareholder and so on. One particularly interesting transaction was a request from the Master of Lunacy to transfer company stock in the name of Mr Edward Hills to a Mrs Kate

Taplein Hills. The company secretary in this case interviewed the Hills family to authenticate the legality of this request. In 1886 the Bishop of Winchester requested a duplicate share certificate because he had mislaid the original. Did the current Bishop of Ely pass a good share investment tip to a friend in Winchester I ask?

As with any commercial company there was always a small band of people unable to pay their way and who either found themselves forced to have a prepayment meter or at worst found themselves in court. In 1891 the Rev Winterfield owed the company £70 16s 8d for gas supplied, a substantial sum in those days and in 1930 the Rev Father Hughes chose a slot meter to replace his credit meter. Messrs Speechley and Beckley were forewarned that unless they paid their arrears they would be 'cut off'. In 1895 Mr Huxley, Mr Rocke, Mr Duich and Mr Woodroffe had county court summons taken out against them for failure to pay gas rental and gas supplied. Mr C Legg and Mr Joseph refused to pay their bills in protest at the 'allotment' meaning salary awarded to the manager. Mr Legg relented but Mr Cutlack bargained a discount of five shillings. In 1933 two over due accounts came to light, one from Mr R Rickwood and Son, and a second for Mr W Rickwood both going back ten years. Negotiations proceeded between parties and after removal of the meter for testing, the Gas Company accepted an offer from Mr W Rickwood of £60 and the matter was closed.

In 1932 the list of arrears detailed F Dobson and J Porter as being unable to pay, as they had no

Ely Gas Employees 1922

Walter Cross, John Bigg and Walter Partridge (top right) Chris Lee, W.G. Lester (foreman aged 39 in shirt sleeves) Tom Brown and John Bigg jnr.

Photograph probably taken in North Yard looking east or south with what looks like a tall vertical cylindrical possibly a washer in the distance and an engine with flywheel may be an exhauster pump in the foreground

Photograph courtesy of G Lester

money whilst J Shephard, C Watson, B Loftus and others had absconded. Bad debts continued over the years, Messrs Rushbrook, Walton, Lett, Burgess and Son, Savage, Ireland, Barnett, Friedman (an evacuee), Kempton and Son, Watman, Drake, Sindall, Ashton, Webdale, Horne, Heath, Merryside, and Burgess having had their debts written off. A Mr Ernest Rouse, the local debt collector, was engaged in 1940 to pursue defaulters such as L.V. Hills and Mr Kempton.

The worst debtor in town must have been Mr John Hawkes, trading as Hawke and Son of Ely, who the minutes record in 1932 as owing an estimated £4,172- 2s- 11d, a mammoth debt sufficient to pay half the cost of the new vertical retort house. Legal counsel was sought at the time and directors conceded there as no useful purpose to be served in filing for bankruptcy and had no alternative but to write off the bad debt. It must have been a catastrophic loss to the company and with the benefit of hindsight such a debt should never have been allowed to amass on this scale. Such a huge debt could not have come from a defaulting gas consumer but might have been from a contractor or supplier to the gas company. The reticence of directors to call in the debt earlier adds to the mystery. Could John Hawkes in 1932 have in any way been related to J Hawke Coal Merchant and for a time sub tenant of the gas company in 1863? Might John Hawke be the son or grandson of J Hawk the former lessee of the Gas undertaking. Might the Coal merchants business have borrowed money against the gas business to subsidise an ailing coal haulage business? There is no proof but what a co-incidence. Indeed, might the early failure of the original gas company and the sale to the National Gas Consumer Company in 1840 have been precipitated by this financial mis-management? Resolving the case, for it is not clear when the problem started, could have taken up to ninety three years, when my father was appointed manager and confirms the dire straits of the company in 1933.

The most consistent late payer must have been in my childhood when a certain very elevated and respected member of the cloth within the cathedral close was consistently in arrears. No, it was not the Bishop, but someone of almost equal standing who had the means to pay and who should have known better! My father talked of him often over the dining table.

The workforce did not escape the impact of two world wars for we read that Mr T. Barnes and Mr T Barman were killed in action in November 1916. The 7/- allowance paid to Mrs Barman, his mother, whilst he was in service was discontinued. At the same time the clerk within the offices, Mr Reader, was 'called up' for service and directors instructed his job be kept open for him on his return. In June of 1916 we read that the works was insured against aircraft attack. J S Lee was called up in 1940.

Employment with the Gas Company was not a job for life. On the one hand labour was in such short supply between 1914 and 1950 in part because of the 'call up' of citizens for the first and second world wars, (1916– 1957/8). The resultant casualties meant that there were sometimes insufficient men to recruit for the yard. On the other hand, the men that were available could not always perform the duties expected of them. The job of foremen seemed particularly fated. Mr George Lester tells me his father G. Lester was sacked by my father, which was slightly embarrassing. The minute books record that J H Brig was dismissed on account of inefficiency and bad conduct in 1934 and lost the tenure of the foreman's house in Back Lane. He was superseded by A Quinney who in spite of pay rises, performance pay and training was fired two years later. Aron Aspley was appointed as his successor only to be dismissed for unsatisfactory conduct and service in 1938. J Skeels, possibly a stoker, was dismissed for insolence where upon his mate, S Scutting,

Two stokers from the Ely works. On the left is Earnest Reynolds who to earn extra money also undertook lamp lighting duties. He died in 1938 when his daughter recounts he was hit by a motorist on a pedestrian crossing. He left a widow and six children aged 2½ to 12½.

Taken it is believed between 1934 and 1939

Photo courtesy of Audrey Longdon nee Reynolds

'Old Bill' Retires

Gas Board Presentation

A PLEASANT CEREMONY took place at the Station-road, Ely offices of the Eastern Gas Board on Tuesday week when all the employees and office staff assembled to express their regard for one of their number who was retiring. Mr. William Taylor, known affectionately as "Old Bill", joined the service of the then Ely Gas and Electricity Co. in 1924, as a stoker. In those days the retorts were of the horizontal type and hand charged. As the works grew and vertical retorts were built with better conditions for labour he had been transferred to the better system. He was now retiring just before another method of gas making was to be started namely the carburetted water gas process for which the plant was nearly completed.

Mr. C. B. Staniforth, the Engineer and Manager, expressed his appreciation of the work of Mr. Taylor, whom he described as reliable, level-headed and altogether a good worker. Good work, he said, was something which all could respect for it gave satisfaction to both master and man.

SYMBOLIC GIFTS

As a token of the respect and regard in which he was held by his workmates, the office staff and management, Mr. Taylor was then presented by the manager with a polished steel garden spade, a windproof cigarette lighter and pen and pencil set. Mr. Staniforth said that the spade would remind him of 28 years of coal shovelling, the lighter of the flames of the furnaces and the pen and pencil of the carbonising report which he ......

Mr. Taylor ...... regret that the ...... telling and tha ...... was now such t ...... not continue to ...... his 65th year wi ...... at the next week ...... sorry that the t ...... to leave.

Finally Mr. S ...... half of the of ...... Chris Lee, for ...... added a few wo ...... for his co-operat ......

resigned in sympathy. All these dismissals occurred under my father's direction, which might say as much about my father as it did his employees!

The company house situated in Annersdale normally occupied by the manager was vacant as Mr Guyatt did not take up the offer of accommodation. It was let to a Mr A E Varell until 1894 who in turn was asked to be relieved of his tenancy, whereupon it was let to a Mr Benton at 15/- per quarter. The following year a Mr Benton was asked for the payment of his rent arrears. In 1907 Mr Benton of Potters Lane was given twelve months notice to vacate his house and yard with arrears owing of £35-10-0d and an annual rental of £17. In 1902 the manager's house nearby was auctioned and sold for £206 to Mr Graven.

The Directors recognised that their role was not merely one of running the company but of fostering good relationships with the public. In 1885 Mr Arthur Hall treasurer of the City School, one of the National Schools, invited the directors to make an annual contribution to the running of the school. They agreed and for many years contributed two guineas. The lighting of the Public Clock in the Market place (now displayed in the Ely Museum) was another example of

> LIBERALITY Mr A Williams lessee of the Ely Gas Works gives his usual Christmas gift, three bushels of coke to 300 poor persons: and to his numerous employees, presents of beef, plumb pudding etc. The gift no doubt is fully appreciated by the recipients.
>
> The Isle of Ely Herald reported 24th December 1881.

Ely Standard Friday 2 January 1953 William Taylor retired after 28 years as a stoker being presented with a garden spade, a cigarette lighter and a pen and pencil set by the manager Mr Staniforth. Second left Mr Secker, far right Mr Ardron and seated centre Miss Redman.— 37 staff were present.

PRESENTATION TO RETIRING COLLEAGUE

170

their giving back to the community. The Archdeacon in his capacity of President of the Institute of the reading room asked directors whether they would be willing to give gas as the company's contribution at a fete to be held in July 1888. They agreed.

Directors in later years maintained the company's gift to the community, for in 1942, they agreed to a request for a reduction in price of gas to the Red Cross Convent Home in the Bishops Palace. In fact they extended the offer to include all three of Elys' hospitals including The Grange and the Isolation Hospital.

In 1891 Dr Beckett reported he had driven his car into an open trench in the road where gas employees had been installing a main and he held the company responsible. Again, directors showed consideration to the GP, who incidentally was probably the grandfather to the Dr Beckett who attended me as a child, and instructed the manager to effect a settlement.

One usually thinks of gas as a fuel for lighting and later heating for the City had very few industrial customers. Mr J N Tibbs asked in 1926 for a reduction in the price of his gas to power his engine. Directors agreed provided he consumed a minimum of 400,000 cu ft per year. Two years later Mr Derbergh was enquiring about a gas supply to the jam factory which eventually declined the service on account of cost and a little later six fish fryers were in use in the town which it is believed used one million two hundred thousand cu ft. between them. In 1944 Mr Bogen of New Barnes Road installed a baking plant using two hundred cu ft per hour.

An unexpected request was made to directors in 1918 in a letter from Messrs Williams, Robinson and Milroy, probably solicitors, asking them to buy out the Soham Gas Company and apply for an Act of Parliament to enable them to run the undertaking. Curious as to the motive the manager was instructed to ascertain the reason only to be met by fierce resistance from Soham Directors who refused to entertain the idea. This suggests there were some very disgruntled shareholders in Soham.

In June 1944 an explosion occurred at the Soham works and staff from the Ely gas works helped restore a supply of gas for consumers. Three months later the Soham works was put up for sale, but Ely directors decided that 'in view of the relatively great distance between the communities and no villages in between whose custom could be picked up with a connecting main, that to purchase the Soham company would not be a good investment'.

Directors monthly meetings were nearly always held in the company offices in Ely but strangely some were convened in London. In 1898 a meeting was held at 30, Free Church Street, London; in 1902 at 5, Victoria Street, Westminster; in 1908/10 at 647, Queen Street, Cheapside, London EC and in 1918 at 6/7, Tower Street, London EC3. Were one or more of the directors members of a gentleman's club in the City or merely bored with their wives or alternatively taking them Christmas shopping, possibly at the companies expense, for the visits were mostly just before Xmas? Who knows, but it is documented in 1921 directors voted themselves an increased allowance of 40 shillings per journey for visits to London. These visits occurred long after the famous Crystal Palace Exhibition held in 1882 which included a large exhibit exploiting the heating properties of town gas . What good reason could they possibly have had to make such a journey? To see the streets of Westminster lit by gas? All subsequent directors meetings were held in the Boardroom in Station Road Ely and none in London.

Cookery demonstrations were all the rage following the increasing numbers of customers buying a cooker. Indeed, cooking soon became the major component of gas usage. Cookery demonstrations were therefore very popular and the first significant event together with a Washing Demonstration was held at the Women's Institute in 1934, widely reported in the Cambridgeshire Times of 9th Feb 1934. This netted appliance sales of £240. Public talks also started to become popular but directors would only agree to such a talk scheduled in the King's School if children were admitted. A subsequent talk on gas meter manufacture was reported in the Cambridgeshire Times on 16th March attended largely by ladies and children. The Manager too gave the occasional public talk and accompanied one with a publicity film on gas.

An Exhibition under canvas with the Local Gas Companies contribution before the days of a showroom   Ely Standard Oct 2nd 1953.

Advertising commenced in the Ely Standard in 1933 with an 8 inch double column every fortnight. A travelling salesman Mr Richmond working for the Gas Stove Company managed in 1934 to sell five cookers, six over-sink water heaters and three irons, so the Directors decided to advertise their own range of products at the Ely Rex cinema at 2/6d per week and also to advertise with posters in prominent places in town, including the outside wall of the coal shed on Station Road and the Corn Exchange.

Advertising posters displayed it is believed on the exterior wall of the gas works facing Station Road thought to have been produced by Mundford Posters.

Later the same year the company negotiated with Lloyds bank to display and floodlight a poster on a house they owned in St Mary Street occupied by Mrs Gotobed, the tenant. The Gas company paid Lloyds Bank £1 per year for the privilege and for Mrs Gotobed 10/- per year, plus a cooker fitted free which would normally have been hired out at 18/- per annum.

The Company Hierarchy in about 1940

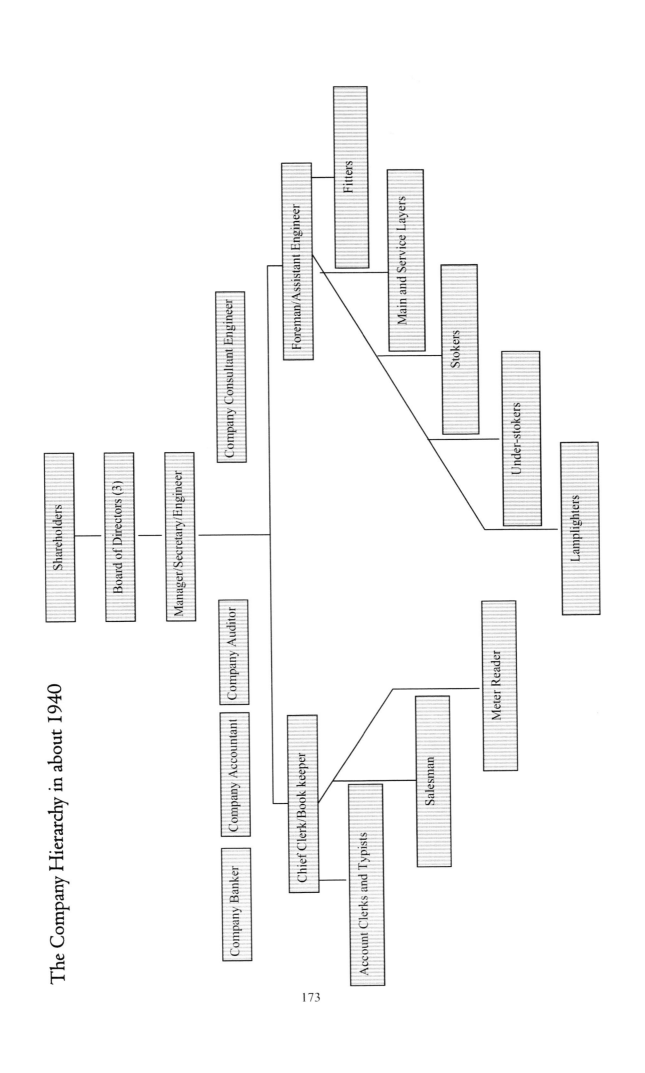

One longstanding problem that even I can recall was the absence of a premises in the High Street in which customers could pay their accounts and select new appliances. As a temporary measure periodic exhibitions particularly of gas stoves were held, the first documented one being in 1886 organised by Messrs Davis and Co and a second at a cost of £5 in 1894. By 1892 an arrangement had been made with George Berridge for use of a room in the Black Swan Inn adjoining the works for use as a showroom for gas stoves at an annual rent of £5-10 shillings. Stoves were now available for the first time on three year Hire Purchase agreements. By 1915 there were 474 stoves in use in the City. In 1933 tentative plans were considered for a Gas showroom at No1 Market Place but then dropped. The manager then provisionally offered the Central Meat Co in the High Street at £25 per annum for use of their window to display gas appliances, but this was rejected as inadequate. Then Mr A.T. Buck of 5, Lynn Road proposed converting his house into a showroom for company use but Directors rejected the idea.

'GOOD BUNCH OF CHAPS' AT ELY

Colleagues gather at Ely 'Holder station' to bid farewell to Mr Archie Collett who retired after 16 years service. Mr Winch Cambridge Divisional Engineer presented a canteen of cutlery and thanked him for his excellent service since he came to Ely from Newcastle in 1947. Originally a fitter, he later became a special servicelayer and mainlayer.
February 1964

From the left—second Walter Partridge, sixth Sid Merry, seventh Harry Martin ?, eighth E. Winch, (Cambridge), tenth Claude Staniforth.

How the gas works was first built, the necessary plant and machinery acquired and coal ordered is beyond my imagination for there was neither a telephone or national postal service when the works was founded. The 'penny post' was introduced six years after the works was established and it was not until 1903 that Directors had the opportunity to consider 'whether the Post Office telephone be entertained'. After initial enquiries they considered the cost of £9-5s-0d too high and deferred a decision. A single payment of £6-3s-4d to the Post Office in 1934 is the only reference as to club when the works might have been connected to the network. Its first exchange number was Ely 84 later changed to Ely 555.

GAS CLUB OPENED AT ELY

CLUB OPENING CEREMONY

Mr Hunter Rioch, general manager of the Cambridge Group of Eastern Gas Board, my fathers boss and Miss Redman from the Ely Office cutting the celebration cake resplendent with an image of Mr Therm. Subsequent meetings of the club were held in the Angel Hotel.
Serving the committee were President Mr Staniforth, Chairman T Staines, vice Chairman T. Young, secretary and treasurer Miss D. Redman, committee Mrs W. Tebb, Messrs J. Martin, A. Collett & C. Clarke.

The Cambridgeshire Times Friday 14th October 1955 & Ely Standard Friday October 14th 1955

Lorry dirvers E. Martin and J. Martin extreme left receiving diplomas for 'driving throughout 1953 without an accident or mishap of any kind', and H.Culpin and L. Cummins each of whom received a St. Johns certificate. Both had concluded a course in first aid. Presenting the awards in the Board Room was Col. G. L. Archer.

Ely Standard November 19th 1954

The manager, Claude Staniforth, a few years after appointment reported to directors that owing to an increase in the amount of work both on the works and district, which required his personal supervision he had needed purchased a motor car to make journeys more quickly. Directors agreed to contribute towards the expense. With a looming petrol crisis in 1942 the manager then asked directors to agree to his having a gas bag fitted to the roof of his vehicle on the grounds that it would be good publicity as well as meet his needs. After deliberation they decided such an expense could not be justified. By 1948 he pleaded his car was in serious need of repair and had decided to replace it with a Standard 14 saloon from Henley's Garage London at a cost of £800. Directors agreed to pay 66% of its cost, the manager to pay the company for his private mileage.

My father in 1942 had plans to move on to another larger works and had to ask directors if they would wave the 'Essential Workers Order' to enable him to do so. The did but he decided to stay.

In 1938 Mr E H Binge was appointed as a salesman remuneration of 5% commission. He came from 'The London Gas Co'. In the space of 13 weeks he sold over 500 varying gas appliances. Mr Secker the District Superintendent was very highly regarded by both my father and the directors.

Peter Crawford was appointed aged fifteen, to the works staff in 1935 as part of the Bishop Laney Charity. He was my fathers 'blue eyed boy'. Five years on he was encouraged to sit the Gas College Exams and directors awarded him five guineas to encourage him. I recall my father telling me that when he did, he came second of all the fitters thought out the country in the national examination. Some achievement for a young man from Ely and a red letter day for the Ely Gas Works. Peter is known to have joined the RAF and sadly went missing on manoeuvres.

Peter Crawford, J Hitch and Allen Normack were all appointed fitters apprentices under the Bishop Laneys Charity.

Salaries in the Industry

Staff on larger works were paid very much more than colleagues on smaller works like Ely where wages were much low.

My father's salary was £369/annum in 1952 rising to £564/annum by 1954 well below the national average. Bold text refers to smaller works.

		1815-1830	1920-1.940
		£	£
Engineer/ Manager	Per annum	**150**-500	**400**-5,000
Assistant Engineer	Per annum	75-200	200-675
Clerk/Bookkeeper	Per annum	**150**-315	132-400
Foreman	Per annum	**110**-200	150-275
Lamplighter	Per week	**5/-** to 14/-	**36/6** to 40/6
Stoker	Per shift	**1/6**to4/3	**7/9** to 14/4
Gas fitter	Per week		**50/10** to 84/4
Labourer day men	Per week	**?** to12/-	**44/-** to 61/-

175

Chapter 23
Other significant events in the Company history

The construction of the RAF hospital brought many challenges as well as significant prosperity to the gas undertaking. In January 1939 the Manager wrote to the Air Ministry to enquire of their need for gas to be told that gas would be used for cooking if the price was right, but they would not entertain gas for heating. The RAF determined their gas need based on a large amount of cooking equipment and the Gas Company immediately realised that the existing 4"pipework was insufficient to ensure a satisfactory gas pressure. Mr Everett, the Consultant Engineer, said even a 6" main from the Lamb Corner could not service the needs of the hospital. The Manager therefore proposed to the Directors that a small gas holder of 1,500 cu ft be built at the hospital costing £1,685. This could gradually fill overnight and meet the peak day time needs of the hospital kitchens. Directors first consulted Mr Everet, before putting the proposals to the Air Ministry with an invitation they pay 25% down payment with the balance spread over ten years. After further exploratory talks Mr Evetts proposed a new 4" high pressure main be laid from the gas works to the hospital and a compressor plant be installed at the works costing in total £2,685. The proposal was again referred to the Air Ministry who agreed to pay 75% of the cost -£2,015. Gas was to be sold at 6½d per therm with a sliding scale of ($^1/_5$ d) rise or fall for every 1/- rise or fall in the price of coal. By 1943 eleven nissen huts, were erected in the hospital grounds and the gas supply was extended to them at a cost of £200.

"Well and truly laid"

MAINLAYING

Over 40 years' sound experience. Skilled and gas-minded workmen. Thousands of miles of mains have been laid by JEAVONS.

E. E. JEAVONS & CO. LTD.
TIPTON • STAFFORDSHIRE
Phone : TIPTON 2161 (10 lines)   Grams : "PIPELINES" TIPTON

The gas pipes which the company usually sourced from Stanton cost 4/6 per yard for 18 foot long pipes and joints 6d per yard. Two tenders were sought for installation and E E Jeavens and Co were awarded the contract at 8/- per yard for laying under roadways to a cover depth of 24". Directors accepted the quote on the understanding work was completed in six weeks. By March 1940 the pipe work was completed and put under a forty eight hour pressure test, during which time it lost only two pounds pressure. (see page 210).The compressor had already been delivered and was commissioned later. By May the gas cooking equipment was installed and gas usage commenced. By July 1940 the hospital was using 3,000 Cu ft of gas per day some 3 % of the works production. Just before the works closure a new arterial gas main was laid from Cambridge via Soham to Ely and then on to Littleport. It had been hoped to use the RAF high pressure pipe and simply extend it from the north end of Orchard Estate to Littleport. Unfortunately, testing revealed it could not withstand the new pressure and leaked like a colander so this section of pipe had to be re-laid.

Whilst the Gas Works sustained no bombing during the last war (1939-1945) Air Raid Precautions were implemented should such an incident occur. In 1939 the Manager reported repair gangs had been formed and trained to deal with broken mains. Helmets, civilian gas masks, special combined coal gas and war gas masks had been ordered as well as gas proof clothing. Fire risks had been minimised by the running of town water mixed with gas liquor to various points on the works. A strong air raid shelter capable of housing the entire staff had been prepared. A steam whistle which used in conjunction with the siren would sound and alert the public of an impending air raid. The introduction of the 'Black Out' when all street lighting was extinguished and house-holders banned from showing a light after dusk, resulted in a 10% drop in gas usage. In 1943 whilst a gas holder was under construction eighty members of the National Fire Service were invited to look over the works after which they were given a talk on gas works fire risks. The concrete tank of an old holder was then converted to hold water for fire extinguishing needs. In 1940 the air raid sirens sounded and employees took to the shelter. At a subsequent board meeting Directors gave instructions that employees could only take cover in the shelter if an air raid actually started.

Beamish Museum

Shortage of labour became so acute that by 1944 two Italian prisoners were recruited. I presume these changed for my father records a German and Italian POW. The following year labour was in such short supply that the manager reported both to the Ministry of Fuel and Power and the Ministry of Labour that the works urgently needed an extra stoker, lorry driver's mate and two prisoners. The Ministry of Labour replied that if the supply of gas to the city was imperilled they would supply military labour and for a fortnight two soldiers were employed as stokers. Company records reveal several monthly payments headed POW Labour. (£46 11s 6d February 1945). The POW must have worked for the company for several years and by 1947 there were four POWs some of whom were not working well, in spite of having been reported to the Commandant but their departure came as a bit of a shock, for in February 1948 the manager was given one hours notice of their withdrawn labour. More importantly joyous news for the prisoners. Owing to the language problems, directors decided not to employ any 'displaced persons' and instead rely on English recruited labour.

Gas companies were on one level very supportive of their many members who were called up for military service and kept their jobs open, usually with a temporary employee until their safe return, in part, I suggest, because the country was so devoid of skilled labour it needed them back. This practice was certainly adopted by the Ely company. At a Board meeting it was emphasised that the company were under no obligation to pay these men's wages and any allowances were at their discretion. Directors decided to grant J S Lee, a single man at the time, who was called up for service a weekly allowance of 10/- but only payable on his safe return back in the employ of the company.

In 1940 the Manager discussed with Directors the Company's liability to pay sick pay, which the company was in law liable to pay. Directors voted that in the event of an employee being away sick for more than a week his employment be terminated but with the offer that once well he could return, but that in the future there would be no further entitlement to sick pay. By 1942 Directors had a change of heart and decided to grant an allowance on account of illness from employees not in receipt of income under the Workmen's Compensation Act ,under the National Health Act on production of a doctors certificate - 15/- for a married man and 10/- for single men for up to four weeks sickness retrospective to January 1941.

In April 1944 a Pension Scheme was introduced to which all employees contributed. The scheme was 'Register of Friendly Societies Ref 363SF'. It took four years to formulate and required the company accountant to verify the company could finance the venture after which pension providers, Friends Provident and Century Life Offices Co were consulted, before Dickerson and Son solicitors in London prepared the final legal paperwork.

Pollution prevention legislation was nothing like as stringent in those days as it is now and the gas company managed to operate largely within the law, - just. Gas liquor, because there was so much of it, became the bane of any manager. In 1935 there was a leakage of effluent into the sewers of Gas House Lane and Directors in their ignorance asked the Manager if there was any means by which the liquid could be made innocuous to fish life and at what cost, presumably so they could treat the material and then pipe it into the river. Up until then liquor was just allowed to run onto a spare piece of land next to the coal house but it seeped below ground damaging trees belonging to Mr Benton living next door and got into the ground of the adjacent swimming pool. Directors agreed to make good damage to council property, compensate Mr Benton modestly and repair a pipe which lead to the river quay so the liquor could be conveyed by tanker to Kings Lynn for processing. Mr Owen Ambrose later consented to much liquor being spread on manure heaps on his land. An agreement was however secured with the Prince Regent Tar Company known locally as 'the muck works', for reprocessing gas liquor which it is believed was conveyed by river lighter to the company's premises situated near the confluence of the rivers Nean and Gt. Ouse at Kings Lynn. In 1932 tar was sold on a seven year contract to Messrs Boulton and Hayward Ltd. By 1934 the works were producing 48,682 gallons per year.

In 1943 tar was reported in the sewer of the Oak Public House in Station Road. After a further complaint the following year from the King Charles in the Oak, Directors agreed it was probably the companies fault and paid the UDC for its clearance. In 1946 traces of tar were reported in the river on the sides of pleasure craft but there was no evidence to prove it came from the works – but where else could it possibly have originated ? In 1947 an interesting altercation occurred between the Surveyor to the Council and the company. The surveyor discovered the entire length of sewer along Back Lane was blocked with a deposit, requiring the pipes to be excavated , cleaned and relaid. Mr Mack, the surveyor, insisted the Gas company pay for the work and that future discharge cease forthwith and no drain connection from the works would be permitted. The directors, one of whom was a solicitor, agreed to pay the cost but only on production of an analysis of the waste. The company could not cease production of waste or change its composition immediately but that the company would be willing to install plant in order to comply with legislation. But he then went on to say that as gas liquor was not classified as 'Trade Effluent' the company was entitled to discharge it into a Public Drain. As a coup de grâce the Directors finished their letter by saying that "Looked at in a sense of proportion the quantity of effluent was so small in quantity to warrant congratulations rather than rebuke and in proportion to the inconvenience caused to the running of the works" and requested re-connection of the works outfall to the sewer. - Round one to the Gas Company.

A little later the Ouse Fisheries Board issued a summons against the Ely Urban District for allowing (gas) effluent to get into the river. Fearing the Company might be 'called to book', the manager with the approval of directors promptly asked Mr Tucker, a local builder, to fit filters to the drain and the company paid one third of the reinstatement costs of the sewer in Back Lane. In 1948 the Ouse Fisheries Board took the Beet Factory and the UDC to the High Court for effluent pollution, material which almost certainly came from the works, but lost their case. My father, I recall, went to London and sat as an observer in the public gallery to listen to the case, fearing that the gas company might be singled out as the culprit. Surprisingly they were not. The same year the manager reported he needed urgently to dispose of 70,000gallons of gas liquor and with the help of Major Fowler found a pit near Wicken Fen, owned by a Mr Bailey of Wicken, who charged £10 per annum for its use. Whilst a tar pipe was laid in 1933 from the works to the river for conveyance of the by-product by boat to distillers, small quantities landed up in Littleport rubbish tip.

The story of the gas filled balloons

It was to be a memorable occasion, never to be repeated in my lifetime and one which I had to mark in my own way. What could I do which the 'world' would notice that I could proudly say, "I did that"?

I needed two accomplices, partners in crime, one with a car plus a ladder and one with 'gas'. Who else should I turn to but my closest friend Peter and our mutual school friend, John. Peter, or at least his father, could supply the gas and John was the proud owner of a Morris Minor traveller. All we now needed was the nerve to 'pull it off'.

Like all school boys the last day of school was one to celebrate, what ever the differing feelings we might have. Mine was one of, 'I've made it, in spite of …..... Look at me'.

Well, instead of burning our school caps on the playground tarmac using an illicit cigarette lighter smuggled into school, we decided to do something rather more public. To hang from the spire of our revered public school, 'The Perse', a bunch of gas filled balloons.

The plot went something like this. On the evening of the day proceeding the last day of term, John, John Wickham that is, took all three of us to the Low Temperature Research Station, situated in Downing College where Peter's father worked. He had access to some cylinders of hydrogen gas. Peter Russell had talked his dad into being in cahoots with the plot and at about 4.30pm all the balloons were inflated and taken to my house in Gilbert Road for later collection.

By 10.00 pm, much to my despair, I realised that the balloons were slowly deflating. By morning they would be flat. Panic! The whole prank would fail.

For once in my life my father came to the rescue. "Why not get them topped up with Town Gas", he said? Town gas is 50% hydrogen. "Oh thanks Dad"! At this point my mother expressed her strongest disapproval and distanced herself from the entire affair. Meanwhile father and I went off to the Cambridge gas works in 'big Humber car', full of sorry looking balloons. On arrival we went to the governor house and whilst father went off to find the night stoker I marvelled at all the machinery around me. The stoker arrived and one by one the balloons were carefully untied, attached to a pipe end and blown up with town gas, something one could not do at home because the gas pressure there would have been insufficient. We had done it! Father drove me home where I waited until the early hours for John and Peter to arrive in the Morris to collect me and the balloons.

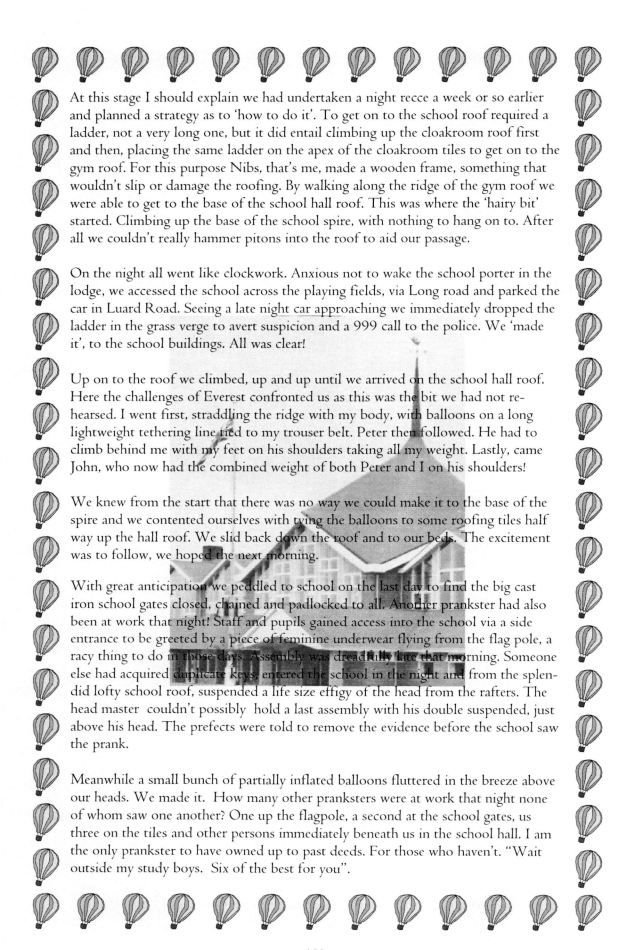

At this stage I should explain we had undertaken a night recce a week or so earlier and planned a strategy as to 'how to do it'. To get on to the school roof required a ladder, not a very long one, but it did entail climbing up the cloakroom roof first and then, placing the same ladder on the apex of the cloakroom tiles to get on to the gym roof. For this purpose Nibs, that's me, made a wooden frame, something that wouldn't slip or damage the roofing. By walking along the ridge of the gym roof we were able to get to the base of the school hall roof. This was where the 'hairy bit' started. Climbing up the base of the school spire, with nothing to hang on to. After all we couldn't really hammer pitons into the roof to aid our passage.

On the night all went like clockwork. Anxious not to wake the school porter in the lodge, we accessed the school across the playing fields, via Long road and parked the car in Luard Road. Seeing a late night car approaching we immediately dropped the ladder in the grass verge to avert suspicion and a 999 call to the police. We 'made it', to the school buildings. All was clear!

Up on to the roof we climbed, up and up until we arrived on the school hall roof. Here the challenges of Everest confronted us as this was the bit we had not re-hearsed. I went first, straddling the ridge with my body, with balloons on a long lightweight tethering line tied to my trouser belt. Peter then followed. He had to climb behind me with my feet on his shoulders taking all my weight. Lastly, came John, who now had the combined weight of both Peter and I on his shoulders!

We knew from the start that there was no way we could make it to the base of the spire and we contented ourselves with tying the balloons to some roofing tiles half way up the hall roof. We slid back down the roof and to our beds. The excitement was to follow, we hoped the next morning.

With great anticipation we peddled to school on the last day to find the big cast iron school gates closed, chained and padlocked to all. Another prankster had also been at work that night! Staff and pupils gained access into the school via a side entrance to be greeted by a piece of feminine underwear flying from the flag pole, a racy thing to do in those days. Assembly was dreadfully late that morning. Someone else had acquired duplicate keys, entered the school in the night and from the splen-did lofty school roof, suspended a life size effigy of the head from the rafters. The head master couldn't possibly hold a last assembly with his double suspended, just above his head. The prefects were told to remove the evidence before the school saw the prank.

Meanwhile a small bunch of partially inflated balloons fluttered in the breeze above our heads. We made it. How many other pranksters were at work that night none of whom saw one another? One up the flagpole, a second at the school gates, us three on the tiles and other persons immediately beneath us in the school hall. I am the only prankster to have owned up to past deeds. For those who haven't. "Wait outside my study boys. Six of the best for you".

Epilogue

The capital value of the Ely gas works and the land it stood on would, fifty years after its demolition be worth many millions of pounds today. Responsibility for the financial viability of the undertaking, engineering knowledge and skill with which to run the plant together with the social responsibility for maintaining a source of power for Ely citizens and the RAF hospital was a huge responsibility. My father, it seems, had a sound knowledge of gas engineering, contract law, government legislation, share trading and marketing that even I have been stretched to keep abreast of the many developments whilst reading the company minutes. It has been said by a senior gas engineer/manager that it was remarkable that a small works like Ely was permitted to expand so rapidly both during and after the war. A tribute to my fathers business acumen. He made so many business decisions concerning the gas works but none of these skills were shared with me. Only after my father's death have I discovered how much he achieved. Sadly, my dad was so absorbed with his work and his first passion preaching in the local Methodist Circuit, that my mother and I hardly had a look in. He was a twentieth century work alcoholic which cost our family dearly. Of the generous salary he received my dad gave away 95% to charities, much of it to Dr Barnardo's. He neither fed or clothed me or my mother. What pocket money he gave me I had to sign for. His estate he gave to charity. Charity did not begin at home.

My mother meanwhile had no interest in my father's work or had any concept of the enormous responsibility that hung on his shoulders. His work had no intellectual attraction and really didn't register as something of any importance. She despised the whole business. Instead, she was preoccupied marking history essays at the Ely High School, the salary of which fed the family, clothed mother and I, and funded my public school education. Neither parent had very much time for me and I became a very frightened child, an emotionally immature adolescent and a damaged adult. The writing of this book has been part of a long and very painful journey to heal the wounds of my childhood.

I expect most readers of this book will by now have realised, that it is not totally about the Ely Gas works, although a lot is said about it. It is, of course, about my lost childhood, the father figure I desperately longed for, but never had. It conceals beneath its pages the enormous pain and the hurt of a little boy who was neither seen or heard, and in the case of my father, rarely touched and never picked up. Someone who was never recognised or acknowledged as to who he was, by either parent. This book above all else is my memorial to my longed for and much loved father, who I really only knew as 'The Manager', when I was a little boy, adolescent and young man. Many, many tears have been shed in the course of my writing.

Claude Staniforth holding in his left hand his bound memories and in his right hand one of the company minute books.

A very mellowed father well into retirement

About the author

Paul Staniforth was born in Ely in 1944 where he received his primary education. At age eight he was sent as a boarder to the Perse School, Cambridge and in 1962 his family moved to the city. He went on to study agriculture at London University, Wye College after which he joined the staff of the Ministry of Agriculture. Most of his career was as an agricultural advisor and following reorganisation he became a Consultant Soil and Water Engineer to the Agricultural Development and Advisory Service - draining and irrigating land, surveying, mapping, pollution control and environmental schemes. In retirement he pursues his passion for fine cabinet making, walking, foreign travel and for making time for people which a goal driven career precluded.

He lives with his wife Esmé and dog Mimi in an idyllic, elevated retreat on the edge of the Norfolk Broads overlooking the River Yare. The village is not on mains gas!

Paul and his wife Esmé who between them brought the book together

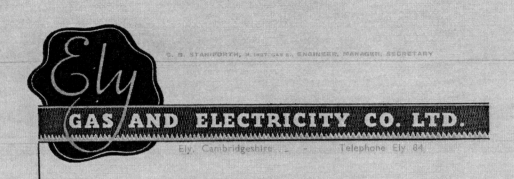

C. S. STANIFORTH, M.INST.GAS E., ENGINEER, MANAGER, SECRETARY

Ely, Cambridgeshire   -   Telephone Ely 84

The Author's Mother

This book would not be complete without further mention of the author's mother, Beryl Staniforth, better known in Ely as Beryl Bufton, her maiden name. She was a long serving teacher of history at the girls grammar school, in Bedford House, St Marys Street and latterly on Little Downham Road. My Mum lived to the ripe old age of 93 and whilst blind for the last five years of life she was very much aware as to the progress of this book. Sadly she died in 2006 just before it was published, but not before fingering the pages of the proof copy. Whilst she had an encyclopaedic memory of European history and scorned local history, she was tickled pink that I, her son, had written a book, albeit a local history book, that I believe I won her over, even though it was about a boring, smelly old gas works!

Beryl Staniforth with bearded son.

The company letter heading. Mid blue type set with small lettering in mid green printed on pale blue-grey Big Ben Bond air dried paper watermarked Big Ben clock and tower

DIRTY OLD TOWN

Song

I met my love by the gas works wall
Dreamed a dream by the old canal
Kissed a girl by the factory wall
|: Dirty old town. :|

Clouds a drifting across the moon
Cats a prowling on their beat
Spring's a girl in the street at night
|: Dirty old town. :|

Heard a siren from the docks
Saw a train set the night on fire
Smelled the spring on the smoky wind
|: Dirty old town. :|

I'm going to make me a good sharp axe
Shining steel tempered in the fire
Will chop you down like an old dead tree
|: Dirty old town. :|

I met my love by the gas works wall
Dreamed a dream by the old canal
Kissed a girl by the factory wall
|: Dirty old town :|
|: Dirty old town. :|

Anon

184

Appendix I

People known or believed to have worked for the Ely Gas Company
(dates where known of appointment + termination of service and /or death D)

Financier

Malam George	Proprietor	1835-

Designer

Malam George	Engineer	1835 -

Lessee's

Cudden John	Lessee	1848-
Bacon John High Constable	Lessee	-1851-1853-
Butcher John	Tenant	
Williams A.	Lessee	1871-

Sub Tenant / plant operators

Broderick William.	sub tenants	
Hawkes John	coal merchants	-1863-

County and General Gas Consumers' Co Ltd

Hills Edward	Agent	1865-1888
	Secretary to Ely Gas	1895-

Directors of The City of Ely Gas Company and later Ely Gas and Electricity Co Ltd.

Robinson Charles T	Director	1871-1880
Neals William M.	Director & Chairman	1871-
Allpress Thomas	Director & Secretary	1871-
Alfred Pitts (engineer)	Director	1885-
Clarke Arthur	Director	-1885-
Bailey James A	Director	-1885-D1891
Williamson Alfred	Director	-1885-D1898
Ambrose Col	Director & Chairman	-1885-D1921
Kitts Alfred	Director & Chairman	-1885-1923
Turkin George	Director	1894-D1898
Cooper G W Rev	Director	1898-1898
Hall Arthur Luddington	Director & Chairman	1898-1927
Trimmer Charles	Director	1921-1923
Ambrose Owen Lt Col	Director & Chairman	1921-1949
Martin Horace Alderman	Director	1923-1949
Archer Goodwin Lt Col	Director	1927-1949

Latterly Chairmanship of the Company was rotated between Directors

185

Engineers, Managers and Company Secretaries

(Company origi-
nally had an engi-
neer plus a secre-
tary, which lat-
terly combined
into one appoint-
ment).

Hardy William	Manager	1873-1880
Sweet Fredrick? ? J In '85 became lessee for Littleport Gas works. D 1890	Secretary & Manager B 1751	1881-85?
Yorston A.J.	Manager	1880?-'88
Foster A J	Manager	1888-1893
Hills Edward	Secretary	1885-1888-
Guyatt Thomas Alexander also Manager of Littleport Gas Co around 1911	Manager	1890-1933
Staniforth Claude B M B I M, M Gas Eng, M Inst Fuel Ass M Sales Man Ass, M Inst Public Light'g	Manager, Engineer & Secretary	1933-1957
Secker Charles Matthew	Chief Clerk then Accountant & Cashier finally Works Superintendent	1928-1959 D1980

Accountants and Auditors

Loss Mr		1885-1893-
Dunnock Mr J A (aud)		-1905
Stonebridge Mr W A (aud)	Capital & Counties Bank	1905-
Bunney Mr John (acc)	Wood Drew & Co	-1918-1968

Solicitors

Mr Beardshall	Messrs Beardshall & Sons	1932

Consultant Gas Engineers

Mr Alfred Williamson	Bankside, London	-1881-
Mr Kitts	Director	1885-
Mr W N Vallon	5, Victoria Street London SW1	1934
M Whaley	159, Palace Chambers, Bridge Street Westminster SW1	-1945-

Foremen (later designated assistant engineers and later still works superintendent)

	Jones J	Foreman	-1890
	Richards	Foreman	1890-
	Lester W. G.	Foreman	-1922-
	Bigg John H	Foreman	-1934-1937-
	Quinney H D	Foreman	1934-
	Richardson	Foreman	
	Aspley Aron	Foreman	1936-1938
	Gould Arthur Kempton Ass M Institute of Gas Eng	General Works Foreman later Assistant Engineer	1938-1954
34 St Marys Street	Hacon Jack	Foreman Assistant Engineer	1954-1946
	Ardron A Eric	Assistant Engineer	1947-1967+

Stokers Fitters Lamplighters Salesmen Clerks etc

Ardron Mrs	Clerk	
Attlesey Ronald	Assistant Stoker	12/57
Bacon James	Stoker	
Barman T	Killed in WWI	-D1916
Barton. Jack H	Lamplighter then Works cleaner.	-1958
Beardshall J		
Binge E. H	Salesman	1938-
Branch V	Fitter/Mains layer	1937-
Big John (jnr)		-1922-
Browne Thomas (Tom)		-1928
Browns J		D 1934
Brunby Dick	Yard worker	1920-?
Bullen L	Fitter from Dublin	1946-
Burton	Lamplighter	-1938-
Clarke E		
Collett Archie	Fitter	1947-1964
Crawford Peter	Gas Fitter trainee	1935-
Cross Walter? William?	Lamplighter then cleaner	1920-1952
Cross Thomas	Born 1849	1893-1923
Cummins L. S		
Day J	Stoker	
Dewing	Stove cleaner	-1933
Elsden P		
Garner G	Collectors assistant	1935D
Gent R.	Office Boy	1941-
George E		
Greggs H R	Lamplighter	1937-1938-
Hitch J	Fitters Apprentice ?	- 1939
Hood P		-1939
Jasman Gerald Neville	Junior Clerk	1937-
Knimsby H J	Fitter improver	-1935
Lane A E	Lamplighter	-1937
Lee Chris J	Stoker	1921-1948
Legge	Junior clerk	1941-
Liles Bob	Stoker	1958
Lovell A N	Stoker	1900
Lucan/Lucas Thomas	(Tom)	-1915-
Martin E		
Martin Harry	Fitter & Salesman-	1935-1958+
Martin J		
Miller Basil Horace	Lorry driver	-1951-
Merry Sid	Main layer pipe tapper	21 years

Newnham H		
Normack Mr Allen	Fitter approx for 3 years	1939-2001D
Oakey George	Stoker	1958
Osbourne N		
Peak Walter	Labourer	1905
Plumb Alf		
Partridge Walter	Fitter	1958+
Reader M		-1916-
Redman Miss Doris	Clerk/Typist	D1958
Reynolds Earnest	Stoker and lamplighter	1934?-D38
Richardson		-1893 D1905
Rickwood		D1905
Scutting S		-1937
Searle E		
Searle Mrs		
Sewell G		
Skeels Jim. C	Mains & Service	-1937
Smith G S	Salesman	1935
Staines T		1956
Starling W		
Stearman Mrs B	Typist	
Taylor W J 'Old Bill'	Stoker	1925-1953
Tebb Mrs	Typist	1951-1957
Thorpe M.	Driver	
Taylor W J	Stoker	
Varell? A E	Tenants of house in Bentons Yard	-1894
Benton	Tenants of house in Bentons Yard	1894-
Wilden A	Coke Yard worker	
Williams A G	Labourer	1937-
Williams A.C		-1957
Youngs T		

188

Appendix 2

Schedule of Street Lamps
attached to Contract between
Ely Urban District Council and the City of Ely Gas Company
dated 1911

BACK HILL AND GALLERY

1	Next to Royal Oak
2	Corner "The Close Garden"
3	Near Cross House
4	Corner Needham School Hall
5	Opposite Hill House
6	At Barton Gate
7	In Barton Road
8	Near Water trough Barton Square
9	Corner of Silver Street
10	Corner of Palace Garden
11	Denary Back Gate
12	West End of Cathedral
13	West end Churchyard
14	South end Green Lane Palace Green
15	At Porchway to High Street
16	East end of churchyard

BRAYS LANE

17	1st lamp on Mr Archers Wall
18	2nd lamp Cattle Market entrance
19	3rd lamp on Garden Wall
20	4th lamp opposite Jam Factory

BROAD STREET

21	Near 'Gravens'
22	West End Victoria Street
23	Middle Victoria Street
24	West End Cutter Lane
24	College entrance (front of 'Snells')
26	West End Ship Lane
27	West End Little Lane
28	Middle of 'Harlocks' wall
29	West End 'Harlocks' Lane

CAMBRIDGE ROAD

30	
31	1st lamp
32	2nd near Parish Room

Not numbered	Lamp Mr Smiths House
32	3rd lamp opposite Eagle and Lamb
33	4th lamp opposite Halls Old Vicarage
34	5th lamp opposite Mr Halls House
35	6th lamp corner of Barton Road
36	7th lamp near Barton Gate
37	8th lamp corner of Wichford Road

CHAPEL STREET

38	1st lamp near Laurel House
39	Middle of Street
40	Opposite Countess of Hunts Chapel

CHIEFS LANE

41	1st lamp Mr Toppings
42	2nd lamp corner of Bernard Street
43	3rd lamp near end of Bernard Street

IN COLLEGE

44	East end of Trinity Church
45	East end of Cathedral
46	South end of Cathedral
47	Near end of Hostel Arm Lane
48	South end Deans Walk
49	Near entrance gate from Gallery

PRICKWILLOW ROAD

50	North end Brays Lane
51	Opposite the Brunnings House
52	Corner of Springhead Lane
53	Near "Rising Sun"

DOWNHAM ROAD

54	Near Wheatsheaf
55	Opposite Chapel Street
56	Opposite Dovecot Close
57	End of Egremont Street

EGREMONT STREET

58	Near Charmichaels
59	Capt Luddingtons Gate opposite R C church

60	Opposite Evanses's	95	Butcher Row
	FORE HILL	96	Opposite Mr Evans Office
61	At Halls gateway	97	North end Chequers Lane
62	Near "Rose and Crown"	98	In Chequers Lane
63	Opposite Hiltons Stores		**NEWNHAM AND NEW BARNES**
64	Opposite Walkers Stores	99	Middle of Newnham
65	Top of Forehill	100	On Slaughter House Wall
	HIGH STREET	101	Opposite Paradise Close
66	At Dolphin Corner	102	Near Neathercoate's
67	South end High Street Passage	103	East end Decons Lane
68	Opposite "Bell Hotel"	104	1st Bohemond Street
69	Corner of Chequers Lane	105	2nd Bohemond Street
70	Opposite Mr Gardiner's	106	1st Decons Lane
71	Lamb Corner	107	2nd Decons Lane
	Lynn Road	108	3rd Decons Lane
72	Back of Lamb stables		**NEWNHAM STREET**
73	End of Market Street	109	Middle Newnham Street
74	East end of Egremont Street	110	North end opposite Rickwood
75	1st lamp beyond Egremont St nr Vicarage Gate	111	1st lamp Nutholt Lane Mr Davison
76	2nd lamp beyond Egremont Street	112	2nd lamp **** Gate
77	3rd lamp beyond Egremont Street		**ST MARYS STREET**
78	4th lamp beyond Egremont Street	113	Opposite Green Lane
79	5th lamp beyond Egremont Street	114	Opposite Mr Comins office
80	1st beyond Decons Lane	115	At "Peacock Inn"
81	2nd beyond Decons Lane	116	Downham Road Corner
82	3rd beyond Decons Lane	117	West end Palace Green
83	4th beyond Decons Lane	118	Opposite St Marys Church
84	5th beyond Decons Lane	119	Opposite Cromwell House
85	6th beyond D' L'ne opposite "Riflemans Arms"	120	Opposite "White Swan"
	MARKET PLACE	121	Opposite "Crown and Anchor"
86	East end of Market Place	122	North end Cambridge Road
87	On "The Limes"		**SILVER STREET**
88	Vineyard Gate	123	1st lamp from east
89	Near "Club Inn"	124	2nd lamp from east
90	Near "White Heart"	125	South end Church Lane
91	Inside Urinal	126	Middle Church Lane
92	Near Brunnings (tobacconist)	127	Corner Parade Lane
	MARKET STREET	128	Near National School
93	"Woolpack" Corner	129	Parade Lane end of Barton Road
94	Near Mr Coates		Illegible entry
	One lamp near Haylocks not lighted		

130	Parade Lane	151	Near "Coopers Arms"
	STATION ROAD	152	Near Surveyors office
131	East end High Bridge	153	Old Hall's Quay
132	West end High Bridge	154	The Hearlock's Quay
133	Hawkes coal yard	155	East end Little Lane
134	Near "Croen"	156	On "Ship" Public House—bracket
135	Near " Railway Tavern"	157	In Ship Lane Mr Abbeys
136	"Angel" Corner		**WEST END ROAD**
137	Middle Annnnesdale	158	1st Lamp
138	Corner Victoria Street	159	2nd St John's
139	River Bank	160	Smith's Mineral Water Factory
140	Opposite Gas Works	161	Hills Lane
141	1st lamp in Potters Lane	162	Near Mr Ascells House
142	2nd lamp in Potters Lane	163	Last Lamp opposite Lavenders
	WATERSIDE	164	St Johns Place
143	Middle of Harlocks Lane		**WEST FEN ROAD**
144	Opposite Bull Lane	165	1st lamp Waterloo cottages
145	In Bull Lane	166	2nd lamp Raynor's Paddock
146	Near "Black Bull"	167	3rd lamp Chiefs Lane
147	Near H????	168	4th lamp Ray????House
148	Almshouses Common Muckhill	169	5th lamp End Hills Lane
149	Hosters Common Muckhill	170	6th lamp Upheards Lane
150	Middle Willow Walk		Entries written in pencil and difficult to read
		172	???? last lamp
		173	Cemetery Road New Barns ***
		174	Cemetery Road 2nd lamp
	Hand written pencil entries difficult to read	175	Cemetery Road 3rd lamp
		176	Cemetery Road ????
		177	Barton Road
		178	8th lamp in Hills Lane
		179	9th lamp in Hills Lane

Tender Document courtesy of Pam Blakeman

Appendix 3

Production Statistics - Cambridge Division 31 March 1955

Vertical retort works **Production Plant**		Wisbech CV.	**Ely** **CV & CWG**	Huntingdon IVC
Production				
Coal gas				
Coal carbonised	tons	14,105	**5,777**	4,501
Therms made	thous th	1,163	**475**	328
Actual calorific value	B.Th.U.	490.5	**488.6**	480.2
Therms/ton	Therms	82.5	**82.2**	72.9
By-products/ton				
Coke used in producer	cwt.	3.77	**1.77**	3.55
Made in ex R H	cwt.	8.42	**9.37**	7.85
Total made	cwt.	12.19	**11.14**	11.4
Breeze used on producer	cwt.	......	**1.78**	....
Made in ex R H	cwt.	1.26	**1.3**	0.07
Total made	cwt.	1.26	**3.11**	0.07
Total Coke used on Producer	cwt.	3.77	**3.55**	3.55
Total Coke & breeze made	cwt.	13.45	**14.25**	11.47
Tar	galls	16.1	**18**	14.9
Benzyele	galls	0.39	....	....
Mixed Gas	%			
Fuel efficiency	%	80.2	**85.8**	62.2
Carbonising Index	B.Th.U	....	.....	.....
Declared calorific value	B.Th.U	500/480	**500**	480
Average Official tests	B.Th.U	489.3	**501.8**	482.5
Actual calorific value after benzol extraction		490.5	**498.6**	480.2
Solid fuel used for steam raising				
Coal used on Boilers	cwt./ton	....	....	0.19
Coke & breeze used on boilers	cwt./ton	0.06	**0.06**	1.33
Total fuel used on boilers	cwt./ton	0.06	**0.06**	1.52
By-products				
Coke				
Used - water gas	cwt./ton	....	....	....
Used - boilers	cwt./ton	0.08	**0.04**	1.27
Used - other purposes	cwt./ton	0.02	....	....
Made for sale to public	cwt./ton	8.32	**9.33**	6.58
Made for sale to public	tons	5,869	**2,694**	1,480
Sold to public	tons	6,248	**2,768**	1,307
Sold to other districts	tons	1.86	....	202
Purchased from other districts	tons	....	....	....

Differing Gas making plant

CV   - Continuous Vertical Retort
CWG - Carburetted Water Gas Plant
IVC - Inclined Vertical Retorts

Production Statistics - Cambridge Division 31 March 1955

		Wisbech	Ely	Huntingdon
Vertical retort works				
Production Plant		C.V.	CV & CWG.	I.V.C
By-products				
Breeze	cwt./ton	....	0.02	0.06
Used - on boilers	cwt./ton	....	....	....
Used – for other purposes	cwt./ton	1.26	1.31	.01
Made for sale to public	tons	892	378	3
Sold to public	tons	899	356	3
Sold to other districts	tons	....	26	....
Purchased from other districts	tons	....	....	....
Total coke & breeze made for sale to public		9.58	10.64	6.59
Gas				
Sold to Public	Thou therms	961.9	391.1	264.5
Sold for Public Lighting	Thou therms	19.2	16.3	4.9
Benzyl extraction equiv.	Thou therms	8.9	....	....
Used on works	Thou therms	4.2	6.6	4.9
Correction to STP	Thou therms	33	10.9	12
Unaccounted for	Thou therms	138.4	51.2	41.8
Total (send out to DCV)	Thou therms	1,168.00	476.1	328.1
% unaccounted for volume basis		11.9	10.8	12.7
Consumer Statistics				
Prepayment No of consumers	No	3,534	1,703	1,227
Prepayment Therms sold	Thou therms	415	186	130
Prepayment Therms sold/consumer	Therms	117.3	108.9	106.3
Domestic credit No of consumers	No	1,992	418	460
Domestic credit Therms sold/consumer	Therms	222	61	51
Number of other consumers	No	111.6	146.1	111.1
Therms sold to other consumers	Therms	483	187	102
Average consumption domestic	Therms	344	161	88
Average consumption all type	Therms	115.3	116.3	107.6
Average consumption ex public light		160.1	169.5	147.8
Industrial load	%	13.7	5.6	10.1
Other non domestic load	%	21.4	33.8	22.5
Output of Gas				
Max. Week to date	Th.cu.ft	6,255	2,891	1,749
Max. Week to date	Therms	31,275	14,455	8,395
Max. day to date	Th.cu.ft	965	445	271
Max. day to date	Therms	4,825	2,225	1,301
Max. day to date (new record)	Date	02/02/54	22/12/50	05/12/50

Annual statistics like those above and to the left were produced by every gasworks in the country from their daily records of production. The annual statistics were latterly collated by the Board of Trade to produce National figures. Very few summary sheets such as these now exist, these few sheets from Ely being the exceptions. My father overlooked throwing these papers away. He used the backs of the sheets on which to draft his sermons.

Appendix 4

Plant changes occurring between 1933 and 1945

Plant capacity	Originally 43 million cu.ft. now 102 million c.f. CV 500	1950?
Retorts	Horizontal two beds reset	1936
	Vertical downwardly heated 54 inch axis	Re set 1936
	Plant demolished and rebuilt as an upwardly heated retort 42 inch? With additional retort added. Capacity 275,000 cu ft/day Plant effectively doubled in size	1941
Producer Gas plant	P G dilution fitted with CO pressure control setting	
Coke breaker and screening plant	Ridi & Bell 5 size coke breaker and grader. De- breezer installed shortly after	1938
Exhauster	Waller 3 bladed replaced earlier one. Rebored Dempster 2 blade	1941
Condenser	Air cooled condenser renewed and a water cooled set to be installed.	1942
Washer	Clapham pump less ammonia washer	
De Tarrer	Whessoe	1945
Purifier beds	4 dry flute purifiers	
Holders	Single lift spiral holder in concrete tank to take 3 lifts 50,000 cu ft doubled storage built Firth Blakeney. Ferro Construction built tank	1942
CWG plant		1950
Booster	Fan Booster driven by geared steam automatically controlled turbine Bryan Donkin capacity 20,000 cu ft per hour raised gas pressure from 5 to 7 inches at works end	1936
Compressor	Holmes Connersville compressor to 4 inch high pressure main to RAF hospital	1940
High Pressure Main	To hospital 1.5 miles 4 inch pressurised by Holmes Connersville compressor with steam and gas engine drive	1940
Low pressure main	Increased length by 35%	
Meter	Wet Connersville	
Un accounted for gas	Fell from 15% to 7%	
Waste Heat Boiler	Spencer Bonecourt 15ft 4½ "	1936
Consumers	Increased by 25%	
Electricity outside commercial supply	Two ring mains installed	1945

Power	Waste heat boiler Changed from tar fired to coke fired. Coke dust 0-3/8 inch. Very few furnaces about in England which can burn such small fuel without choking the flues	
	To meet demands during winter of 1945 Cannel coal used diluted with producer gas. Help from the Fuel Research Board to find a suitable Cannel coal from Derbyshire, S. Yorks & W. Yorks. Only two other works in the country known to be using Cannel coal regularly	
Finance	Dividend raised from 0% to 10% legal max Value of stock in 1933 was 40 per 100 nominal. Upon Nationalisation this had risen to £202 10s 0d	
Thermal efficiency of works	Increased by 20% to 84%	
Meter scrapping programme	No meter over 15 years old or 7 years from repair	
Pension scheme	Available for all employers without distinction. Sick pay scheme	1944
New steam main	4 inch round works	1940
Weighbridge	30 ton 30ft by 8 ft platform	
Rateable Value	On appeal to the quarter sessions this was reduced from £850 to £150	1934

Ely Standard January 4th, 1952

Ely Standard December 3rd, 10th, 17th 1954

Financial and production changes between 1933- 1945

1	Dividend rise from 0% to 10% (maximum permissible by law)
2	Credit balance on revenue account raised from £400 to £4,000 a rise of 900% paid up capital £27,000
3	Capital per million cu ft gas sold reduced from £750 to £450
4	Many thousand pounds of outstanding debts and loans paid off. Also £30,000 spent out of revenue on major repairs and new plant and now £4,000 cash in bank and no increase in paid up capital.
5	Gas output increased by 6% and still rising 43 to 69 million cu ft.
6	Price of gas halved on two part tariff to which more than 50% of consumers subscribe after only 12 months. Gas price reduced from 14d to7d / therm.
7	National wage increases have been awarded. Sick pay, free gas and working clothes also provided by firm. Generous superannuation scheme for all grades introduced. Special mess room and washing facilities provided.
8	Overall efficiency of works raised from 60% to 74% and still improving 85% possible. Fuel Expenditure index of 20.
9	Unaccounted for gas fell from 12% to 4%. (In 1936 it was 13.7%)
10	Rateable value reduced on appeal by 80% from £850 to £150.

Appendix 5

Indenture of Claude Staniforth as an Articled Pupil

This Indenture made the Twelfth day of August One thousand nine hundred and twenty four Between Claude Bertram Staniforth (Hereinafter called the Articled Pupil) of Number 187 Stafford Road, Southtown, Great Yarmouth in the County of Norfolk of the First part JOHN EDWARD STANIFORTH of the same place (the father of the said Claude Bertram Staniforth) of the second part and the GORLESTON AND SOUTHTOWN GAS COMPANY (hereinafter called the said Masters) having their Offices at The Gas Works, Southtown, in Great Yarmouth aforesaid of the third part WITNESSETH that the said Articled Pupil of his own free will by and with the consent of his said Father Doth put and bind himself Articled Pupil with and to the said Masters to serve them as Articled Pupil from the twenty Fifth day of August 1924 until the full end and term of THREE YEARS to be fully complete and ended and to learn the art Profession or Business of Gas Engineering and Gas Works Management AND this indenture also witness that the said Articled Pupil agree to perform a reasonable amount of clerical work for the Masters during the said term to the satisfaction of the said Masters' Engineer and Manager and for the consideration aforesaid the said Masters agree to pay to the said Articled Pupil the Weekly sum of Twelve shillings and sixpence during the first year Fifteen shillings during the second year and One Pound during the third year during the Continuance of the said Articles AND they the said Articled Pupil and his Father COVENANT with the said masters that the said Articled Pupil shall and will during the said term well and faithfully serve the said Masters as an Articled Pupil in Art, Profession, or business of Gas Engineer and Works Manager and as aforesaid and their lawful commands willingly to obey and shall not do or commit or suffer to be done or committed any waste, damage or other injury to the property or goods of the said Masters or lend them to any person without the consent of the said Masters and shall not unlawfully absent himself from the service of the said Masters during business hours AND FURTHER that he the said John Edward Staniforth will at all times at his own expense provide the said Articled Pupil with good and sufficient Meat, drink, board, Lodging, clothing, medicine, medical and Surgical attendance

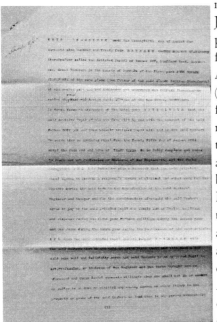

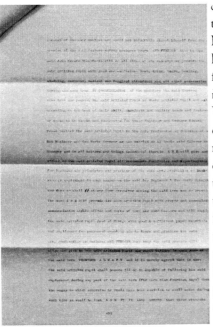

the promises the said Masters will take and receive the said Articled
Pupil as their Articled Pupil and will according to the best of their
skill, knowledge and ability teach and instruct or cause to be taught
and instructed (by their Engineer and Manager Edward Frost Keeble)
the said Articled Pupil in the Art, Profession or business of a Gas
Engineer and Manager and in all matters and things incidental thereto

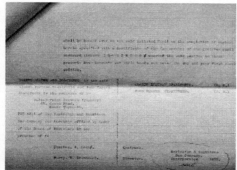 AND will give and afford the said Articled
Pupil all reasonable facilities and opportu-
nities for learning the principles and practices of the said Art, Profession or business
or employment in such manner as the said
Gas Engineer & Gas Works Manager now
does or shall at any time hereafter during
the said term use or practice the same
AND will provide the said Articled Pupil
with proper and convenient accommodation at the office and the Works of them
the said Masters and will supply the said Articled Pupil free of charge
with good and sufficient paper materials and appliances for the purpose of enabling him to learn and practice the said art, Profession or
Business and Further that the said Masters will allow and give to the
said Articled Pupil one weeks holiday in each year of the said term
PROVIDED ALWAYS and it is hereby agreed that in case that the
said Articled Pupil shall become ill or incapable of following his said
employment during any part of the said term (for more than Fourteen days) then the wages to which otherwise he would have been
entitled to shall cease during such time as shall be lost AND IT IS
ALSO AGREED that these presents shall be handed over to the said
Articled Pupil on completion of the terms herein specified with a
Certificate of the due service of the Articled Pupil endorsed on theon
IN WITNESS of the said parties to these presents have hereunto set
their hands and seals the day and year first above written.

SIGNED SEALED AND DELIVERED by the said
Claude Bertram Staniforth and John Edward
Staniforth in the presence of: -

Walter Frank Stevens (Cashier)
45, Crown Road,
Great Yarmouth.

THE SEAL of the Gorleston and Southtown
Gas Company was hereto affixed by Order
Of the Board of Directors in the presence of :-

Charles. S. Orde   Chairman

Harry. T. Greenachre   Director   Gorleston & Southtown
                                            Gas Company Incorporated 1876

Indenture of William Lester as an Apprentice

This Indenture Witnetself that William Lester 18 years of age on June 20 last doth put himself Apprentice to William West to learn his Art and with him after the Manner of an Apprentice to serve from the 1st day of august 1900 unto the full End and Term of Three Years from thence next following to be fully completed and ended During which Term the said Apprentice his Master faithfully shall serve his secrets keep his lawful commands every where gladly do he shall do no damage to his said Masters nor see to be done of others but to his Power shall tell or forthwith give warning to his said Master of the same he shall not waste the Goods of his said Master nor lend them unlawfully to any he shall not contract Matrimony within the said Term nor play at Cards or Dice Tables or any other unlawful Games whereby his said Master may have any loss with his own goods or others during the said Term without Licence of his said Master shall neither buy nor sell he shall not haunt Taverns or Playhouses nor absent himself from the said Masters service by day unlawfully But in all things as a faithful Apprentice he shall behave himself towards his said Master and his during the said Term

And the said William West in the consideration of the sum of 10/0/- ten pounds to be paid in two instalments four pounds at signing and six pounds in November following, shall pay him the weekly wage first year three shilling per week second year four shillings and six pence per week and the third and last year six shillings per week the number of hours per week to be 56½ and all over time to be paid and shall teach his said Apprentice in the Art of Tinman Gasfitter & C…. which he useth by the best means that he can shall teach and Instruct or cause to be taught and instructed Finding all necessary tools & C. His parents to provide all food lodging clothes and all other necessary arising there from

And the true performance of all and every the said Covenants and Agreements either of the said Parties bindeth himself unto the other by these Presents The Witnets whereof the Parties above named to these Indentures interchangeably have put their Hands and Seals the First day of August and in the sixty third Year of the Reign of our Sovereign Lady Queen Victoria by the Grace of God of the united Kingdom of Great Britain and Ireland QUEEN Defender of the Faith and in the Year of our Lord One Thousand 900

> Signed and delivered
> In the presence of

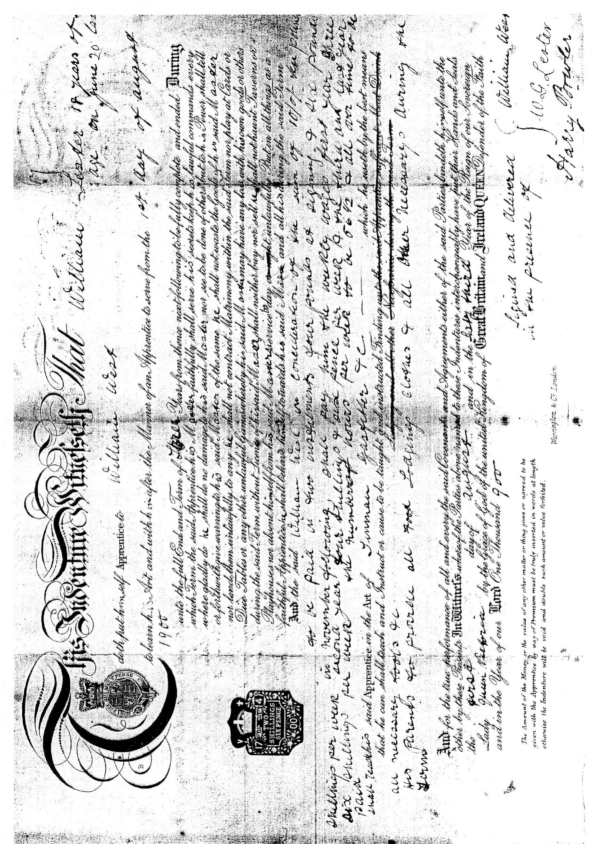

Bibliography

City of Ely Gas Company Deeds Cambridgeshire County Council Archives
Bidwell's Map of Ely 1851 Cambridgeshire County Council Archives
Board of Trade Company Registrations 1871 - BT31/34117/5284 & BT 31/34118/5284. C° No 5284.
Candle Lighting David J Eveleigh Shire Publication No 132, 1985 ISBN 0-85263-726-8
Cambridge Chronicle 1762-1934 Local History Collection Cambridgeshire County Council
City of Ely Gas Company: Gone but not Forgotten by Audrey Denton Life Magazine 1986 periodical article.
Department of Trade and Industry http:/www.
Domestic Utilisation of Gas by R.N. Le Fevre 1961.
Domestic Utilization of Gas Parts 1, 2 by Norman Smith & R.N.Le Fevre.
Ely Bill heads by Pamela Blakeman Published by the Ely Society ISBN 0-90361-608-4
Ely Cathedral Market Town 1900-1953 by Mike Rouse & Reg Holmes 1975
Ely Gas Company Directors Minute Book 1871-1884 Untraceable presumed Lost/Destroyed
Ely Gas Company Directors Minute Book 1885-1910 Cambridgeshire County Council Archives
Ely Gas Company Directors Minute Book 1910-1930 Cambridgeshire County Council Archives
Ely Gas Company Directors Minute Book 1930-1938 Cambridgeshire County Council Archives
Ely Gas Company Directors Minute Book 1939-1946 Cambridgeshire County Council Archives
Ely Gas Company Directors Minute Book 1947-1949 National Gas Archive Warrington – National Grid
Ely Gazette 1898-1912 Cambridgeshire County Council Local History Collection
Ely Standard 1913-2003 Cambridgeshire County Council Local History Collection
Ely Weekly Guardian 1889-1898,1905-1909 Cambridgeshire County Council Local History Collection
Ely & Cambridge Gas Works. Memoirs by Ronald William Attlesey [unpublished private collection]
Fenland Barge Traffic 1972 by John K Wilson and Alan Faulkner Robert Wilson Publication
Heritage Research Centre Ltd http:/www.heritageresearch.com/manufactured_gas
Historic Gas Times - Newsletter of the Institution of Gas Engineers & Managers
Gas Act 1948 Ch 67
Gas Analysis by A. McCulloch 1938.
Gas Light and Coke Company London 1812-1895. by Stirling Everard 1949
Gas Lighting by David Gledhill Shire Series No 65.
Gas Orders Confirmation Act 1881 Chapter ciii Cambridgeshire County Council Archives
Gasworker Ancestors. How to find out more about them ISBN 0 952 4607 X David E. Loverseed 1994 containing
    over 200 cross references to other gas history publications
Historical Index of Gasworks 1806-1957.
Iron & Steel Catalogue 1932 from Dunlop& Ranken Ltd.
Information about Ely circa 1900 Cambridgeshire Libraries History on the Net [Kellys Directory of Cambridgeshire].
Kemper's Engineer's Year Book 1942
Kings Manuel of Gas Manufacture Sections 1-10
Local, Personal & Private Acts, 44&45 Victoria 1, ref HL/PO/PB/1/1881/44&45VI127 dated 1881. House of
    Lords Record Office.
Malam Family (gas industry) by Golisti, Kenneth O. M. (Malam),1996. Foster Library [Lincolnshire Archives]
Manchester Guardian Gas Industry Supplement 1923
Modern Gas Works Practice by Alwyne Meade 2nd edition 1921
Murdoch Centenary Lecture to the Institute of Gas Engineers by E. F. Armstrong (Trans Inst Gas Eng 1938-9)
New Light Dawning. Gas engineering in the first half centaury of the Industry
    by Ken Golisti & Barry Wilkinson 1992
Board of Trade listings of Companies National Archives Kew
Ordnance Survey Map 1886 Cambridgeshire County Council Archives
Ordnance Survey Map 18** National Grid Gas Archives Warrington
Ordnance Survey Map 1900/1911 Cambridgeshire County Council Archives
Ordnance Survey Map 1904 Cambridgeshire County Council Archives
Ordnance Survey Map 1925 Cambridgeshire County Council Archives
Ordnance Survey Map 1970 Cambridgeshire County Council Archives
Photographic Collection Cambridgeshire County Council Local History Collection.
Precious monuments? Gas & John Grafton: New Technology comes to Cambridge, Periodical - Local History Mar/
    April 2004 by Allan Brigham.
Reports of Gas Association 1937, 1939.
Retort House Technical Control by A. R. Myhill 1945.
Robinson's Commercial Directory of Beds, Buck, Cambridgeshire, Hunts, Norfolk, Suffolk with Oxfordshire 1839.
Self Instruction for Students in Gas Engineering Advanced1921.

Technical Data on Fuel by H.M. Spers1935.

Terrace's Notebook for Gas Engineers and Students by John Terrace1948.

The Development of British Gas undated 1990?

The Efficient use of Fuel by HMSO 1944

The Ely Gas Company by Claude B. Staniforth manager 1983 unpublished but reproduced in full in
    'Can you smell gas?'

The City of Ely Gas Company Ltd - Public Utility Plan of 12th November 1880, Cambridgeshire County Archives ref
    Q/Rum/97 [n.d.]

The Gas Adventure at Whitby 1825-1949 by K.O.M. Golisti revised 1995 ISBN09521950 3 8

The Gas Engineer's Chemical Manual1886

The Gas Engineer's Pocket Book by H O'Connor 1898

The Gas Journal Directory 1937, 1954, 1963.

The History of the Gas Light & Coke Company 1812-1949 Stirling Everard 1949 Earnest Benn Ltd reprinted by A
    & C Black (Publishers) 1992 ISBN 0-7136-3664-5

The Independent 25th April 2006. 'A Window of Victorian Britain'.

The Science and Practice of Gas Supply by Arthur Coe Volumes 1,2,3.

The Theory of Industrial Gas Heating by Peter Lloyd 2nd edition 1938.

Wallace Collection Local History Collection Cambridgeshire County Council

Woodall & Duckham Ltd, Gas engineers & retort manufacturers 1905-1979 minutes, corporate records, financial
    records, list of plant erections, technical drawings, publicity material etc. Glasgow University Archive

Workshop Practice Volume 1, 2, 3. by E. A. Atkins 1929.

Sources of Research Material

Cambridge Local History Collection

Cambridgeshire County Archive

Ely Standard newspaper

Fakenham Town Gas Works Museum

Glasgow University Library

John Doran National Gas Museum Leicester

Lincolnshire County Archive

National Archive Kew

National Grid Transco Gas Archive Warrington

Norfolk County Council Archives

Norfolk County Council Millennium Library & http://noah.norfolk.gov.uk/,

Northumberland University Gallery

Oslo (Norway) Gas Works Archive

Snibston Discovery Park/Museum & National Coal Board Colliery

Beamish Open Air Museum

Documents and/or information not found

1   Memorandum or Article of Association

2   In the absence of a Parliamentary Act, then a Deed of Settlement establishing the first company in 1835.

3   Minute books covering the period 1871- 1885

4   The original shareholders of the Ely Gas Company founded in 1871

5   Company Share Register if one existed separate to the Minute Books.

6   Company Accounts, Annual Reports, Employment Records.

7   Inaugural Brochure if one was produced by Woodall Duckham commemorating opening of the new retorts

8   The table tennis bats, net and ping pong ball from the Board Room

Glossary

Bijou	Smallest commonly sized gas mantle
Boys Calorimeter	Used in the works laboratory for measuring the heat value of the gas produced
B. Th. U.	British Thermal Unit. A measurement of heat
Breeze	Coke dust
Caking	Coal in the retort fused together to form a solid mass. Oxide did the same in the purifiers. An ideal coal for coke production was said to 'cake' well to form a solid pieces of coke measuring six to 12 inches as distinct from a coke dust. Coke was later crushed and sieved to size.
Calorific value	The heat value of the gas measured in British Thermal Units per cubic foot
Ceramic	As in radiant fire. These were the heat reflectors to be found in domestic fires.
De Tarrer	Plant for removing tar mostly by cooling or for residual tar mist, electrically
Exhauster	Plant to remove gas from retort and pump it round works through purification plant and eventually to the gas holders
Fitter	Employed to visit clients and connect up domestic appliances to the supply
Flue	Chimney or exhaust vent for burnt gasses
Gas Liquor	Wash water from the scrubbers. A black unpleasantly smelling liquid high in ammonia.
Hang up	Occurred in the vertical retort when coal failed to slide through by gravity and had therefore to be dislodged by rodding from the top
Incandescent	As in gas mantle which glowed white in the heat of the gas which burnt inside the envelope
Lamplighter	Persons from the works who manually turned on and lit the street lights each evening and turned them off later the same night. Latterly they wound the clocks and cleaned the glass
Lift	Necessary to convey coal bogey to the top of retort house to empty coal in to vertical retort
Number two	The most commonly sized gas mantle
Purifier	Plant for removing sulphur from the gas
Producer	Furnace for manufacture of producer gas from interaction of steam on red hot coke
Producer gas	This was piped to the sides of the vertical retort and burnt in a semi enclosed space around the retort raising the temperature of 1,200° Centigrade.
Pyrometer	A portable device for measuring high temperatures in retorts
Rodding	Practice of poking the coal in a horizontal or vertical retort to stop the coke forming a solid mass and preventing its removal when all gas had been extracted
Stoker	Yard worker responsible for filling the retorts with coal and removal of coke + other tasks
Scurfing	After a period of time coal in the retorts would leave behind on the inner walls a film of pure carbon which if not removed would cause the coal to hang up. Scurfing was a process of burning off the carbon and was undertaken when the retort was empty of coal but still under fire.
Station Governor	Plant for providing 24 hour control and adjustment of the gas pressure to the district
Therm	A measure of heat. In the case of Ely works there were 500 therms to a cubic foot of town gas.
Under fire	Meaning the retorts were being heated by the burning of Producer gas
Water gauge	Gas pressure which ranged from 0 to say 6 inches was measured on a simple 'U' tube filled with water.

Chronological History of the Company

Date	Works History	Social History
1816		Death of Napoleon. Littleport and Ely Bread Riots 24 condemned to death but commuted for most to transportation but for 5 who were hung at Roswell Pits
1827		Navigation Improvements to River Ouse just north of Ely
1829		Opening of first railway Liverpool to Manchester
1830		King William 4th. Poverty and illiteracy widespread thought out Britain: Invention of Telegraph. Transport- stagecoach or boat. London to Brighton railway built.
1831		Chartism Political Reform 1830-1840
1832		Cholera kills 20,000 in England: Outbreak of the disease in Ely: Great Reform Act giving Freemen and Freeholders the right to vote
1833		Act of emancipation - abolition of slavery in British Empire
1834		Poor Laws: Parishes sanctioned to build Workhouses
1835	Ely Light Company Works believed to have been built by George Malam: Leased on an annual basis to him and others between 19/8/1835-1842	Charles Darwin lands from H M S Beagle on the Galapagos Islands.
1836		King William 4th Ely workhouse opened on a site in Cambridge Road.
1837		King William 4th /Queen Victoria Houses of Parliament lit by gas supplied at a very much higher pressure (four inches water gauge) than the rest of the country.
1838		First railway
1839		
1840	Works put up for sale. Believed to [...] buyers.	Repeal of Corn Laws :Introduction of Penny Post: Invention of match: Traction engines used for road haulage: Railway mania all over Britain. Buckingham Palace lit by gas
1841		
1842		
1843		
1844		
1845		Irish Potato famine. Railway opened Yarmouth-Norwich and Brandon-Cambridge
1846		Robert Peel PM Cholera kills 70,000 in England
1847		Ely corn exchange built
1848	Ely citizens declined to buy works. Works re-Conveyance between County and General Gas Consumer's Co Ltd and J Cudden +an other	Public Health Act 1848 established Local Boards of Health responsible for street lighting

ELY LIGHT COMPANY PRIVATELY OWNED

Year	Historical events	Gas works history
1849	Public Library Act: End of Mini Ice Age 1550-1850: Country covered by telephone lines	
1850	Window tax repealed formerly half rate: Kaffir War Great Exhibition. First cigarette sold in Britain	
1851		John Bacon Lessee: Bidwells Map of Ely showing gas works site
1852		
1853	Cholera kills 10,700 in England	Indenture of 14/2/1853 concerning land S of Back Lane for £500 from Dean & Chapter of Ely
1854	Outbreak of Crimean War	Replacement of entire gas making plant
1855		
1856	Cessation of Crimean War :Invention of Safety Match	
1857	Indian Mutiny	
1858	Darwin's Evolution of the Species	
1859		
1860	American Civil War commences. 50% of children in England die before 5 years of age.	
1861		
1862	East Anglia Railways and other companies amalgamated to become Great Eastern Railways	William Broderick +John Hawkes living in Benton's Square believed to be sub tenants & works operators. John Butcher the tenant.
1863		County & General takes works lease?
1864		Indenture 30/6/1864 purchase freehold of site £8,525 between John Bacon, Robert Monro Christus (Angus) and County and General Gas Consumer Co. 16 Retorts.1/7/1864; re-Mortgaged to John Butcher interest 5% for £4,525.
1865	Slavery in Africa finishes: American Civil War ceases	Edward Hills Agent to County and General Gas Consumer Co. 1/7/65 John Butcher transferred security £6,016-13-4d + interest to James Cudden barrister and Frances Thatcher Grey's Inn Square.
1866	Cholera outbreak in London	
1867	Reform Act 4½-7½% of male population could now vote	
1868		County and General in Chancery on a petition of Crawford a coal supplier. The company was ordered to be wound up. Liquidators appointed were Henry Stephenson consulting gas engineer + William White accountant.
1869	Suez Canal opened	Conveyance (of the mortgage) between John Bacon and the liquidators.
1870	Fosters Education Act Elementary education for all in Board Schools	

Overlay annotations:

PRIVATELY OWNED BUT LEASED TO LOCAL CITIZENS WHO SUB LEASED TO PLANT OPERATORS

BOUGHT COUNTY AND GENERAL GAS COMPANY WORKS RUN BY PLANT OPERATORS

BUT SUBSIDUARY OF GENERAL GAS COMPANY RUN BY PLANT OPERATORS

The diagonal watermark reads: **CITY OF ELY GAS COMPANY PUBLIC LIMITED COMPANY WORKS RUN BY PLANT OPERATORS**

Year	Company events	World / general events
1871	Formation of the City of Ely Gas Co on 10/1/1871. Conveyance of company in liquidation to Stephenson Clarke for £9,750 dated 1/5/1871. Stephenson Clarke sold gas works to City of Ely Gas Co for £11,500. Directors were William Neal (Ch), Charles Robinson + Thomas Allpress Company Secretary: Company financiers bankers and co-partners of Cambridge but business in Ely were Ebenezer Bird Foster George Edward Foster Charles Finch Foster Shareholders meeting Borrowed £3,000 on lease of Land in Cambridge to buy scrubber, purifier, boiler and engine:	
1872		Secret Ballot and licensing hours introduced. Penny Farthing in general use.
1873	Mr William Hardy manger	
1874		
1875	A Williams lessee: William Hardy manager	Invention of Telephone
1876		
1877		Ely Voluntary Fire Brigade formed.
1878	Edward Hills becomes secretary to Ely Gas Co	Afgan war commenced
1879		Thomas Edison invents electric light bulb
1880	Manager Mr Yourston Foreman Mr Arnold?? Robinson (Ch) ??	Rail traffic increases by 900% between 1850-1890
1881	Parliamentary legislation - Ely Gas Order Issued 300 £10 shares: First Site Plan:	Eiffel Tower built
1882		Founding of Marks and Spenser
1883		
1884		National Reform Act - All could vote
1885	Stokers beer allowance stopped New horizontal retorts: Complaints about gas quality: Start of 2nd Minute Book.	Spectacular explosion of one of Londons largest gas holders(1 mill c.f.) killing 11 and maiming many more.
1886	Manager Mr Foster	
1887	Directors arranged for two Star lights to celebrate Jubilee	Victoria's Jubilee County Agricultural Show held in Ely
1888	Mt A.J.Foster manager. Foreman Mr Richards :Horizontal Retorts re-built :accident on works	
1889		Boer War 1889
1890		1850-1890 Emigrants to North America rise from 1.5 to 3 million Fourth rail bridge opened
1891	Two bench of sixes horizontal retorts built	
1892		

206

Year	Ely Gas Works events	General / National events
1893	Manager Mr Guyatt: Complaints about smell from works	
1894	Public complaints about loading liquor onto barges	Local Government Act set up Urban District Councils
1895	76 slot meters in use by 1986. Wireless telegraphy invented.	Turnpike Trusts wound up 1864-1895. First petrol car on British roads.
1896	One setting of seven horizontal retorts commissioned: Council complains about quality of gas	
1897	First experimental gas meters in Ely	Men working in Ely gas works given 3 days holiday/year
1898	Two Cornish boilers installed. Street lights with mantles	
1899		Second Boer War 1899-1902
1900	Manager Thomas A.Guyatt. ?'s chimney heightened	First Zeppelin flew. Radio telephone invented.
1901	Vertically guided gas holder ? installed	Queen Victoria / King Edward 7th
1902		King Edward 7th
1903	Office block built: Regulating controller installed	
1904	Acquired adjacent land	
1905	Bench of 8 horizontal retorts installed	
1906		
1907	2nd hand station meter installed 1,000cu ft /hour	Ely High bridge rebuilt over the River Ouse.
1908	Workshop built	
1909		
1910		King Edward 7th Tea Bag invented
1911	Cockley washer fitted	
1912		Titanic sank on maiden voyage.
1913	Renamed Ely Gas and Electricity Company Ltd	
1914		
1915	180 public lights: 1,293 meters including 705 slot meters:	
1916	Therm introduced as a unit of heat for gas 1916-20	
1917	Rebuilt Waddles retort: demonstration benches of fours	
1918		
1919		
1920	National Coal Strike: Works ran on Derby coal	
1921	2nd year of Coal Strike: Working day shortened from 12 to 8 hours	
1922	2nd hand exhauster pump from Wellingborough fitted	
1923	2nd hand exhauster pump from Torbay Gas Co fitted	
1924	Rail strike disrupted coal deliveries but not to Ely	

CITY OF ELY GAS COMPANY PUBLIC LIMITED COMPANY WITH SHAREHOLDERS

ELY GAS AND ELECTRICITY COMPANY PUBLIC LIMITED COMPANY WITH SHAREHOLDERS

Year	Ely Gas & Electricity Company	World / National events
1925	Gas holder erected: Woodall-Duckham Vertical retort built: 4 railway wagons bought	Old Age Pensions inaugurated
1926	Another National Coal strike: Silesian coal acquired for Ely	General Strike 4-12 May
1927	Vertical Retort House built :Emergency coal from Camb'ge	Worst Harvest since 1879
1928	Mr C Secker book keeper: ; 10 ton tar condenser erected	
1929	Four railway trucks bought	Unemployment rose to over 2 million
1930		
1931	Leak in gas holder crown: Tar burner installed: UDC complains about excessive H²S in gas	
1932	Water leak in holder: 2nd gas holder collapses : Mammoth bad debt of £4,172 written off	Britain paid off 19 million war debt to USA
1933	Manager Claude Stanforth Foreman J Brigg Refurbished 2 bed of 6; Horizontal ret's held in mothballs: Gas explosion on West Fen Rd	Hitler becomes Chancellor of Germany.
1934	Foreman Mr Quinney: All automatic street lights + mantles	Mr Therm introduced. Hitler becomes Fuhrer.
1935	New gas holder: Top of Woodall-Duckham vertical retort rebuilt	
1936	Foreman Mr Aspley New Coffin Boiler. Coke breaker	George 5th/Edward 8th/King George 6th Ely shopping week. 20,000 visited Brays Lane K. jam factory. Queen Mary finished record voyage to USA 5days.23 hr.57mn
1937	Dismantled 2 old holders: Waterjacket boiler fitted	King George 6th Cost of armaments £1.5 billion
1938	Foreman A K Gould	Markham (Chesterfield) pit disaster 79 dead
1939	Start 5th Minute Book: Annual make? Sales 2,377,000 cu ft from 2,924 tons of coal Sales 36,620,000 116 customers including 1,584 with slot meters: 8 miles of main 74 street lamps. Gas 1/2per Therm:1/3d per therm for slot meters:	Outbreak of World War Two: Severe Flooding in Ely and the Fens. Petrol rationing announced. Gov announce plans for war damage to property
1940		
1941		
1942	Woodall Duckham retorts rebuild and adapted from ... to 4 retorts	
1943		
1944	Woodall Duckham retorts extended from 4 to 6 retorts	
1945		
1946		
1947	Start 6th Minute Book: Spirally guided gas holder erected ???	
1948	Ely Gas & Electricity Co Nationalised: Government owned Total sales 80,000,000 cu ft make 91,000,000 gas 1/6 per Therm slots 1/7.5d per therm	N.H.S. introduced. London North Eastern Railways Nationalised to become British Rail.

ELY GAS AND ELECTRICITY COMPANY PUBLIC LIMITED COMPANY WITH SHAREHOLDERS

NATIONALISATION BRITISH GAS EASTERN REGION

1949	Installation about now of Carburetted Water Gas plant
1950	
1951	
1952	
1953	
1954	Showroom No 9 High Street opened on a lease
1955	**NATIONALISATION**
1956	**BRITISH GAS EASTERN REGION** Foreman/Assistant Engineer Mr E Ardron
1957	Gas production ceased 20th January: Town Gas supplied from Cambridge via Fordham and Soham. Main extended to Littleport. Supplies later converted to Natural Gas: A gas holder demolished
1958	North Sea gas came in about 1969 but this information is not verified.
1959	
1960	Works demolished.

Note on page 174

I am informed that the pressure loss in the pipe of two pounds is ridiculously low and it would have failed the test. However on checking the minute book this figure is definitely correct. This leads me to ponder. Did my father make an error. I think not. More likely that his information is correct and that in the following 20 years pipe installation improved because leakage rates reduced possibly as a result of better pipe couplings.

My fathers figures would account as to why the pipe failed so dramatically when pressure tested again for part of the planned supply main to Littleport.

From

The Ely Gas & Electricity Co. Ltd.,
ELY, CAMBS.

To : A tribute to the Citizens of Ely past and present

Who helped set up of the Ely Light Company

patronised its services, worked for the company

and who benefited enormously from it.

36392

Per With love **CARRIAGE** Paul Staniforth 7th October 2006 **19**